Imagined Societies

In many countries in Western Europe, the demand for immigrant integration has inevitably raised questions about the "societies" into which immigrants are asked to integrate. *Imagined Societies* critically intervenes in debates on immigrant integration and multiculturalism in Western Europe. Schinkel argues that the term "multiculturalism" is not used primarily to describe a type of policy or political philosophy in countries such as the Netherlands, France, Germany, or Belgium, but rather is used as a rhetorical device that promotes demands for "integration". He analyzes the ways in which such demands are ways of imagining the very idea of a "host society" as "modern," "secular," and enlightened. Starting from debates in social theory on social imaginaries, and drawing on public debates on citizenship, secularism, and sexuality and on the social science of measuring immigrant integration, this book presents a highly original study of immigrant integration that challenges our understanding of the concept of society.

WILLEM SCHINKEL is Professor of Social Theory at Erasmus University Rotterdam. He is a member of The Young Academy of the Royal Netherlands Academy of Arts and Sciences and a well-known intellectual in the Dutch public sphere.

Imagined Societies

A Critique of Immigrant Integration in Western Europe

WILLEM SCHINKEL
Erasmus University Rotterdam

CAMBRIDGE
UNIVERSITY PRESS

CAMBRIDGE
UNIVERSITY PRESS

University Printing House, Cambridge CB2 8BS, United Kingdom

One Liberty Plaza, 20th Floor, New York, NY 10006, USA

477 Williamstown Road, Port Melbourne, VIC 3207, Australia

4843/24, 2nd Floor, Ansari Road, Daryaganj, Delhi – 110002, India

79 Anson Road, #06–04/06, Singapore 079906

Cambridge University Press is part of the University of Cambridge.

It furthers the University's mission by disseminating knowledge in the pursuit of education, learning, and research at the highest international levels of excellence.

www.cambridge.org
Information on this title: www.cambridge.org/9781107129733
10.1017/9781316424230

First published 2017

A catalogue record for this publication is available from the British Library.

Library of Congress Cataloging-in-Publication Data
Names: Schinkel, Willem, 1976– author.
Title: Imagined societies : a critique of immigrant integration in Western Europe / Willem Schinkel, Erasmus University, Rotterdam.
Description: New York : Cambridge University Press, 2017. |
Includes bibliographical references and index.
Identifiers: LCCN 2016040373 | ISBN 9781107129733 (hardback)
Subjects: LCSH: Social integration–Europe, Western. | Europe, Western–Emigration and immigration. | Immigrants–Cultural assimilation. | Multiculturalism–Religious aspects.
Classification: LCC HN373.5 .S335 2017 | DDC 305.8–dc23 LC record available at https://lccn.loc.gov/2016040373

ISBN 978-1-107-12973-3 Hardback

Contents

Acknowledgments   *page* vi

1 Immigrant Integration Imaginaries in Western Europe   1

2 Imagining Society: Social Theory and/as
   Social Imagination   35

3 Measuring Society: Moral Monitoring and the
   Social Science of "Immigrant Integration"   68

4 Transformations of Racism and the Rise of Culturism   112

5 Traditionally Modern: Contemporary Frameworks of
   Sexuality and Religion   156

6 The Uses of Citizenship   192

7 Social Science: Between Moral Monitoring and
   Public Sociology   218

Bibliography   236
Index   260

Acknowledgments

This book has grown out of several years of giving academic and public lectures on immigrant integration and social theory. It has benefited from the many audiences at those occasions. Parts of this book have been presented in lectures and seminars at New York University, Cambridge University, Oslo University, the University of Amsterdam, and the Université Libre de Bruxelles and at several conferences of, among others, the International Sociological Association and the European Sociological Association. I have benefited greatly from discussions there. Important parts of the work for this book have been part of the European Research Council–funded project "Monitoring Modernity: A Comparative Analysis of Practices of Social Imagination in the Monitoring of Global Flows of Goods, Capital and Persons" (ERC Starting Researcher Grant, project number 283679).

I have had the opportunity to work on this book in several stints abroad, twice as visiting scholar at New York University, in particular at the Institute for Public Knowledge (IPK). Special thanks are due to IPK's former director, Craig Calhoun, who generously provided the opportunity and who also critically commented on parts of the manuscript. His exceptional breadth of scholarship and his generous sharing of his expertise have been inspirational. A stay at Humboldt University Berlin, made possible by Rahel Jaeggi, has likewise been beneficial to writing this book. The reviewers for Cambridge University Press were generous in their comments, and they have helped make this a better book. John Haslam provided professional guidance throughout for which I am grateful.

Parts of the research in this book have been made possible by an ERC Starting Researcher Grant by the European Research Council, for the project "Monitoring Modernity" (grant number 283679). At Erasmus University Rotterdam, I have been greatly inspired by the members of the Monitoring Seminar. Jess Bier, Sanne Boersma, Eva van Gemert, Maja

Hertoghs, Friso van Houdt, Irene van Oorschot, Rogier van Reekum, and Anne Slootweg continue to form a highly intelligent, interdisciplinary group of thinkers that constantly allows me to learn and to develop my own thoughts.

Parts of Chapter 3 have previously been published as "The Imagination of 'Society' in Measurements of Immigrant Integration," *Ethnic and Racial Studies* 36(7): 1142–1161 (2013). They are reprinted here with kind permission of Routledge, Taylor & Francis Group.

Parts of Chapter 5 have previously been published as "The Nationalization of Desire: Transnational Marriage in Dutch Culturist Integration Discourse," *Focaal – Journal of Global and Historical Anthropology* 59: 99–106 (2011) (doi:10.3167/fcl.2011.590108). They are reprinted here with kind permission of Berghahn Books.

Parts of Chapter 6 have previously been published as "The Virtualization of Citizenship," *Critical Sociology* 36(2): 265–283 (2010) (doi:10.1177/0896920509357506). They are reprinted here with kind permission of Sage Publications.

At home, Marguerite van den Berg has been a source of love and inspiration. I'm so glad our son, Daniel, and our daughter, Ella, are part of our life to share in that love. I dedicate this book to the three of them.

1 *Immigrant Integration Imaginaries in Western Europe*

Immigrant Integration in Western Europe

In many countries today, debate rages on who really belongs to society and who doesn't. Specific to Western Europe in the last few decades is an increasing emphasis on the opposition between the national society and immigrants in need of "integration." In public discourse, this has been made explicit in recent years as a move from a supposed "multiculturalism" toward "integration." In all cases, a particular notion of "society" is put forward in the sense that it is always already unproblematically presupposed, although its unproblematic character is maintained only through the problematization of what it excludes. Often, this image of society is at once a national society, which is presumed to have particular historical roots, while it is also a society claiming certain universal values, such as liberty, tolerance, and democracy. Critiques of "failed immigrant integration" in mass media, state policies, and politics, as visible, for instance, in Belgium, Denmark, France, Germany, Norway, the United Kingdom, and the Netherlands, articulate the national society over against an "outside" of "nonintegrated." But French "unintegrated" immigrants, for instance, are not part of Germany or Belgium, so where are they when they are "outside"? What does it mean to assume that *here* is a society that, also after immigration, by and large remains what it is so long as immigrants, who are *there*, can be "integrated" in it? What invisible barriers separate "immigrants", who reside within the territory of the nation-state, from "natives"? Which conceptions of citizenship are needed in order to assume the simultaneous presence and nonpresence – or not-yet-presence – of immigrants in society? Why does "integration" always only concern those generally regarded as "others," that is, immigrants, mental patients, criminals, and so on? Which conceptions of culture are active in the imagination of society and the call for adaptation or assimilation by immigrants? If, as it has generally

1

functioned, "society" is a sociological container concept, encompassing all of social life, then what is its residue? Does society overlap with the group of people bound by culture or religion? Or is it perhaps more fruitful and realistic to say that societies are riven by difference and sometimes conflict? Could it be that the imagination of society under the sign of immigrant integration is a way of "whitewashing" Western European societies, of purifying them according to ideal images entertained by dominant middle classes? Is "integration" not a political way of separating what dominant groups want from parts of everyday social life they don't want but that are nonetheless inescapably a part of that life? And, amid all of this, what should the role of social science be? What should the status of "immigrant integration" be in social scientific research? And what role should be given to the concept of society in social theory?

By asking such questions, this book critiques what I shall call *immigrant integration imaginaries*. That is, it both foregrounds the sociological assumptions in the imagination of societies and their unintegrated immigrants and it critiques the ways in which the concept of immigrant integration renders the imagination of society possible. In a time when the very idea of bounded national societies is contested, immigrant integration can serve as a prism though which processes of boundary maintenance and social closure can be observed. One of the ways in which Western European national societies (re)articulate their identities is by highlighting what supposedly does not properly belong to them. By imagining what they are not, an image of what they are becomes available for meaning making and (or, perhaps, including) for governing. They do so by invoking "integration," a concept stemming from a vocabulary ideally suited to articulate boundaries and internal cohesion. The concept of "integration" allows the identification of what does not belong. Western European societies diagnose themselves as under threat from immigrants they perceive as "not yet present in society," although these immigrants are part and parcel of the social process in these societies. Immigrants present in the nation-state are considered as still "outside society," just like imprisoned criminals are said to eventually "return to society," as if prison were not a constitutive part of society. Such ways of seeing, and the practices with which they are connected, are productive to the extent that they identify what "society" is and who properly belongs to it. Immigrant integration becomes the object of scrutiny in elaborate knowledge forms that

I shall call forms of *moral monitoring*. A critical look at moral monitoring reveals that the asymmetries reported by social scientific studies of immigrant integration in Western Europe are a priori introduced into them. They operate, for instance, with what I shall call a *dispensation of integration*, meaning that only the extent to which nonnatives are "integrated" is researched. Thereby, it is assumed that there exists a "society" that is whole and healthy, and that only immigrants are in some ways at a remove from it. Small wonder that the findings of such studies reflect exactly that. When feelings of "belonging to society" are measured only among immigrants and their children, any feelings of not quite belonging become visible only for such persons, now coded as "ethnic groups" lacking in "integration." The dispensation of integration highlights a crucial aspect of integration imaginaries: it makes clear that the difference at stake is *not the difference between well-integrated persons and not well-integrated ones*, but between *those for whom integration is not an issue at all and those for whom it is*. The dispensation of integration thus contributes to a constant effort at "unmasking" those who are merely "passing" (Garfinkel 1967) as true members of society. You may encounter "them" on the street, but they are not really "in" society. They constitute today's "vagrants" and "psychotics," who were deemed "nonproductive liabilities" by Robert Merton. What he called "asocialized persons who are *in* society but not *of* it" (Merton 1968: 142–144) very much resembles the way immigrant integration and society figure in dominant forms of social imagination. Such unmasking efforts strengthen the ideological plausibility of the dominant imagination of society, for if it is possible to unmask the fake membership of society immigrants, and if it is possible to show, by means of social scientific scrutiny, their fictive Europeanness, then *imaginaries of "society" and of "Europeanness" themselves are naturalized as really existing beyond the status of imaginary fictions*. The legitimate definition and limits of "society" and of what it means to be "European" are therefore at stake in Western European discourses of immigrant integration and in the often accompanying denouncements of "multiculturalism." Theoretically, what is at stake is the difference between the two theorists just mentioned: Garfinkel's emphasis on passing and performativity and Merton's emphasis on a delineated society with integrated parts. The latter will appear here in the form of contemporary social scientific accounts of immigrant integration. The former will be developed in the direction of the performative effects of forms of social imagination.

This book seeks to visit those sites at which society imagines itself by problematizing itself. It looks for the discursive spaces in which society imagines itself as endangered, as wanting in "integration" and "cohesion." In recent decades, immigrant integration has evolved into a primary vehicle for the imagination of national societies in Western Europe. Integration imaginaries, as I will call modes of imagining society through the integration of, mostly but not exclusively, immigrants, always imagine society as under threat, as facing problems, and they operate through apparatuses of meaning making that bear striking similarities to forms of medical monitoring. As I will argue in Chapter 2, "integration" is a concept that comes out of a long history of organicist thought in which society is rendered analogous to a human body. These days, then, diagnoses of immigrant integration abound, often on the basis of extended forms of monitoring. In part, diagnoses of society have been produced by social science; in part they spring from public debates over the nation, citizenship, or religion. But these debates have increasingly come to overlap each other in debates of immigrant integration, which has in recent decades become one of the main issues around which collective self-reflection has centered. The social science of immigrant integration constitutes one of the most interesting sites of investigation in this book. It is one field in which "society" is actively imagined. Where immigrant integration is measured, "society" is the measure. Measurements of integration, which go on to play an important role in policy and political discourse, construct an image of society. One example of such image construction concerns measurements of integration in the Netherlands, which presuppose the "secular" character of Dutch society. In this measurement of immigrant integration, "secular" is defined simply as "not religious." This means, in effect, that one million (self-defined) Muslims in the Netherlands are, by definition, not well integrated and thereby reside at a certain distance from society. Of course, it also means that Christians would not be members of society, but Dutch integration research focuses on specific groups of "non-Western immigrants." So while the standard of "society" is never measured as such, it is used as a yardstick by which to measure, and judge, immigrants and their position vis-à-vis society. The same logic is active when measuring the socioeconomic position of migrants and doing so in terms of their "integration": why would a relatively low socioeconomic position (read: class position) mean one is "less integrated" in society? Why would a certain class background be a reason to conclude that a person exists at a certain distance from "society"? Society, in this logic, is constructed as a closed body that may be inhabited or invaded by foreign influences that remain essentially "outside" the social body. So it is quite common in discourses of immigrant integration to assume that, while immigrants are "here," they yet remain "outside society." Underneath the usually unquestioned acceptance of "society" as a kind of container of social life lies a continuous work of boundary maintenance and of the sorting out of belonging. Under the guise of description, the social science of integration produces a thoroughly prescriptive account of society. And when politicians from both the left and the right call for an overcoming of "cultural, ethnic and religious divisions" by furthering "integration into society," they reproduce a similar imagination within the political system.

What this book therefore does *not* seek to do is to analyze "immigrant integration." It does not seek to understand how far certain "ethnic groups" are "integrated" or to what extent others are not and what the causes of such (lack of) integration might be. Rather, my aim is to analyze the phenomenon of a society observing itself in terms of such integration – a society that appears only able to observe itself through the articulation of its difference to that which isn't properly "integrated." For while the main case chosen here is that of immigrant integration – which is by far the most salient of contemporary discourses of integration – it is not the only existing one. In fact, "integration" has become something of a master concept identifying all who in one way or another appear "unadjusted to society." The unemployed, the poor, the young, the elderly, those who do not use computers, those convicted of crimes, and those in mental institutions, to name a few categories, are subject to "(re)integration in society." Public concern over immigrant integration, then, is one possible lens through which the social construction of the national society, as well as its contestations, can be perceived. In recent years, that public concern has largely taken the form of a denouncement of "multiculturalism" in countries such as Germany, France, the Netherlands, Belgium, Sweden, Denmark, Norway, and the United Kingdom. But did these countries ever share a multiculturalist policy? They hardly did, and so we should not take the similarity in the many denouncements of multiculturalism as indicating a really existing multiculturalism. Multiculturalism in Europe has rather been a political ploy. More specifically, what Western European countries share is a rhetoric of what can be called *multiculturealism* that functions as a mechanism of exclusion. Multiculturealism is a rhetoric that insists that there was a multiculturalism, which failed, and that we should be realists about this instead of politically correct. In current debates in Western Europe, "multiculturalism" is not primarily a type of policy, and neither is it a political philosophy. Most of all, it is a rhetorical trope of recent invention. Denouncing a multiculturalism that in most cases never existed, often even in the form of a confession ("yes, we were naïve multiculturalists, but now we have become realists"), proves a particularly potent means of instituting hegemonic constructions of national society versus nonbelonging cultural aliens.

A Study in Social Imagination

This book is titled "Imagined Societies." These two words correspond to two related claims. The first is that what can be called social imagination is a key process in all social life. As such, this title shares affinities with Anderson's *Imagined Communities* (1991) and Ezrahi's *Imagined Democracies* (2015). The second is that "society" is not an entity that exists independently of its imagination. For a society to exist, to have effects, and to make a difference, it needs to be imagined. And as a consequence, the difference "society" makes and the effects it has are effects of the imagination. But what does that mean? Does it mean society is a mere "phantom of the imagination"? What is the substance of social imagination? The way I use social imagination here is intended to make use of both connotations that traditionally accrue to the imagination. The first is, indeed, that it concerns imagining things that are absent. In this sense, *imaginatio* became the scholastic translation of what Plato had discussed as a *phantom* or *fantasy* (Casey 2000: 15–16) – a connection still evident in Husserl's treatise on fantasy (2006: 84–85). This connotation recurs throughout the conceptual history of the imagination. At the same time, the concept of imagination has often contained a creative potential, even a potential to create institutions. According to Maguire, in Pascal, and later in Rousseau and Tocqueville, the imagination "is the basis of the self's appearance in the world, as well as the primary medium of relation between the self and others. Imagination is the agent of persuasion and often the creator of law, justice, and happiness in the world, especially through acts of writing and reading" (Maguire 2006: 10–11). Such an institutional creativity is much more evident when imagination is used in the sense of social imagination. This occurs, for instance, when Benedict Anderson (1991) considers nations to be "imagined communities." For Anderson, nations need imagination, for instance, through mass media, because of their scale. They cannot be perceived the way one could know and be visually familiar with all the members of a small community. Anderson highlights how education and media systems therefore become crucial vehicles for the imagination of the nation. From a slightly different angle, Cornelius Castoriadis has discussed "social imaginary significations," by which he means a certain type of performative creation that works through the imagination. That is to say that it "cannot be accounted for by reality, by rationality, or by the laws of symbolism ... it has no need to be clarified in concepts or in representations in order to exist; it is operative in the practice and in the doing of the society considered as a meaning that organizes human behaviour and social relations, independently of its existence "for the consciousness" of that society" (Castoriadis 1987: 141). For Castoriadis, there exists a "magma" of significations that is not preordered into what he calls an ensemblist-identitarian conception of society, but that is rather immanent to society (Castoriadis 1987: 175–177, 367, 370). For my purposes here, it is important to note that what Castoriadis calls the "imaginary institution of society" not only refers to lofty ideals of the communal questioning of the social and moral bond. It also produces a Master Signifier that orders social space along power differentials.

More recently and influentially, Charles Taylor has analyzed modernity in terms of its "modern social imaginaries." By such imaginaries, Taylor intends "the ways people imagine their social existence, how they fit together with others, how things go on between them and their fellows, the expectations that are normally met, and the deeper normative notions and images that underlie these expectations" (Taylor 2004: 23). In other words, Taylor argues, a "social imaginary" is to be considered as what philosophers have called a "background," which involves the fundamental assumptions made in social life. By speaking of "imaginaries," Taylor wishes to draw attention to the fact that people indeed "imagine" the broader social context in which they are enmeshed, much like nations, in Anderson's account, need to be imagined because they cannot be "seen" or engaged with in their entirety. Taylor also notes how social imaginaries are "carried in images, stories, and legends" (Taylor 2004: 23). Examples of social forms occurring under modern social imaginaries that Taylor discusses in his book are the market economy, the public sphere, and the self-governing people. He thereby indicates that social imaginaries, and modern imaginaries in particular, are complex. For he argues that under conditions of modernity, "society" is no longer necessarily imagined as an equivalent to the polity:

There will be more than one way in which the same body of systematically interacting human beings can be considered as forming an entity, a society. We can speak of them as an economy or a state or a civil society ... or just as a society or a culture. "Society" has been unhooked from "polity" and now floats free through a number of different applications. (Taylor 2004: 79)

Yet despite the fact that "society" can thus be imagined in a variety of ways that are at times contradictory, Taylor's conception of social imaginaries veers toward a consensus-driven concept that foregoes struggle and conflict over the dominant forms of social imagination, as well as the conflict inherent in the domination exerted by existing social imaginaries. First of all, while Taylor admits that "society" needs imagining, it at the same time forms the apparently stable basis or context of imagination. This becomes apparent when Taylor describes a social imaginary as "what enables, through making sense of, the practices of a society" (Taylor 2004: 2). Clearly, "society" occurs twice in Taylor's account, both as that which needs to be imagined in order to be and as that within which this imagining takes place. Consider, for instance, the following description of a social imaginary: "the social imaginary is ... shared by large groups of people, if not the whole society" (Taylor 2004: 23). And such a "shared" background operates in particularly consensual ways, especially when, as Taylor says, "the social imaginary is that common understanding that makes possible common practices and a widely shared sense of legitimacy" (Taylor 2004: 23). My approach here, while inspired by Taylor's account, differs from his in two ways. First of all, it seeks to highlight the often violent character of dominant social imaginaries. As Castoriadis also emphasizes, rather than being akin to relatively unproblematic, Durkheimian collective representations, social imaginaries are forms of domination, and as such they may also be contested. Rather than "shared" or "common" understandings to which "legitimacy" accrues quasi-automatically, they involve struggle and, often, active juxtaposition. Rather than unitary images of social life, they may involve dual images of, on the one hand, a "society," and on the other "immigrant groups in need of integration in society." And their imagining such oppositions may be forms of governing by division. The second way in which my approach to social imagination differs from Taylor's social imaginaries, and, a propos, from Castoriadis's description of social imaginary significations, is my refusal to accept "society" as the context of the imagination. If "society" exists only in and through a work of imagining, it is theoretically unsatisfactory, at the end of the day, to assume that this work takes place within the confines of "society."

For this reason, I shall take my cue in this respect from Niklas Luhmann's systems theory, which deals explicitly with the paradoxes and the concomitant blind spots that occur when "society" describes itself, supposedly, from within itself. According to Luhmann, social systems involve forms of self-observation and reflexive self-description that involve not only the making of boundaries between themselves and their environment – as all social systems necessarily do – but also the "re-entry" of the distinction between system and environment in the communications that make up the social system. As Luhmann says:

> self-descriptions constitute an imaginary reality. Otherwise they could not solve the logical problems of self-implication. But that doesn't preclude the acceptance of their projections in the social system, especially as there are no other ways of self-assessment. (Luhmann 2002: 203)

Luhmann thus calls "self-descriptions" those "imaginary constructions" that signify the unity of a social system (Luhmann 1997: 867). Precisely because "society" is not a neutral descriptor, the abstract notion of "social system" is helpful here. It avoids the duplication that ensues when it is assumed that *what* is imagined (society) is also that *in which* the imagination occurs. Social systems do not operate, according to Luhmann, on the basis of an objective grasp of their environment. Rather, that environment is always a system-internal construction. In other words, social systems operate through a crucial work of social imagination.

At this point, it is good to circumscribe what I mean by the concepts of immigrant integration imaginaries, social imagination, and image. For Luhmann, such imagination takes place at the level of communication. For Taylor, it involves images, stories, and legends. Here I shall often use the notion of "image," but not in the immediate, commonsensical sense of a figure given to binocular visual perception. Images can be mental, but, more importantly here, they can be ideogrammatic, narrative, or discursive as well. They entail recognizable configurations of persons, actions, signs, and objects that can travel across different carrier media. Immigrant immigration imaginaries are associative webs of meaning and of contestation in which such images figure. By "social imagination" I mean, in a more limited sense, the professionalized and routinized forms of producing images that constitute the core of, in this case, immigrant integration imaginaries. In this book, the professional context of social imagination largely concerns social science itself. Precisely because immigrant integration imaginaries are intricately connected to notions of society, they are crucially connected to the core concerns of social science. Sociology, for instance, has since its inception centered on the imagination of precisely that object which emerges from the imagination of immigrant integration: society. Both in social science and in social life at large, then, "society" has been a highly consequential form of imagination. Those considered "outside society" because they are "not well integrated" undergo real effects from this, and these effects are not the result of an objective position that is then merely named in neutral terms as "unintegrated."

Social imaginaries, then, are not "mere phantoms"; they are fundamental to the ways we orient ourselves in social life toward each other and toward "the other." But to say that "society" is an object of a social imagination is to say that it does not constitute a readily observable entity or domain "out there." Maurice Blanchot's approach to the imaginary is helpful in clarifying what the status of its objects is. For Blanchot, one of two versions of what he calls the imaginary involves a distance to the object imagined (Blanchot 1988: 341–355). It highlights its absence, but that absence is the only way in which the presence of the object announces itself. Therefore, for Blanchot, the imaginary deals with a real whose only positivity operates by means of negativity. In a quasi-organicist language typical, too, of integration imaginaries that we shall encounter at various points in this book, Blanchot accordingly likens an image to a corpse, the presence of which (its body) signifies an absence (life). An image, he concludes, is both here and nowhere. The same goes for images of "society" and "integration." In his *Autobiography*, Malcolm X remarks: "'integration' is an *image*" (Malcolm X 1964: 277). But he at the same time notes how that image does *work* for – in his case – Northern liberals in the United States: "it's a foxy Northern liberal's smoke-screen that confuses the true wants of the American black man" (Malcolm X 1964: 277). Certainly in today's European context, integration does even more: it crucially contributes to that other image, "society," at once so problematic in times of "European integration" but vehemently defended everywhere as a fundamental social milieu. To take seriously that society is an effect of a social imaginary is to depart, once and for all, with the notion of society as the collection of individuals, or norms, or institutions that exists out there. That notion is not only commonsensical, but it is also very much at the heart of social theory and social science. If the hopelessly unmodest aim of this book is to modify the ways we imagine this thing we call society, then that aim always relates both to social life and its forms of governing and to social theory and social science.

A Critique of Immigrant Integration Imaginaries

It should come as no surprise by now that I believe immigrant integration imaginaries should be treated with suspicion. They should be rendered susceptible to critique. That brings me to a key concept in the subtitle of this book. Critique is understood here in the Kantian sense of a search for conditions of possibility. In this case: what makes an imagination of a society and of immigrants in need of integration into that society plausible? How are such conceptions able to become part of the stock of everyday meaning, even though they bear no reference to directly observable phenomena, and even though they are suffused with inconsistencies and black boxes and are at least as much prescriptive concepts of government as they are descriptive concepts of social science? I use "critique" also in a sense more akin to the tradition of "critical theory," which builds upon the Kantian understanding of "critique." Critical theory has often taken certain forms of imagination as its object of analysis and critique. Primarily, of course, imagination as ideology has been critiqued. The connection with fantasy is evident here as well, for instance when Žižek writes:

"in order to effectively liberate oneself from the grip of existing social reality, one should first renounce the transgressive fantasmatic supplement that attaches us to it" (Žižek 2000: 149). Here I shall take this second sense of "critique" to refer to the mediation in the imagination of what is actual and what is possible. That means I distance myself from prevailing images of immigrant integration. In this book, it will not be a given that "societies" exist and that these societies are faced with immigrants that could, and should, somehow be "integrated" in them – just like I will not accept the by now dominant rhetoric of multiculturealism, which imagines a fictional multicultural past. And bounded notions of culture or ethnicity in which individuals share and that enable their lumping and splitting will not be my tools but my objects of analysis. As Rogier van Reekum says in his authoritative account of recent debates on Dutchness and citizenship: "all of these differences are being made, are in-the-making" (Van Reekum 2014: 26).

This critical attitude ipso facto extends to social science. If such differences are indeed not stable containers of identity but continuously in the making, then the use of identitarian, differentiating concepts in social science raises the question to the making of what social science contributes. At the most fundamental level, the issue for sociology has been succinctly stated by Charles Tilly, who said in 1984 on the idea that "society is a thing apart":

Sociology's greatest victory as an academic discipline brought its greatest defeat as an intellectual enterprise. Persuading others that a distinct realm called "society" and distinct entities called "societies" existed freed sociologists to justify their studies. Those premises justified sociology as at once essential and independent of philosophy, psychology, or biology. Although human beings created society, once in existence society had its own laws. . . . That accomplishment, nevertheless, gave sociologists and anthropologists a terrible burden: the task of delineating structures and processes of fictitious entities. (Tilly 1984: 20–21)

The approaches I build upon in particular, such as those by Luhmann and Foucault, are characterized by the fundamental starting point that social science is part of its research object, and that hence there is no objective footing or neutral starting ground to be found in an encompassing concept such as "society." A consistent explication of this starting point entails the bracketing of all statements that posit "society" as something we are all encompassed by or embedded in. That social science is part of its research object does not warrant the idea that it resides "inside" society. Rather, what it does is place limits on the very ability of social science to posit any encompassing objects. It necessitates the recognition of a "blind spot," as Luhmann would say, or the difficulty of writing an archaeology of the present," as Foucault emphasized. All imagination of "society," then, does not consist of descriptive statements of some "thing" existing beyond its expression. Rather, it consists of often prescriptive statements that are part of a continuous work of social imagination. This book is therefore not concerned with questions such as "How might immigrants best integrate into society?" Instead, it analyzes the specifics of the social imagination that expresses itself through such statements. I'm not primarily interested in debating the social science of immigrant integration on its own terms. I'm more interested in *analyzing* the social science of immigrant integration. What is more, I do so critically, because I highlight the contradictions in the social imagination in which it partakes, as well as the forms of violence it effectuates.

One might counter that such a theoretical posture is a comfortable armchair position that never engages with the messiness of empirical reality or with the real problems facing immigrants. My answer to that is fourfold. First, it is not that easy to take up this position from within privileged institutions, which is why it has hardly been adopted at all in recent years, because it is met with resistance by champions of a thing called "empirical reality" at every step of the way, often in curious entanglement with a thing called "policy relevance." Second, the analysis I offer has its very own empirical object, which consists of the ways in which the imagination of social science is bound up with larger social imaginaries, and with immigrants, nation-states, citizenship policies, and forms of racism – all of these are perfectly legitimate objects of research, also when the social science thus analyzed feels uncomfortably objectified by it. Third, there is a real political urgency in doing this kind of work. In the practice of everyday life, the social science of immigrant integration feeds into forms of government that are often racist (specifically, as I seek to show in Chapter 4, culturist). The social science of immigrant integration is hardly a neutral, descriptive science. Exposing this is not only helpful for discussions internal to social science. It is also necessary to critically scrutinize the contributions social science makes to the perpetuation of violent divisions in social

life, such as that between "society" and "nonintegrated immigrants."
And, fourth, I believe the theoretical instance I adopt here is actually
more useful in contributing to forms of emancipatory politics for
immigrants in Western Europe and possibly elsewhere. The real problems facing immigrants have to do with poverty and unemployment,
with asymmetrical access to schooling and labor markets, with asymmetrical forms of citizenship, with forms of racism, and with social
imaginaries that quasi-permanently problematize those who do not
conform to an image of "modern, secular society." None of these
problems, not even the basic ones recognized by nearly all social
scientists, such as unemployment, are aided whatsoever by *adding to
them* an imagination of integration. Immigrant integration in fact
increases the burden placed upon the shoulders of immigrants. Not
only do they have to cope with relative unemployment and a host of
other problems, but their unemployment also means they are not well
integrated and thereby reside at a certain distance from "society." My
position with respect to the practical use for emancipatory politics, or
what is called in more depoliticized terms the "policy relevance" of the
social science of immigrant integration, is that emancipatory struggles
are better served by a position that does not add a layer of symbolic
meaning to being unemployed and other problems. Such an added
layer actually does not do anything whatsoever to render these problems more effectively solvable. One can combat unemployment. But
how does one combat "lack of integration in society"? How does
recoding them in terms of "integration" make social problems more
readily solvable? What is more, how does recoding having a certain
labor market position or having a certain religion into being at a
remove from "society" help emancipatory struggles in any way?
How do power imbalances get to be "tackled" more easily or effi-
ciently by first adding insult to injury in this recoding process? How
does it in fact not aggravate things, by adding a form of imaginary
expulsion from the field in which one is always already situated in
various problematic ways that require improvement and emancipation? Especially when the ways of measuring immigrant integration
ensure that there will always be such a lack as soon as one is an
immigrant with, say, a Muslim background, it becomes clear that
measuring "immigrant integration" does not do anything at all in
helping immigrants lead a dignified life. Quite the opposite, this book
aims to show the ways in which such measurement is to be seen as

contributing to a social imagination that is intricately entangled with forms of governing immigrants and their descendants through the perpetuation of power differentials. The Immigrant integration, as this book seeks to illustrate, *sustains* rather than *softens* forms of what are conventionally called "social exclusion" – which is likewise a concept I shall not accept at face value but analyze in terms of its presuppositions and its effects.

That immigrant struggles are not helped by the prevailing ways of measuring immigrant integration but rather by forms of critical scrutiny of such measurement practices also became clear to me after having published a first book on the issue nearly ten years ago (Schinkel 2007a). Written during a boom in the attention to the issue of immigrant integration, it received a lot of attention not only by those interested in arming themselves with arguments against the predominant right-wing view on issues of immigration, citizenship, culture, religion, and immigrant integration (which mixed these all together). It was also met with what I can only describe as relief by many who felt themselves objects of such popular concerns. Immigrants as well as people whose partner had immigrated to the Netherlands often wrote me or talked to me at lectures and debates throughout the Netherlands and Belgium, saying they found in my work on these issues tools to understand their own situation and concepts to articulate what they could previously not utter. The same goes for local and national-level policy makers who had long felt uneasy about the direction of immigrant integration policies. I have no illusions about the importance of my work here, nor do I claim that it took a white Dutch scholar to finally make immigrants understand their own positions. But I am convinced that this type of work has practical uses in daily life, because it seeks to connect the imagination of immigrant integration with larger social imaginaries. It seeks to see through hegemonic forms of social imagination, not by exposing the univocally real, but by highlighting the fact that social imagination is never univocal, that it is malleable, and can be changed and appropriated. This book is dedicated to the critical work required to foster such change and such forms of appropriation of the prevailing forms of social imagination. In doing so, it stands in direct and deliberate contrast to the "policy-relevant" forms of social science that, as mere forms of state thought without a genuine interest in analyzing social life and its modes of imagination, merely perpetuate the inequalities of the status quo.

I am therefore not interested in the state of "immigrant integration," since I doubt the neutrality of the meaning of this, but I am interested in the particulars of the political imagination of immigrant integration and the imagination of society it renders possible. My focus is on the features of such imagination, on its effects, on the realities it renders plausible, and on the alternatives it blots out.

What Happened to the Netherlands?

To get a better handle on the stakes in immigrant integration imaginaries, I propose to first zoom in on the Netherlands, which I take to be, with many others, an exemplary case of the problematization of immigrant integration in Western Europe. To be clear, my focus in this brief section is on the very recent history of the problematization of immigrant integration as it has been and is productive in (re)articulating dominant conceptions of "society." I am specifically concerned in this book with the first decade of the twenty-first century, as it constitutes the threshold of the present. As will become apparent in coming chapters, there are important parallels with Dutch colonial history, especially in what was formerly called the Dutch East Indies. So when I ask here, by way of introducing the setting, what happened to the Netherlands, that qualification of the time frame covered is important to bear in mind. While immigrant integration discourse occurs in varying shapes throughout Western Europe, the Dutch case has recently been considered of particular interest due to its perceived shift, over the last few decades, from a tolerant to a rigorously assimilationist country, which in some respects has given it the "forerunner" role many Dutch imagined it to have when it came to its "progressiveness" in earlier decades. Again, it is important to remember the limited historical reach of such ideas, since they blot out not only the Dutch colonial history but also the role the country played in the international slave trade (Blackburn 1997; Hondius 2011). In the more recent debates, the Dutch case is in a sense extreme because of its fierce debates, including its early critique of multiculturalism, its highly bureaucratized social scientific measurement of immigrant integration, and its heavy focus on national identity and culture in recent policies and formulations of citizenship. It offers a prime case of a self-perceived bounded unit fearing loss of boundedness and cohesion. And, although it is in certain aspects an extreme case, it is also an exemplary case in that it is "extreme" only on dimensions present in most other Western European countries. This is the case, for instance, with respect to the problematization of "culture" and of "Islam," and more specifically it concerns notions of secularity and sexuality in which "modernity" is seen as exemplified by acceptance of homosexuality. This is a development that in the Netherlands, as Judith Butler has said, "has been brewing for some time" (Butler 2010: 106). From another American source, similar notions of Dutch immigrant integration avant-gardism can be heard. A cable by the U.S. embassy in The Hague, accessible through Wikileaks, that provides general thoughts on the Dutch and on the U.S.–Netherlands relationship states:

A new, but potentially serious factor in Dutch domestic politics is its large, poorly integrated Muslim population, currently numbering just under 1 million, or 5.8 percent of the population. ... While the problems of Dutch integration captured international headlines following the van Gogh murder, the Dutch believe they have an early start on the rest of Europe in seeking creative ways to address these concerns. Their strong interest in sharing and soliciting ideas has opened up opportunities for Embassy and USG outreach and consultations throughout Dutch society, providing insights into a growing problem throughout Europe. We expect our experiences here will provide good indications of broader European trends.[1]

Whether or not the Dutch are actually "ahead" in addressing such "concerns" is not of concern here. What is relevant is rather that the underlying logic of what happens in the Netherlands serves as a prism for a wider Western European situation (in this respect I concur with the departing U.S. ambassador quoted here). First, let me give a rough sketch of "what happened to the Dutch."

The route that the Netherlands has taken to a public sphere dominated by such a discourse is surprisingly short. In the 1990s the Dutch public image of what is called, since 1989, "allochthons," and specifically "non-Western allochthons," changed drastically, even though, it is important to say, this does not mean that significant changes in policies or attitudes necessarily ensued. The year 1989 is a symbolic one, of course, and it could be taken here as a marker for an inward shift in public discourse. Simplifying matters greatly, one interpretation of an increased public scrutiny of immigrants and their integration is

[1] Wikileaks Reference ID 05THEHAGUE2309.

that with the disappearance of an enemy without (communism), the search for enemies within gained strength. At least as likely, though, are demographic and structural factors. Certain groups of what used to be known, in the decades after World War II, as "guest workers" appeared to stay during the 1970s and the 1980s, and at the same time the oil crises and an ongoing deindustrialization led to increasing unemployment and welfare dependency among migrants and their children. Also, during the 1970s, postcolonial migrants from Surinam arrived in relatively large numbers up to the independence of Surinam in November 1975, and beyond that until 1980. Similar to the way Germany was late to realize it was an *Einwanderungsland* ("immigration country") (this was only officially acknowledged by Angela Merkel in 2015), it became clear during the 1980s that the Netherlands was an "immigration country." Initially, policies focused on socioeconomic mobility, but around the beginning of the 1990s they gradually became critiqued as naively "multicultural," and the idea was that there were many problems with the allochthon population that this multiculturalism suppressed out of left-wing political correctness. This political correctness was replaced by a multiculturealism that boasted (and still does) the courage to "call things by their real name." Multiculturealism in a very real sense invented a "multiculturalism" that, as will be more elaborately shown in Chapter 4, never existed. In fact, "multiculturalism" first becomes a current concept in public discussions of immigrant integration *after* its supposedly all-embracing reign in policy and in the public sphere. The multiculturealism that defines itself in terms of a realist awakening vis-à-vis multiculturalism in a sense secures its discursive legitimacy by inventing a history with which it claims to break. Whereas the explicit public critiques of "multiculturalism" in Germany, the United Kingdom, and to some extent also in France are more recent, in the Netherlands "multiculturalism" became a crucial discursive figure in the 1990s and in the early years of this century. This took effect to such an extent that, today, one will hear most anyone speaking about immigrant integration first securing a speech position by distancing oneself from the former multiculturalism that was blind to the existing problems. Multiculturealism was most influentially explicated (and instituted) in a newspaper essay by journalist Paul Scheffer. His essay, entitled "The Multicultural Drama" (2000), contains all the characteristics of multiculturealism: a critique of a politically correct ignorance of problems and a call for cultural adjustment and discussion of cultural incompatibilities, specifically between "Islam" and "the West" (Scheffer 2000). Such issues have gradually become intertwined with policy practices targeting specific "ethnic groups," focused, for instance, on crime among "Moroccan" and "Antillean" youth.[2] Restrictions on immigration were implemented, such as in terms of income demands when marrying someone from outside the country. Specific urban neighborhoods, starting in Rotterdam, implemented similar income demands (120 percent of the official minimum) to bar immigrants. Initially, as the European Committee on Racism and Inequality (ECRI) recognized in its 2008 report, what later became known as the "Rotterdam Law" was explicitly intended to bar non-Western allochthons (ECRI 2008). When this proved legally untenable, the measure shifted to an income demand, which constituted a form of indirect discrimination that continues today. Meanwhile, citizenship courses incorporated much more strongly cultural demands. A "thick" identification with the nation became more explicit during the years 2000. This resulted in the drafting of a "Historical Canon" and the institution of a Dutch "national Historical Museum." Both were called for in the 2007 Cabinet policy paper on immigrant integration. The 2011 Cabinet paper *Integration, Bond, Citizenship*, though proclaiming "a new perspective," offers a rehash of many of the themes present in the debate since the late 1980s and early 1990s. Again, it is stated that the "Cabinet explicitly distances itself from the relativism enshrined in the concept of multiculturalism. ... Integration concerns integration into Dutch society" (Dutch Cabinet 2011: 5).

A *burqa* bill, proposed by right-wing populist Geert Wilders, was passed by Parliament in 2005 (before the Belgian ban in April 2010 and the French ban in September 2010, effective in April 2011). It proposed banning use of the *burqa* in public life, but legal obstacles hindered its effectuation up to 2016, when a ban on face-covering clothing in public space and institutions was passed. Meanwhile, Wilders had also proposed a tax on the wearing of the *hijab* (as he said, this would be a tax comparable to an environmental tax: the polluter pays, where in this case, public space would be

---

[2] Some examples are the "Integral Approach Antilleans" in Rotterdam (as of 2005) and the "Moroccans Letter" by the Dutch Cabinet (2008). Chapter 4 provides a more thorough discussion of policy changes in this field.

visually "polluted" by the *hijab*) or a ban on the wearing of coats with hoods that would, supposedly, make Moroccan delinquents invisible to surveillance cameras when hiding under their hoods. When less populist parties respond by saying that debate should focus on actions, not on clothing, they cannot escape the ratification of the fact that the groups targeted in such discussions are indeed "groups" that "cause problems." Moreover, all too often, a critique of extreme and populist politicians serves to hide the fact that the entire political spectrum has shifted: the extreme right politician Hans Janmaat was convicted for enunciations in the 1980s that have in the meantime become conventional for Cabinet members – a fact that gives all the more plausibility to multiculturalism's claim to break with political correctness. A 2008 Cabinet letter to Parliament, informally entitled the "Moroccans Letter" (*Marokkanenbrief*), for instance, emphasized the problems of crime relating to young Moroccan boys. It related these problems to the boys' traditional and authoritarian upbringing, only to emphasize a few lines further that often these boys' fathers were hardly at home and sometimes parents were altogether lacking. And then there are some issues that continue to be seriously debated by conventional political parties. One is the issue of forced abortions for Antillean single mothers. As one former minister and member of the Dutch liberal party[3] (Jorritsma, VVD) said: "forced abortions are a bridge too far, but we can talk about forced sterilization."

In 2004, Theo van Gogh, a Dutch filmmaker and public figure who frequently spoke in harsh terms about "Muslims," "Moroccans," and their integration in Dutch society, was murdered by a young man of Dutch-Moroccan background. When in the days following his murder, which soon came to be regarded as an act of "terrorism," Minister Rita Verdonk of Immigration and Integration Affairs was asked whether Van Gogh's murderer was not, by all common standards, well integrated (educated, did volunteer work, and with no criminal record), her reply was "Well, apparently not!" This response may serve as a prism for the anxiety surrounding immigrant integration.

---

[3] The VVD, or People's Party for Freedom and Democracy, is "liberal" (at least in theory) in the sense of John Stuart Mill's liberalism. It promotes small government and free markets, takes libertarian views on certain issues, such as abortion and euthanasia, but is at the same time conservative and right-wing when issues of immigrant integration are concerned. It is traditionally one of the main players in Dutch politics, often being part of ruling coalitions.

The translation of a religiously or possibly politically motivated murder into "terrorism" signifies the extent to which an act is set apart when committed by a Muslim. When in 2002, a Dutch animal rights activist shot Pim Fortuyn, the maverick populist politician, the act was mostly seen as a murder committed by an individual. In the case of Van Gogh, however, the Dutch "Moroccan community" was called upon to distance itself from the act. The very idea of having to distance oneself from a crime, of course, implies an initial proximity to and affinity with it. But what is perhaps more striking is the minister's response: "apparently not!" This illustrates one of the prime functions of the concept of "integration." Integration cleanses the domain of "society" from unwanted elements. The murderer of Theo van Gogh, so this reasoning goes, was *apparently* well integrated, until it became clear that he wasn't after all, and that he hadn't been all along. In other words, the moment one commits a crime it becomes clear that one was all this time not really a member of society. As a nonintegrated individual, one was in fact in need of "integration into society." This amounts to a purified image of society. Society is a Durkheimian domain of moral purity, which Durkheim called the "ideal society." In other words, such a society has no problems. It knows no crime, no poverty or unemployment, and so on. For as soon as such problems appear, they are attributed to individuals deemed "not integrated." Such individuals are thereby readily recognizable as not (yet) members of society.

The minister's statement is not an isolated case. It is one example that exposes the logic of contemporary immigrant integration imaginaries. Migrants are pitted against a society that is conceived as unscathed yet threatened. Despite immigration, society has remained exactly the same. So when migration has led to the existence of one million Muslims in the Netherlands, the idea is that society hasn't changed a bit. Rather, there are now one million people "at a certain distance from society." When I say "the idea is," then that goes to mean that this is the common way of speaking of and of imagining immigrant integration. Both the dominant political discourse and the social scientific measurement imply that "Dutch society" remains unchanged, and that migration brings people onto the nation's territory but not into "society." It is no wonder, then, that the Netherlands has been given widespread attention, both as an example for other countries' policies and as a site of academic research. Not only is the Dutch renationalizing tendency an example of the constitution of "glocality" (Lechner 2007a, 2007b), it also provides a prism of larger European debates concerning immigration and "Islam" (Buruma 2006; Geschiere 2009) or of the possible workings of "cultural trauma" (Eyerman 2008). Debates on "Britishness" and French discussions of republican values, as well as policy changes in the definitions and requirements of citizenship in various Western European countries, are but a few examples of similar phenomena. Throughout Western Europe, a shift toward a discourse of assimilation in policy, politics, and public debate has been noted to have taken place in the 1990s (Brubaker 2001).

The Netherlands thus provides a good example of the severity of this shift, which has itself been a continuous reflexive aspect of integration imaginaries. It is often taken as the prototypical case of a Western European country formerly "multiculturalist" but now increasingly assimilationist. This change took effect to such an extent that, today, most anyone speaking about immigrant integration first secures a legitimate speech position by distancing him- or herself from the former multiculturalism that supposedly turned a blind eye to the existing problems. What is more, the Netherlands is considered an early example of the assimilationist turn. *The New York Times* went so far as to say that "the sometimes violent European backlash against Islam and its challenge to national values can be said to have started here" (Erlanger 2011: A6). That does not mean the multiculturealists have a point. Rather, I argue that "multiculturalism" is, paradoxically, a *performative effect of its denouncements*. It served as a discursive technique that opened up the space for an openly assimilationist vocabulary, which is not at all to say that assimilationism did not underpin integration policies before that time. In part, given the exemplarity of the shift toward multiculturealism, and in part given its role in intellectual debate on "multiculturalism" both on the left and on the right (from Judith Butler and Tariq Modood to Francis Fukuyama and Christopher Caldwell), the Netherlands offers what Merton called a "strategic research site" for an analysis of the ways in which images of bounded national societies emerge in integration discourses.

And yet all of this needs further qualification. While it is true that the Netherlands is a good case to study the severity of the shift toward assimilationism, this is mostly the case because the Netherlands has been *imagined* to have undergone such a severe shift. However, ideas of decisive shifts in attitudes toward non-natives need to be met with suspicion. "What happened to the Netherlands?" is a question often asked nowadays, and it reproduces the imagination of a once tolerant society that has grown less so. But for the same reason "multicultural-ism" never was a policy reality in the Netherlands, it is questionable whether a decisive shift has been made. The Dutch "integration policy" of the 1980s was, as I will argue, in fact an assimilationism from the start. So if a shift to the right has occurred in the last two decades, it is not a shift toward assimilationism per se. In fact, the whole issue of whether or not the Dutch – or anyone else, for that matter – have become more or less "tolerant" is not really relevant for my purposes here. It is a problematic question anyhow, informed by a liberalism that assumes societies to exist on the basis of shared values, consensus, and toleration. And so I choose not to expand on the "empirical" answer to the question what has happened to the (tolerant) Netherlands; I remain agnostic about this, or rather I think the question is misplaced in the first place. Rather, the imagination of a severe shift is what makes the Netherlands a key case here. That imagination, rather than current "tolerance scores" gleaned from surveys and polls, is what is closely tied to a work of configuring "society" as a social imaginary.

The Argument: Culture, Modernity, and Citizenship as Programs of Society in Integration Imaginaries

My question is how we can see the imagination of society in what can legitimately be said in integration discourses, and in what is predomin-antly seen as illegitimate speech, for instance, as "multiculturalist" or as "old politics." I take "integration discourse" to comprise a discourse with a specific "order" and with concomitant tropes and forms of censorship. Next to, for instance, the crafting of actual images of immi-grant integration, such as graphs and tables (Boersma and Schinkel 2015), integration imaginaries depend strongly on what is usually called discourse. When I refer to discourse, I mean it in the Foucaultian sense of an order of speaking (Foucault 1971), which therefore always extends beyond "mere text" toward a varieties of practices and, ultimately, toward the settlement of the boundaries of what is, at any given moment, imaginable. I do not subscribe to the idea that there were several competing discourses when their competition is sought, for instance, in political terms (left/right) or, as Uitermark (2010) has done, in terms of policy approaches (culturalist/pragmatist). When I refer to a "dominant discourse" I mean to describe the possibilities and limits of the entire realm of discursive imagination. Rather than concluding that two sides of a disagreement, for instance, regarding the degree to which immigrant integration demands should be assimilationist, constitute competing discourses, I conclude that such disagreement constitutes a legitimate conflict within the same order of speech. Discourse does not refer to discursive positions, but to the order of various, oftentimes competing, positions. And it pertains as much to what is said as to what cannot be said. When new disagreements emerge, the entire space of discursive imagination has morphed. Today, for instance, Dutch politicians can openly speak about the forced sterilization of Antillean women as a measure to prevent Antillean youth crime. Many might vehemently critique the option, but they are nonetheless drawn into a discursive practice in which the issue is a real, and legitimate, possibility. That possibility is indicative of a shift in discursive parameters and rules of censorship. The culturist imagination that rose to dominance in the early 1990s persists today, and its development will be traced in more detail in Chapter 4.

What I call discourse is thus a field of social imagination in which the limits of the legitimately imaginable are defined and negotiated. For this reason, I will often alternate between "integration discourse" and "integration imaginary." Discourse, in its Foucaultian sense, is indeed much more than text, as it structures the sayable and the seeable. That is, it circumscribes the realm of social imagination, and it constitutes a set of practices in which social imagination is most visibly actualized. Discourse is regulated through rules of inclusion (of legitimate topics and opinions) and exclusion (censorship and readymade attribution and stereotyping of illegitimate topics and opinions). My focus on "discourse" runs into the to some extent justifiable critique that I leave out of consideration the interactional practice of everyday life. Nor do I present an analysis on the basis of one of the existing discourse methodologies. But that is because my interest lies in the more Foucaultian sense of discourse as a collection of symbols and speech rules that are immanent to certain very specific practices of cultural production. I focus on a few sites of such production. Since my interest is in the relation between social science and such processes of production, social theory and the social science of integration are my first site of investigation. Then I discuss the way certain concepts of integration and society are present in policy and in public debate about the role of religion in the public sphere. My reason for thus focusing on certain specific sites of the production of the social imaginary is precisely that it is this imaginary. I wish to take one step back behind the assumption that "society" is a social assemblage of some sort in order to investigate the workings of various sites of production of that assumption. In so doing, the social imaginary, that is, a set of symbols, as well as the rules of their expression that are immanent to their production and functioning, necessarily have to be the starting point. If we, as I propose we do for the moment, suspend the belief in the idea that "society" designates a bounded set of people and practices, then what remains is precisely what will be the starting point here: the *idea* of "society." In a sense, then, I use "discourse" and "imaginary" in a way very similar to the way Niklas Luhmann speaks of a "semantics." By this he means a repertoire of meaningful and practically relevant forms (and by "forms" he means distinctions that enable observation) that has historically evolved in close relation to sociostructural changes (Luhmann 1997: 200).

The idea that there is a dominant integration discourse does not mean that there are no speech positions outside that discourse or that it doesn't encounter resistance. Yet precisely the fact that it does affirms its dominant status. Moreover, the dominant discourse regulates the topics and the issues that are deemed legitimate to disagree about in the public sphere. This explains the dominance of issues related to *culture* and *ethnicity* (both as causal factors giving rise to "cultural incompatibilities"), issues of *religion* or *secularism* and *modernity* and the proper definition of *citizenship* (the place of Islam in the public sphere, the compatibility of "Islam" with liberal democracy), issues of *gender* and *sexuality* (the veil or headscarf, female subordination, forced marriages, female circumcision, sexual practices, the raising of children), issues of *nationality* (what constitutes national identity, who qualifies for citizenship and when, what is the Dutch historical and cultural canon), and, last, issues of *security* (crime, nuisance, terrorism).

I am thus primarily interested in integration discourse as a prism of the social imagination of society. In other words, the question is: while being a *product of* social life, what does the concept of society *enable* or *produce* in social life? As becomes apparent in contemporary discussions of citizenship (Chapter 6), when seen from the perspective of a sociology of the state (or, broader yet, in the context of contemporary governmentality) "society" operates as a *medium of governing*. It is the performative effect of the substantivist claim that "society" is a pregiven entity. The unfolding of social inside/outside articulations in the medium of "society" takes place in everyday practices of engaging the "other" as well as in mass-media, political, and social scientific constructions thereof. Yet in an age of mass migration and of diasporic public spheres, such claims are continually contested. I thus aim to illustrate the functioning of *the medium of society*, which is coded in terms of inside/outside. The imagination of "society" and its assumed "outside" are made possible by the emergence of topics related to discursive repertoires I call *programs*. Who does and does not belong to "society" is discursively worked out in various programs relating to immigrant integration, the most significant of which are culture, modernity, secularity, sexuality, and citizenship.

These programs find discursive expression in the form of a *diagrammar* that allows for the separation of society's inside and outside by means of an asymmetric reference to integration, ethnicity and faulty citizenship. The diagrammar of immigrant integration is a way of sorting out, of classifying those who belong and those who do not. As the word "diagrammar" indicates, it is a *grammar of separation*: it separates "good" and "faulty" forms of culture and citizenship, and acceptable and nonacceptable practices of secularity. Most chapters in this book are concerned with fleshing out the diagrammar of integration. They seek to unravel the often implicit logics that separate members of "society" from those portrayed as no quite belonging, as remaining "outside." My focus in the following chapters is threefold. After discussing the theoretical and historical roots of integration imaginaries, I discuss the contexts of the social science of integration, of integration and citizenship policy, and of public and political debate concerning, for instance, the role of religion in the public sphere.

Culture, ethnicity, secularism, modernity, citizenship, gender and sexuality, the nation and security – all can be regarded as specific "vehicles" of society, and to some of them separate chapters are devoted. For it is through the thematization of these issues that the observation of "society" is constituted. These themes therefore require careful consideration in this book. They embody the connection between integration discourse and the social imagination of society. Loosely drawing upon Niklas Luhmann's work on systemic semantics,

I shall regard them as *programs* that serve to identify both sides of an inside society/outside society code. In the context of immigrant integration, programs selectively link *issues* (e.g., crime, the oppression of women, school dropouts, residential segregation) to larger *themes* (e.g., culture, ethnicity, religion, citizenship) using "immigrant integration" as their connector. Programs are thus named here after the themes that are mobilized in the articulation of specific issues. For there to be a "program" in this sense means that repeated connections between issues and themes are brought about, and that their link is provided by "immigrant integration." The discursive diagrammar of integration facilitates the attribution of speech, practice, and membership to either side of the inside/outside binary. The diagrammar of integration discourse can be regarded as the repertoire of discursive techniques through which integration is legitimately imagined. It is the "logic" of discourse that enables discursive attributions along an inside/outside scale in discussions of immigrant integration. Thus, religion can be regarded as one program that enables the discursively mediated imagination of "society," but it does so through a diagrammar that construes it as "dogmatic," "fundamentalist," or perhaps "traditional" only in the case of certain "ethnic groups." These programs are intricately woven together. Talk of "culture" soon becomes talk of "religion," which may be opposed to "modernity" and construed as conflicting with sexual freedoms. The programs of culture, secularism, ethnicity, sexuality, security, and the nation in a sense provide the tapestry on which lines of discourse are woven and within which practices, for instance, in the realm of policy, can be actualized. But they often appear individually, for instance, when Christian politicians critique culture but not religion, or religion but not sexuality and emancipation. On the other hand, combinations may occur that facilitate unexpected coalitions, for instance, when second-wave feminists fight alongside conservative politicians to critique the oppressive character of "Islam." The diagrammar of integration discourse then facilitates, in all these cases, the attribution of practice and speech to either the "inside" of "society" or to its "outside."

The discursive reworking of various issues and themes is possible on the basis of existing immigrant integration imaginaries, with their opposition between "society" and its "outside." But it is at the same time the everyday form in which such imaginaries are reaffirmed. All the diagrammatic sorting that takes place occurs on the basis of "society" as a medium of separating inside from outside. But that discursive reworking of issues and themes (programs) also reaffirms and reestablishes the prevailing realities that are imaginable. As noted above, Castoriadis and Taylor still seem to assume, in a rather circular way, that the imagination of society occurs within society. That circularity is reminiscent of all the classical theoretical circles in which "man" and "society" were squared, and in which, oftentimes, "the individual is defined by society" and "society" simultaneously "comprises individuals." My attempt is to relocate that circularity, and in fact to "flatten" it, and to point at the social imagination of society as an "input" of integration discourse that is, at the same time, reaffirmed as a "product" of such discourse. Another way to say that is to say that imagination and discourse are immanent to each other. Integration discourse is one site at which social imaginaries gain substance, or are actualized, and imaginaries of society vis-à-vis its outside remain active by being discursively attached to a variety of issues (e.g., headscarves, language tests, citizenship requirements) and themes (e.g., culture, ethnicity, citizenship, national belonging). Imaginaries, as Taylor says, form "backgrounds," but the backgrounds need to be regularly activated, to be mobilized in the "foreground," in order to retain their potency in defining the limits and the affordances of what it means to be inside or outside of a thing called society. Next to, for instance, the production of visual images, discourse is one practice in which imaginaries become mobilized, if one will, materialized. In this book, my focus is restricted to this discursive mobilization and reaffirmation of integration imaginaries and their imagination of "society." The strength of integration imaginaries lies in their current power to draw together vastly differing discursive objects, ranging from culture to the economy, and to do so in different national contexts where, despite discursive differences and policy differences, certain fundamental tenets of imagining immigrant integration are nonetheless shared, as is their shared effect of rendering the very idea of a "national society" sayable and seeable. That is the main reason for taking "immigrant integration" as a lens to study the imagination of society.

Ethnicity and Culture

Ethnicity is conceived in both a narrow and an essentializing way in integration discourse. It is roughly equaled to one's nationality of birth, or the nationality of a parent. As analyzed in Chapter 3, definitions of ethnicity are put forward by state-led research institutes. Yet as Arjun Appadurai has noted, global commerce and media have blurred the image of ethnicity as tied to certain locales. As he says, ethnicity "has now become a global force, forever slipping in and through the cracks between states and borders" (Appadurai 1996: 41). I argue that that is precisely why today we witness efforts by the state to control ethnicity. In a sense, ethnicity becomes part of a logic of government. I shall in this book outline the contours of a governing through integration, which at the same time comes down to a *governing through society*, since "society" is always the mirror image of that which is to be integrated. By rendering its obverse observable, "society" becomes an identifiable object, as well as an object one can identify with. State-initiated attributions of ethnicity play an important role here. They are part of what can be called a *domestication of difference*. This entails both the taming of difference defined as potentially subversive and the incorporation of such tamed differences into the home of the nation. Difference, once domesticated, becomes "diversity," a marketable value ridden of possible antagonistic elements. That is, it is difference formatted to a certain version of liberalism – a liberalism that never really encounters practices and opinions that test its limits and push the liberal paradox of tolerance. Precisely because of the liberal exclusion of everything that might question its "neutrality," it is no exaggeration to say, as Wendy Brown has remarked, that liberalism engages in a "forthright engagement with fundamentalism" (Brown 2006a: 24). While proponents of "Dutch" liberalism advocate an individualized treatment of citizens inspired by that liberalism, things are different where Muslims are concerned. Then it is "ethnic communities" or "a religious community" that is addressed, as when the Moroccan community is asked to distance itself from the murder of Van Gogh. Or in general, one is an individual that bears responsibility for one's integration, yet one also shares a collective responsibility for faulty integration due to one's "culture."

The concept of *culture* thus figures in important ways in integration imaginaries. This is all the more relevant here, since "societies" have often, for instance, in the Durkheimian-Parsonian tradition, been characterized in terms of "cultures." Conceived in essentialist terms, a distinction is made in matters of integration between "the dominant culture" (as, for instance, Dutch "Judeo-Christian-humanist culture"

or the French "culture of *laïcité*") and "foreign cultures." The opposition between "culture" and "cultures" finds discursive expression in
the way culture is evaluated. Culture determines behavior, but only in
the case of "non-Western cultures." Especially since the early 1990s,
culture has appeared in integration discourse. In a sense not only has
this meant a shift in focus from economic issues to cultural issues, but it
has also meant a depoliticization of discourse. Paradoxically, just at
the time when "integration" became a hotly debated political issue,
integration discourse depoliticizes that debate both by refusing to take
socioeconomic relations into account and by individualizing *and* cul-
turalizing integration issues. This puts those subject to demands of
"integration" in a paradoxical position. Integration is first of all individualized. That means it is not the integration of society that is
explicitly at stake, but the integration of a specific individual. Thereby,
responsibility for the issue of integration is attributed to the individuals
in need of integration. But in a next step, if that individual is deemed
not properly or fully integrated, that responsibility is *de-individualized*,
since one's "ethnicity" or one's "culture" is seen as the most important
causal factor leading to faulty integration. This combination of individualization and deindividualization is one element of the diagrammar of integration discourse, the substance of which will be discussed
extensively in Chapter 3.

   In the case of "the dominant culture," one can witness a further
transformation of "culture" into "Culture." This Culture is not simply
"a" culture, but "the" culture of Enlightenment. That means it determines behavior without constricting the freedom of the individual.
That is to say, it determines through freedom, as the will does in the
Kantian analysis of practical reason. This determination through freedom of the one Culture (that can, by appeal to reason, legitimately
claim universality yet at the same time recognizes its "national" character) stands in stark contrast to the unfree determination by particularist cultures in the plural. That is how liberal democracies can
problematize various practices in depoliticized ways under the heading
of culture without having to admit that liberal democracy is, itself,
culturally constituted. "Culture" is thus explicitly conceived as an
organic whole that is faced with various external cultures. But, paradoxically, it is conceived as a whole that is organic in precisely such a
way as to be liberal and "individualist," that is, as not preoccupied
with organic closure and wholeness in either a "pre-modern" or a

totalitarian way. In fact, the organic wholeness of the society characterized by such a "Culture" is the ultimate Durkheimian dream of
organic solidarity – its wholeness is preserved by the performance of
responsible liberal citizenship by its individual members. The ways in
which the program of culture is actualized in integration discourse are
analyzed in Chapter 4, where the concept of *culturism* is introduced to
make sense of a discourse of alterity that has racism at its core.

Sexuality, Secularism, and Citizenship

In conceptions of culture and in the issues mediated by the invocation
of culture lies a connection with the program of *modernity*. What is
"British," "French," "Danish," or "Dutch," and hence what the
nationally bounded substance is that the immigrant is to be integrated
into, is at the same time "Western" and defined by its being "modern."
The process of integration then amounts to a process of becoming
modern. When such modernity is invoked, the assumption is often that
"modernity" exists in one form only that is shared by Western societies, although these are said to differ in that they, such as Germany or
the United Kingdom, "still" have an arrangement in which religion and
politics are not completely separated, as they are presupposed to be in,
for instance, the United States or France. In the case of the Netherlands, one can similarly hear that modernity is incomplete because
there is still the possibility of founding a state-subsidized school on
religious grounds. For the same reason, a successful political campaign
was launched in 2013 to scratch the prohibition of blasphemy from
Dutch criminal law. This occurred in 2014, when Parliament also
asked the government to investigate whether religions needed separate
protection in some other way, opponents feared that this might lead to
a regression back into what was conceived as a less complete stage of
modernity. So while there are differences in degree, "modernity" is
treated as a shared heritage of Western societies, and this is why it can
serve as a measure by which to judge others (in the case of immigrant
integration but also where problems of "Third World development"
are concerned).

"Modernity" is a program that can be actualized in various ways.
Chapter 3, for instance, illustrates how migrants' "modernity" is
measured in social science. Another way in which "modernity" functions is in connection to the program of *religion* and/or *secularism*,

dealt with in Chapter 5. The notion of the secular has particular
relevance here. For "religion" is attributed to the "nonintegrated"
whereas "society" is characterized by "secularism." Yet as Talal Asad
(2003) has convincingly argued, there is nothing particularly nonreli-
gious about "secularism." Rather, it is a particular form in which
liberalism effectuates a transcendent mediation of collective imagination. It operates, according to Asad, through the political medium of
citizenship. Here I shall take religion (and, therefore, secularism) and
citizenship to be programs that allow the processing of topics on the
basis of which clear-cut divisions between "society" and the "nonintegrated" can play out. The diagrammar of integration discourse in a
sense allows for the coagulation of "society" and its binary opposite on
the surface of discursive programs such as "modernity." That is why
"modernity" is not to be treated as a description, that is, as an existing
state of affairs, but as something that is, as Asad says, "aimed at"
(Asad 2003: 13). It is not a clear-cut object in itself, but in a sense a
projection, a "project," as modernity indeed explicitly is for various
academics. I take that to mean that it functions as a program that
facilitates the counterfactual projection of "society" through the discursive thematization of various issues in light of this program. This
program furthermore claims to be of descriptive import, whereas it is
in fact much more prescriptive, "aiming at," in Asad's words. The
secular, as Craig Calhoun and colleagues have argued, is more than
simply the "absence of religion"; it needs to be understood as a
presence (Calhoun, Juergensmeyer, and VanAntwerpen 2009). While
there are many ways to understand the meaning of concepts such as
"secularism" and "religion," it is here understood in the way it functions in the construction of society. This is an admittedly restricted
view of such phenomena, but one that picks up on one important way
in which these function. From this perspective, secularism operates
in the same plane as religion, as a program that allows for the attribution of inside/outside values through topics debated with a view
to the secular and the religious. Secularism is part of a larger self-
problematization of "society." It can be regarded as part of the larger
program of modernity. Increasingly, modernity is mobilized as what
"non-Western immigrants" really lack. It is connected both to secularism and sexuality, thus giving rise to what Joan Wallace Scott (2009)
has called *sexular modernity*. The program of modernity is thus a more

encompassing program, comprising thematizations both of secularism and of sexuality.

Chapter 6 deals with the program of citizenship. Citizenship has been of renewed interest for a few decades now, and "globalization," in various guises, has no doubt been the main reason for reconsidering this mechanism of belonging developed by modern nation-states. That development had rudimentary beginnings after the Peace of Westphalia in 1648, but its completion took at least three more centuries. Yet, as T. H. Marshall (1963) has influentially argued, depending on the dimensions one cares to distinguish in citizenship, it was incomplete even in the second half of the twentieth century. Reconsiderations of the nation-state's main mechanism of in- and exclusion have been spurred by the fact that mass migration has led to more fluid boundaries of nation-states. Much of the homogeneity that was at least assumed present in Western nation-states has been problematized in the last few decades. The cultural dimension of citizenship has gained renewed attention, and, partly in the face of intermediate forms of citizenship such as "denizenship" (Hammar 1990), there have been debates about the expanding or reformulation of citizenship, for instance, in the form of "multicultural citizenship," "transnational citizenship," or "cosmopolitan citizenship" (Bauböck 1994; Soysal 1994; Kymlicka 1995; Habermas 1996; Dower 2000; Balibar 2004; Benhabib 2004; Modood et al. 2006; Van Houdt 2014). With respect to Europe, "European citizenship" is much debated as well (Delanty 2007). Nonetheless, recent redefinitions of citizenship by Western European states are rather more indicative of what Saskia Sassen has called renationalizing moves than of a denationalizing process (Sassen 2006: 2). Chapter 6 therefore deals with the recent transformations of citizenship in citizenship policies. For one, citizenship has appeared in the second half of the 1990s as synonymous to "integration." That means discourse on citizenship is implied in all the workings of integration discourse. This has given rise to a *moralization of citizenship*. On the basis of a differentiation between *formal citizenship* and *moral citizenship*, this chapter illustrates the relative weight given today to the latter. For the most part, this involves a discourse of moralization under the heading of "active" or "responsible citizenship" – an ideal of citizenship that is mainly problematized in the case of immigrants and their offspring. Citizenship, then, has appeared as the program most immediately linked to the state through which a differentiation between "society" and its "outside" is reproduced. I propose we reconsider contemporary debates on the status of citizenship through this lens: like many debates about culture and secularity, it acts as a way of fixating the boundaries of various national societies that are increasingly uncertain of the whereabouts of these boundaries.

Chapter 7, which concludes, discusses the implications of this analysis for social theory and for the public role of social science. It positions social science in the context of an EU-wide neonationalism and pleads for bringing internal social scientific conflict into the open so as to mobilize and empower a variety of alternative publics that do not wish to understand themselves using prevailing integration imaginaries. A public social science is able to provide a variety of publics with the materials to recognize the contingency of their own position. The public role of social science can and should be more than the moral monitoring that integration measurement amounts to, and it is in the interest of social science itself to invent its own public uses anew.

2 | Imagining Society: Social Theory and/as Social Imagination

Social Science and the Organicist Imagination

When people decry immigrant integration in daily contexts, when politicians do so, when journalists report on the integration of immigrants in Western European nation-states, or when social scientists measure immigrant integration, they use a concept they did not invent. In fact, "integration" is an old concept that is part of a longstanding type of imagination. In this imagination, the image of the body takes center stage. The name by which this type of imagination is usually known is *organicism*. Its roots stretch back to Greek, Chinese, and Indian axial age thinking, and the history of its reception (its *Wirkungsgeschichte*) is equally long and pervasive. The roots of much of social science, certainly of sociology, lie in a nineteenth-century boom in organicist thought. My claim is, however, that we have still not entirely moved out of the organicist imagination. The concepts we inherit from it, such as "society" and "integration," have certainly changed, but my claim is that their ambience remains. Charles Taylor offers a typical account of organicism by locating it in premodern times and commenting that "the modern idealization of order departs radically" from it (Taylor 2004: 12). But from what? From the idea that, as Taylor summarizes some key aspects of organicism, "the organism seems the paradigm locus of forms at work, striving to heal its wounds and cure its maladies. At the same time, the arrangement of functions that it exhibits is not simply contingent; it is 'normal' and right. That the feet are below the head is how it should be" (Taylor 2004: 12). To say, on the basis of this account, that the organicist imagination is irrelevant today would be all too easy. The contingency of functional differentiation may not be questioned per se (Luhmann 1997), but one foregoes an entire history of biopolitics when one forgets that the effort at wholeness and the governing of life for the procurement of the normal have been integral to modernity (Foucault 2004a, 2004b;

Van Houdt 2014). In fact, philosophers such as Deleuze and social theorists such as Luhmann have long argued against what they assumed to be still prevalent organicist notions. Such notions are the idea of a society as a bounded whole, consisting of individual parts, which has a more or less clearly demarcated order and identity.

Most of social theory has distanced itself from such presuppositions, and yet they continue to inform the basic outlook, often implicit, of social scientists. Sociologists will tend to say their research object is, or resides within, "society." And when they have a hard time specifying what they mean by that, they rely on implicit assumptions that they draw from age-old organicist imaginaries. The social sciences moreover have a long history of explicit concern with norms, normalization, and social pathology. As I will discuss in the next chapter, C. Wright Mills critiqued the "social pathologists" of his age, who problematized whoever did not conform to middle class norms, and whose work in fact very much resembles colonial science and administration, for instance, in the case of Dutch measurement of the morals of Europeans in the East Indies (Stoler 2002, 2009). These, in turn, resemble current practices – whatever their differences – of measuring immigrant integration throughout Western Europe. My argument is thus that many of the silent presuppositions that come along with concepts such as "society" and "integration" remain wedded to organicism. Because they are active at the level of the social imaginary, they are rarely expressed, and yet they are easily uprooted. While the next chapter seeks to do so for contemporary social scientific measurements of immigrant integration, the current chapter looks at the history of the organicist imagination and highlights its links with social theory. It then discusses several attempts to get rid of the concept of "society" in social theory, and it concludes by presenting the theoretical case against the organicist remainders in the imagination of society.

Parts and Wholes: Entities with Identities and Orders with Borders

In the dominant Western imagination, society has been imagined as both an *assembling concept* and a *container concept*. It delimits and selects members of a set. Like any limit or boundary, the concept at the same time separates and connects or contains, and it at the same time produces the image of an inside and an outside. But precisely because inside and outside are at the same time a *consequence of* the working of "society," they cannot be regarded as separate terrains that conform to a realist opposition between "society" and its "outside." And so, as I argue in this book, when the sociology of immigrant integration opposes "society" to groups and individuals that are "not (well) integrated," it contributes to the imagination and thus the very formation of "society," even though it claims to describe as given the object and its environment, its transformations and its identity. The same goes for social theory more generally: it has itself been part of a more encompassing social imagination. So instead of debating the merits and shortcomings of specific conceptions of society in social theory, this chapter attempts to critically tease out the main elements of the imagination of society as articulated in social theory and social science.

Strictly speaking, the history of the Western concept of "society" starts somewhere in the seventeenth century, it really takes off in the eighteenth century with Montesquieu and Rousseau, and it gains social scientific centrality in the nineteenth century with authors like Comte, Spencer, Sumner, Schäffle, and Von Lilienfeld. But the history of a concept does not begin with the first appearance of the word. The concept of society bears the connotations of its forebears. Some of these forebears and related concepts are the Greek concepts of *koinonia* and *polis*, the Roman concept of *res publica*, the early medieval concepts of *societas*, *universitas*, and *corpus mysticum* and their subsequent development, and modern concepts of commonwealth and community. A "history of society" is not my aim here (it would be a book in itself, or several books), but I do wish to highlight a key feature of the ways in which society has been imagined. Most importantly, a particular metaphysics keeps reappearing in concepts of society and its precursors. Such concepts are almost invariably conceived in terms of a part/whole scheme. In other words, a *mereological metaphysics* pervades concepts of collectivity in social and political thought. Mereology, as the study of parts and wholes and their relationship, exists in the conceptual history of society in various forms. Two main forms are *organicism* and *mechanism*. Even though, as historian John Tresch has convincingly shown (2012), organicism and mechanism at times coincided, these differ in that the former accords primacy to wholes, whereas the latter prioritizes the individual parts of a whole. In social and political thought, organicism has dominated, no doubt partly because, as Mary Douglas (1996: 72–91) has argued, the human body has throughout history been the most plausible image of a natural order. It could thus be seen as a microcosm embedded within larger bodily *cosmion*. Mechanicism existed in certain forms of scholastic nominalism and mainly in modern materialist and libertarian theories. Modern social science has roots in organicism, and it has since developed a range of more mechanicist alternatives, yet these all retain significant organicist connotations in that they are ambivalent about the status of the whole. Even nominalist social theories seem to at the same time adhere to a container concept of society, which is hard to defend in nominalist terms. Certainly, the social science of immigrant integration analyzed in this book starts (and ends up) with a part/ whole conception of society.

Crucially, closely related to the centrality of the part/whole scheme is the imagination of *wholeness* that adheres to "society." This too becomes readily identifiable in the ways immigrant integration and the society in which it is thought to occur are imagined. Etymologically, "whole" and "health" are connected, and both are connected to *Heiland* (*messias*) (Nederveen Pieterse 2001: 132ff.), which inserts a certain messianic input into the concept of a whole corresponding to the *teleological* character that such wholes have often been credited with. Such teleology may consist in a latent form, where it refers to the maintenance of existing wholeness. An entire history of organicism links the "whole" of society to its "wholeness" in terms of its health. Nikolas Rose has thus, for instance, remarked:

medicine has been bound up with the ways in which, since the end of the eighteenth century, the very idea of *society* has been brought into existence and acquired a density and a form. ... Society, as it is historically invented, is immediately accorded an organic form and thought in medical terms. As a *social body* it is liable to sickness: that is to say, it is problematized in the vocabulary of medicine. (Rose 1994: 54)

In another, less explicitly organicist sense, the wholeness of the whole of society is contained in the connotations of companionship that remain active in the concept. When the modern concept of "society" appeared, it denoted limited assemblies of companions and friends. The Latin concept of *societas* is likewise connected to *socius*, meaning "companion." Until today, therefore, "society" remains characterized by this character of collective assembly, and what it assembles is said to have something in common, a shared bond, a mutual sympathy, an integrated set of values, that is, something that corresponds to the substance of friendliness or companionship that sets "society" apart from its outside. It may be that a state is conceived as a necessary warrant for the maintenance of societal bonds of friendship, as it is in Hobbes (Dean 2007: 40), but "society" maintains its closure on the basis of some form of sympathy, however abstract (such as a shared set of normative orientations). On the basis of the mereological imagination of parts and wholes, and of the wholeness of both, the notion of "society" has conventionally come to refer to some kind of *entity with an identity*, and to some form of nationalized *order with a border*. In the social science of immigrant integration, everything hinges on the imagination of its identity, which occurs on the basis of the assumption of its order and the visualization of its border. Immigrant integration itself thereby operates as a mediating or coordinating concept, and as such, it too stands in a long line of historical imaginations.

Sociology, then, could have been named "societology," the name Sumner coined for it. Sociology has acted as iconographer of the social body of "society." And when needed, it has acted as chief physician. From British ameliorism to studies of "social exclusion," from Durkheim's "therapeutic" role of the sociologist to Bourdieu's "clinical" approach, and from the "social pathologists" critiqued by Wright Mills to contemporary sociology of immigrant integration, sociology has often tied its own fate to the health of society (compare Luhmann 1984: 505). If conventional accounts situate the birth of sociology in the nineteenth century, we should not forget that this was the century that worshipped "society" as a super-organism. As political theorist Sheldon Wolin has noted:

the century turned to "society" which became the symbol of its intellectual preoccupations, the source of a new *mystique*, the *Magna Mater* of an age that wanted desperately to commune. ... The century endowed society with a status as distinctive as that previously accorded the political order, surrounding it with the affectionate metaphors that another age had reserved for the church, personifying it as the life-force ultimately shaping politics, economic life, and culture. (Wolin 2004: 323)

And the nineteenth century could fall back on a long history that had merely been briefly interrupted by purely mechanicist thinking. For as Tawney has said: "From the twelfth century to the sixteenth, from the work of Becket's secretary in 1159 to the work of Henry VIII's chaplain in 1537, the analogy by which society is described – an analogy at once fundamental and commonplace – is the same. ... It is that of the human body" (Tawney 1922: 35). Tawney here uses "society" in a somewhat anachronist sense, but this only illustrates how what came to be "society" rested on earlier notions of *societas*, *corpus mysticum*, *corpus politicum,* and *universitas* that were thoroughly organicist.

My claim is that the icon of "society" exerts a decisive hold on social imagination until today. We should not forget that, despite textbook canonizations of what Jonathan Turner has called Saint Marx, Saint Durkheim, and Saint Weber, the earliest sociologists were rather Saint-Simon, Comte, and René Worms in France – all of them organicist thinkers. In Germany, the organicists Hans Scherrer and Otto Caspari were the first to teach what they called *Sociologie* in Heidelberg in 1870 (Weingart 2000). Apart from them, thinkers like the Swiss Lorenz von Stein, the Austrian Alfred Schäffle, the Russian Paul von Lilienfeld, and the German Ludwig Gumplowicz were influential organicist social theorists in Germany. In Britain, Spencer's evolutionist organicism was dominant, along with that of Hobhouse, Kidd, and Geddes. And in early U.S. sociology, Sumner's organicism was followed by Lester Ward's less explicit organicism, which – and this is the key point – did not preclude him from speaking of society as a "social organism" (Ward 1921). These, and many others, have largely been written out of the textbooks, partly because their theories were often eugenic in nature or application, but they were the generations that coined sociology's key concept of "society." This concept, empty and theoretically useless save for its existence as a form of social imagination, is only meaningful if, however latent, certain organicist presuppositions of a social whole consisting of parts are taken on board. It would take another chapter, or even a book, to sort out the organicist genealogy of "society" in the history of sociology, including the many internal differences among organicist thinkers (for instance, regarding the question whether the "parts of society" are individuals or institutions). I therefore summarize the point by citing accounts of two contemporary social theorists from widely differing theoretical strands. While explicit organicist accounts have largely faded, according to Manuel DeLanda, the organicist metaphor nonetheless lingers on in the presuppositions of contemporary thought:

But a more sophisticated form of the basic metaphor still exerts considerable influence in most schools of sociology, and in this form it is much more difficult to eliminate. This version involves not an analogy but a general theory about the relations between parts and wholes, wholes that constitute a seamless totality or that display an organic unity. (DeLanda 2006: 9)

Cornelius Castoriadis has come to surprisingly similar conclusions when he discusses the origins and implications of assumptions of social wholes and their parts:

the only schema available to inherited thought for conceiving of a whole that is not a system *partes extra partes*: the schema of the organism. A schema that, despite the rhetorical precautions that are taken, in fact returns more often than is thought, even today, in discussions on society. (Castoriadis 1987: 179)

"Rhetorical precautions" – indeed, we shall encounter those in our discussion of sociologies of immigrant integration. Thoroughly steeped in organicist assumptions that steer their racist outcomes, they operate, as I seek to show, in a theoretical mist, unaware of the theoretical, logical, and practical import of the assumptions they borrow from the organicist tradition.

Sociologically speaking, it is therefore relevant to distinguish between a *primary* and a *secondary* way of speaking of "society." In its *secondary* meaning, which has been dominant, "society" refers to a social aggregate, compound, or constellation. Here, "society" is an object or entity of some sort (for instance, of intersubjective value subscriptions). This secondary conception is a metaphysical use of the concept of "society." It has ancient roots. We find, for instance, in St. Augustine the definition of "society" (a "commonwealth" or "people") as "the association of a multitude of rational beings united by a common agreement on the objects of their love" (Augustine 1972: 890). For Augustine, it is moreover the *unity* of society that equals the *health* of the people. His concept is one of assemblage and containership: a multitude of beings (be they rational beings, believers, individuals, or subjects) is assumed to constitute "society." Such presuppositions have often been reproduced, and centuries later similar notions abound, albeit now attached to "national societies." We find Proudhon, for instance, claiming that "society" consists of "the sum total of relationships; in a word, system" (quoted in Wolin 2004: 325). The basic intuition that in the end informs nearly all conceptions of society (no matter how theoretically sophisticated in other respects) is that, as John Dewey states: "society is composed of individuals: this obvious and basic fact no philosophy, whatever its pretensions to novelty, can question or alter" (Dewey 1950: 148). And while Dewey, in his *Reconstruction in Philosophy*, deems it crucial not to think in the rigid terms of "the state" and "the individual," the rather unsophisticated abstraction of "society" is hard to get around for him and for most others. I will not give an exhaustive overview of the prevalence of this type of social imagination in contemporary social theory (this, too, would require another book). My claim is that container concepts of society are a form of common sense in social science and philosophy. They in the end often, but not necessarily,[1] come down to wholes consisting of *people*, as in Gellner's description of "*society* which is, by definition, a human group persisting over time" (1970: 133). This is, in one form or another, how "society" is described to students of sociology.[2] I leave to the reader the assessment of the extent to which this secondary use of "society" is, indeed, a constituent element of the prevailing form of sociological imagination. As I illustrate in the next chapter, it certainly holds sway over contemporary analysis of "immigrant integration."

Over against this secondary meaning of "society" stands its *primary* sense, in which "society" is regarded as a claim to such compound objecthood, or as a specific type of social imagination. Often, it is a self-imagination. That does not mean that we should start believing in the existence of the self that the imagination claims. Rather, we should take it as an imagination that claims the imagination is performed by the "self" (the social compound or collective) that is thus imagined. This may sound confusing, but it's actually much more down to earth than the assumption that "society" refers to an entity consisting of such different things as individuals, actions, communications, values,

---

[1] Systems theorists in the wake of Luhmann's work deny membership of society to "people" or "humans," though that does not mean they do also not use "society" in the sense of a container concept. See, for instance: Fuchs (2001: 4).

[2] See, for instance, one of the currently best-selling international English-speaking introductions to the discipline: Macionis and Plummer's *Sociology: A Global Introduction* (2008). The front matter of this edition includes an interesting "history of society," in which "society" becomes a primordially existing object, rather than a product of sociological assemblage: "sociology came into being in the wake of the many changes to society wrought by the Industrial Revolution in the last few centuries – just the blink of an eye in evolutionary perspective."

rules, institutions, feelings, objects, and so on. What it means is simply to assume that the *imagination* "society" is really that: a historically contingent form of social imagination.

Integration: A Coordinating Concept

Concepts of society have thus often had the form of a relation between a whole and its parts, and they have been in need of a supplemental, *coordinating concept*. This supplement has often assumed the form of a concept circumscribing, if often merely naming, a mediating process between parts and whole. The reason why this supplement can be called a "necessary supplement"[3] is that the part/whole distinction has been crucial throughout the history of western social and political thought. Hence, there has always been the need for a harmonizing or coordinating concept that takes care of the relationship between parts and whole. In a sense, such a coordinating concept always described a certain way in which "society" was self-productive, since the part/whole distinction "doubles" society: it describes it once as a whole and once as a collection of parts. The theoretical problems of this ordering scheme will be more fully addressed in Part 3 of this book. But the mediation between parts and whole should, in a definite sense, be seen as a way in which society is redoubled or folded back onto itself. Today, the main concept that fulfills this function is the concept of "integration." But this coordinating concept has its precursors too. They can be found in the Greek concepts of *homonoia* and *sympatheia*, the Roman and early Christian concept of *ordinata Concordia*, and in modern concepts such as sympathy, for instance as used by Adam Smith, or *consensus universalis*, as used by Comte.

The main problem such coordinating concepts speak to is how to incorporate the in-dividual (that which cannot be divided) into the social whole. Some (though not many) solutions have come out of

---

[3] I here allude to the concept of the "supplément" as espoused by Derrida. For Derrida, concepts require supplements because they can never be wholly closed in themselves. They necessarily depend on the invocation (often silent) of other concepts. In his discussion of Rousseau's *Émile* and sexuality, he, for instance, describes how masturbation functions as a "dangerous supplement" in a regime of sexuality and how, according to Rousseau, writing is a dangerous supplement of speech as education is of nature (Derrida 1974). Similarly, Derrida (1981: 67–186) notes how writing is an "originary supplement" (*supplément originaire*), despite (or precisely as visible in) Plato's condemnation of it as *pharmakon*.

what we call "classical" social theory, most prominent being Durkheim's ideas on socialization. Socialization is a process through which the part is invested with some portion of the whole, while the whole is invested with the part. How this takes place, nobody knows, for beyond vague notions of primary socialization or education, which make it unclear exactly how a social system enters the mind, and vice versa, this process remains obscure. In the twentieth century, many of the "compromises" between objectivism and subjectivism or between structuralism and finalism have put forward some form of mutual influencing. Thus, to name a few of the most prominent attempts, reconciliations between "structure" and "agency" were put forward (Giddens, Archer), "meta-levels" were introduced (Bhaskar), "field" and "habitus" were construed as "objectively adjusted" (Bourdieu), and "communicative action" in a "life-world" was opposed to "strategic action" in a "system" (Habermas). Whichever route was taken, the organicist problem of reconciling whole with parts was taken as the basic theoretical issue in social theory. In some form or another, these approaches have stayed within the vicinity of the Hegelian "law, that the exterior is the expression of the interior" (Hegel 1970: 202).[4] Often, auxiliary constructs such as ordering systems opposed to society (the state) or value systems were deemed necessary as guarantees or even as mediators between parts and whole. And often, a differentiation between "society" as a factual and "society" as a counterfactual given would ensue. For the concept of society is to present a unity in diversity, a site of integration amidst differentiation. Durkheim's novelty lies in the coining of a unitary concept to designate differentiation, to presuppose that differentiation is not opposed to but *is* integration. But Durkheim was only able to do this by distinguishing between a "real" and an "ideal" society. By moralizing the concept, credit for its *contemporary* existence is bought in the *future*. Other, sometimes less moralizing approaches embodying a similar reconciliatory mechanism are Weber's description of society in terms of distinct value spheres, Simmel's description of the *coincidentia oppositorum* of money, Adam Smith's and Von Stein's conceptions of the division of labor, and Spencer's organic laws of integration and differentiation.

---

[4] Thus, George Herbert Mead could remark that "the Romantic philosophy pointed out that the self, while it arises in the human experience, also carries with it the very unity that makes society possible." Quoted in Shalin (2003: 299).

To a large extent these ways of reconciling parts and whole blotted out the question whether it makes sense at all to posit some kind of social "whole." The presupposition of such an identity has socio-theological overtones. As a basic theoretical issue, the whole/part problem would be productive if it concerned an identity whose onto-logical status wasn't problematic in itself, which is hardly the case with the "whole" of "society." Rather, we have here, at the basis of social theory, a circular argument (and circular arguments are of course often to be found at the basis of a discipline or theory): the basic theoretical problem of social thought is in a sense legitimized with reference to the existence of a society, whose plausibility rests, in turn, on the possible solutions to the basic theoretical problem. The consequence is that in social thought, as Luhmann has stated, "the foundational concept itself has never fulfilled a foundational function" (2005a: 279). Instead, it has served to delimit a field of research. The end result has been that sociology and social philosophy, whatever their take on the nature of society, have invested its very idea with plausibility, they have been performing as the professional iconographers of society. They have done so by adding to the imagination of a container concept a mer-eological metaphysics of parts and a whole, and by subsequently inventing coordinating concepts mediating between these. Currently, integration is a key coordinating concept. And in the current historical juncture of European nation-states and their concerns over immigra-tion, "immigrant integration" has become a key site for the imagin-ation of society.

Habeas Corpus? Critics of "Society"

Are there ways out of "society," this Alcatraz of social theory? When some form of social body has usually been presupposed, the obvious question would be to produce this body: habeas corpus! Various authors have argued that this is in fact impossible, or that it used to be possible but isn't any longer. Let's survey some of the terrain these critics have covered. In recent critiques of the concept of society, three types of argument exist. One is that recent social developments, such as globalization or postmodernization, have rendered the category of society useless. Let's call this argument the "argument from globaliza-tion." A second is that society was a useless category to begin with: the "argument from uselessness." And a third agrees with the second, but holds that "society" did have its, often highly political, uses: the "argument from political use."

The Argument from Globalization

Many critics of the concept of society presuppose that the notion has *lost* much of its appeal as a category of social thought. They then presuppose that it used to function as such, but that social life has changed in ways rendering it obsolete. They point at qualitative changes or at quantitative changes so big they amount to qualitative changes, and they suppose these changes mean it's time to move beyond the concept of society. "Globalization" is the key concept here. Indeed, most of the time processes of "globalization" are conceptualized as added to "societies" (Luhmann 2005b: 68), and where they are not, the idea is that "society" was long a legitimate ultimate concept encompassing the social. The presupposition of an increased heterogeneity of the world was, for instance, reason for Clifford Geertz to discard the notion (2004: 578). Likewise, the increased density, mobility, and network character of a "globalized world" is considered reason to shift, as Urry, for instance, does, from "societies" to "mobilities" (Urry 2000). But such approaches unjustly assume that the fact that social life "flows" is something new. Apparently, "society" was a relevant category before our age of "mobilities" and "flows." But the idea that reality "flows" is as old as Heraclitus, and also rigid visions of reality can be seen as modes of process. Whoever holds that the social has become *more* processual confuses "change" and "process." Both continuity and change are possible on the basis of process, and there was every reason to adopt a conception of the social attuned to "flow" and "process" long before globalization inaugurated specific types of flow. The same goes for Ulrich Beck's assertion that society is now (in times of globalization) a "zombie-category" (2002a, 2002b). It is dead but still lingers in social science, mostly for lack of alternative. But zombies used to be alive, and so the notion of a "zombie-category" implicitly subscribes to an image of society as a social body. Like Urry, Beck concludes that "society" is *no longer* a relevant sociological master category, and this means that for a long time, it was. In debates concerning the relevance of society in times of either globalization or postmodernization, Zygmunt Bauman has perhaps most explicitly drawn the conclusion here:

a sociology geared to the conditions of postmodernity ought to replace the category of *society* with that of *sociality*; a category that tries to convey the processual modality of social reality ... and a category that refuses to take the structured character of the process for granted – which treats instead all found structures as emergent accomplishments. (Bauman 1992: 190)

Bauman claims that what should especially be broken with is "the assumption of an '*organismic*', equilibrated social totality." Such a totality is informed by

the vision of a principally co-ordinated and enclosed totality (a) with a degree of cohesiveness, (b) equilibrated or marked by an overwhelming tendency to equilibration, (c) unified by an internally coherent value syndrome and a core authority able to promote and enforce it and (d) defining its elements in terms of the function they perform in that process of equilibration or the reproduction of the equilibrated state. (Bauman 1992: 189)

There is much of value here. One can argue that such notions of society are hardly explicitly endorsed, but the reply would be that nearly everyone either assumes society unproblematically and is thereby wedded to identitarian presuppositions or explicitly operates within the space opened by such presuppositions, navigating between (degrees of) unity and disunity, cohesion and dissolution, integration and disintegration. But in Bauman's case too, it is important to emphasize that the social *always* consisted of emergent "accomplishments" (compare Garfinkel 1967: 11). It has not become "more processual" in character. Former social realities may have been more characterized by continuity, but the continuous "accomplishment" of that continuity was always processual.

Typical of this first line of reasoning for the uselessness of the category of society is the name of the symposium, held in Paris in 2003, "Does the Prospect of a General Sociological Theory Still Mean Anything (in Times of Globalization)?" This made explicit that the question was whether society was *still* a relevant category, and that if it wasn't, this had to do mainly with "globalization." A number of important sociologists were asked the question "Do you think that the object of sociology had a link with the concept of society and that the latter had no real existence outside the ideal of the nation-state? ... Could "global society" become a new frame for sociology?" (Caillé 2007: 180). An overview of the symposium was published in the *European Journal of Social Theory*. Two outspoken critics of the

concept of society can be found there. The first is Touraine, who is
among those who thinks that society used to be valuable but is less so
today. The second is Harrison White, whose view I shall discuss in the
next paragraph, as his answers reach beyond the scope of the symposium in that he never found the category of society useful to begin with.

Alain Touraine states that the concept of society was relevant in the
age of the sociological classics. According to Touraine (2003, 2007),
"society" was a modern invention. Society held the individual actor
and his or her social environment both at a distance and together in an
institutionally controllable fashion. However, classical sociology could
not hold in the midst of increasing social change, ranging from the
student movements in 1968 to the American civil rights movements,
and crossing these movements squarely was the process of economic
globalization. At the same time, social life became increasingly defined
in cultural instead of institutional terms. The self increasingly defines
itself in terms of cultural identities and not in the institutional-
economic terms that were current in the age of Marx (position in the
apparatus of production), Weber (position in occupational structure),
and Durkheim (position in the division of labor). In its turn, according
to Touraine, the economy has started to undermine society by creating
a field of social relations that does not stick to national boundaries and
that is dictated more by "the market" than by (national) government
policies. In this respect, Parsons was really the last "classical sociologist," and there is no place for society in the postclassical era of
sociology. Nonetheless, Touraine reintroduces the concept of society
at the end of his contribution to the Paris symposium. He then states:
"our society is less and less a society of the subjected and more and
more a society of volunteers" (Touraine 2007: 191). Apparently (and
regardless of the empirical and normative value of this statement)
Touraine can't do without the category of society after all. And
besides, Touraine makes clear that society certainly was a useful sociological category before the culturalization of social life and the economization of the world. There are problems there, since the very rise of
nation-states can be seen as a cultural form of identity politics, but the
main point is that Touraine holds that the concept of society referred to
an actual entity in the age of the sociological classics, but doesn't
anymore – although he still uses it as such. These problems, most
prominently the idea that the uselessness of society as a consequence
of social change, implying its former usefulness, and certainly its

reintroduction and continued use, may have to do first of all with the fact that the "argument from globalization" may have a limited historical horizon. After all, globalization has been under way for centuries, and the plausibility of nation-states and national societies themselves was a product of this process. Secondly, the argument from globalization may simply be not quite fundamental enough in a theoretical sense. So let's review some positions subscribing to the argument from uselessness.

The Argument from Uselessness

In his contribution to the Paris symposium, Harrison White states that while preparing for the symposium he concluded that the concept of society actually didn't play any role whatsoever in his work. For White (2007), "society" is a "mirage," which means, as he says in the new edition of *Identity & Control*, that we "can disregard notions of an overarching 'society'" (White 2008: 1). White admits preferring to speak of "structures" or, better yet, "networks." Here he comes close to Charles Tilly, whose first of eight "Pernicious Postulates of Twentieth Century Social Thought" holds: "'Society' is a thing apart; the world as a whole divides into distinct 'societies', each having its more or less autonomous culture, government, economy, and solidarity" (1984: 11). In White's theoretical work, intended to be a foundation for a network approach, he looks for the ways in which actors try to define and sustain identities through control over other identities amidst a network in which they need to maintain footing while control is being exerted upon them. This way, White can effectively do without the notion of "society" as an encompassing frame. Two qualifications can, however, be made here. First, according to White, all great theoreticians in sociology previously made use of the concept of society "because none were Tikopians or Swat Pathans or Tallensi; instead all were, like us, living in a civilization which had come to make use of the term as a convenient place holder" (2007: 198). But one wonders whether "civilization" doesn't emerge here as ultimate explanatory context. What use is it to get rid of the category of "society" only to replace it, when we wish to refer to grand processes and even to explain the "sociology of society," to "civilization"? Second, and more important, is the fact that "society" may be a "mirage," but it cannot be denied that it is a very effective mirage. For this reason, I believe it is proper to consider society as a form of social imagination or as what Castoriadis has called a social imaginary. In other words, a sociology that discards the category of "society" for theoretical reasons, must not forget its empirical relevance as a category of social imagination. What must not be forgotten is the *productivity* of "society" in terms of what White might perhaps call a "story," but which I more broadly conceive as a form of imagination that often involves the production of images through forms of monitoring and surveillance. "Society" may not be the basic entity of social life, and it may not be an encompassing home to all that is social, or at least a national address thereof. But it is, or rather does something, it is an active principle, and this activity should be accounted for in social theory and social science.

First, let's consider another critic of conventional concepts of society in social theory. In several of his works, Bruno Latour aims his critique on "society" at what he calls the "modern constitution." Latour deems this contract or settlement defining of modernity, even to the extent that this settlement gives us the false feeling of modernity as a break with what happened before and what happens elsewhere. It is characterized by the distinction and opposition between "nature" and "society." Partly on the basis of work by Tarde, Whitehead, and Serres, Latour develops an "actor-network theory" in which he pays attention to what he calls, in Whiteheadian vocabulary, the "articulation of propositions." "Society" is replaced with "network" or "collective" by Latour, but so is "nature" (Latour 1999, 2005). Against social constructivist conceptions of arbitrariness and artificiality on the side of society, and determinacy and objectivity on the side of nature, Latour claims that both domains are actually intertwined, giving rise to a proliferation of "hybrids," which he also calls, using a concept by Michel Serres, "quasi-objects." Similarly, his "actors" aren't the actors of conventional sociological action theory, but "actants," a concept he adapts from Benveniste to describe the active potential of humans and non-humans alike. The "social" is replaced by "associations" in Latour's work (1999: 304; 2005: 5, 11). I won't elaborate further on the details of this proposal (but see Schinkel 2007b), but I wish to pay some attention to the definition of "society" given by Latour, which is interesting here. In *Pandora's Hope*, Latour describes "society" as follows: "The word does not refer to an entity that exists in itself and is ruled by its own laws by opposition to other entities, such as nature; it means the result of a settlement that, for political reasons, artificially divides things between the natural and the social realms" (1999: 311; compare 2004: 249). Latour is thus an exception in that he not only describes what is wrong with the concept of "society" (it artificially divides between a "social" and a "natural" world that are actually indiscernible in actor networks), but he also has a take on the way "society" functions. He makes a distinction between "society" as an entity of some sort (the conventional sociological position) and "society" as the outcome of a modern contract, in which "society" functions as a description of a domain artificially separated from the rest of the world. Of course, there is a problem here, for Latour's description of "society," as quoted above, has all the characteristics of a "social constructivist" debunking of "society." After all, it is something that *artificially* divides the social and the natural, and it does so for *political reasons*. These are formulations that, with a different substance, appear to emerge straight out of the idiom of orthodox Bourdieusian relational sociology. And yet Latour's notion of "society" goes some way in the direction of treating it as a description that has performative effects, so in a sense he takes an intermediary position between the argument from uselessness and the argument from political use. These effects, though described by Latour as "political," are not elaborated upon by him, mostly because they interest him less than do the actor-networks, the collectives or "imbroglios" he traces.

The Argument from Political Use

One approach that is equally critical of the centrality of "society" in social and political theory and that does go some way to developing an idea of its productive aspects is Laclau and Mouffe's conception, developed in *Hegemony and Socialist Strategy: Towards a Radical Democratic Politics*. According to them the ontology of the social is always already political. The social is always the site of some form of hegemony, by which they understand a particular social force (for instance, neoliberal capitalism) that assumes the representation of a social totality (compare Laclau 2000: 56; Laclau and Mouffe 2001: x). According to Laclau and Mouffe, the social can by definition not be "occupied" by particular forces, and yet the continuous antagonism between such forces, claiming universality, leads to a particular hegemonic occupation of the space of the social. Hegemony thus always concerns a contingent articulation within the discursive space that they take the social to be. The totality of the social, represented within the form of hegemony articulated at any point, necessarily remains incomplete. And the antagonism between social forces will sooner or later give rise to another contingent articulation of hegemony – something Laclau and Mouffe actively seek to promote as an option for the left. Laclau and Mouffe apply this to the concept of "society" as well: "the incomplete character of every totality necessarily leads us to abandon, as a terrain of analysis, the premise of *"society"* as a sutured and self-defined totality. "Society" is not a valid object of discourse. There is no single underlying principle fixing – and hence constituting – the whole field of differences" (2001: 111; compare 130). In other words, Laclau and Mouffe depart from the concept of "society" as an exhaustive descriptor of all things social. No one label, so they assume, can capture the social in totality. Some remarks need to be made here. First, Laclau and Mouffe adopt what can be called a "negative ontology": they define the social on the basis of a lack. For they say, "if the social does not manage to fix itself in the intelligible and instituted forms of a *society*, the social only exists, however, as an effort to construct that impossible object" (2001: 112). This illustrates very well the role played by "society" in social life according to Laclau and Mouffe. But in so describing the productive effects of the signifier "society," they appear to psycho-analyze the social. The social becomes something that has a lack, something that longs for a "society" but never reaches it, a social suffering from a kind of broken heartedness. Hence they speak of the fixation of relations within "nodal points," a concept with which they translate Lacan's "points de capiton."[5] But how productive (perhaps even: how radical) is it to abolish "society" as an analytical category, only to then define the social as impossible love for "society"? "Society" appears to linger on in their theory in a not fully historicized but ontologized version, as a desire of the social to complete and total closure within "society."

A second point is that there is much inconsistency here, as "society" is presupposed at many points throughout *Hegemony and Socialist Strategy*. For instance, that which is unable to be identical to itself

---

[5] Lacan hereby refers to privileged signs (*signifiants*) that fix the meaning of a signifying chain. For Laclau and Mouffe, this concerns points within a discursive field that are privileged in the representation of the field as a whole. In other words, it concerns points wich facilitate the play of differences within such a signifying field.

remains "society" (Laclau and Mouffe 2001: 113). And "society" remains the domain *within which* antagonistic forces struggle over the hegemonic representation *of* "society" (2001: xiv). For as Laclau and Mouffe argue: "our approach conceives of universality as a *political* universality and, in that sense, as depending on internal frontiers within society" (2001: xiii). In the end, Laclau and Mouffe switch between a reflexive use of "society" as a social signifier that plays a certain productive role in social life, and "society" as an entity to which they refer as a shorthand, both in the examples above, but also when they, for instance, speak of "industrial societies" (2001: 159–160). At such points, the substance they give to "society" seems wholly forgotten, and "societies" appear once again as neatly discernable social blocks.

A third point, finally, places limits on the usability of Laclau and Mouffe's theory in the case of national societies emerging as observable objects in discourses of immigrant integration. Their thinking is rooted in Carl Schmitt's ontological, existential, and even quasi-natural notion of antagonism (Schmitt 2002: 27). Laclau and Mouffe deploy a similar primordiality of the social antagonism (compare Mouffe 2005). They thereby depart from a purely materialist form of Marxism (they claim to be "post-Marxists"), and they introduce the sphere of symbolic representation into the idea of antagonism. The danger of applying such reasoning can be the naturalization of conflicts and, in the context of immigrant integration, the construction of culturist oppositions. Just like, according to Laclau and Mouffe, a hegemonic articulation retroactively creates the interests it purports to foster, it is possible for an articulation to retroactively construe the antagonism it supposedly springs from. There is a political value in assuming antagonisms (such as a "clash of civilizations" or "cultural incompatibilities" or a "multiculturalism" versus a "realism"), and hence the theorist cannot start from an acceptance of the hegemonic frame of antagonism. In fact, the antagonism may be a *result* of an articulation – an articulation that constructs a frame of antagonism to legitimize itself. The presupposition of the antagonism as always necessarily *preceding* a hegemonic articulation may then simply be the uncritical acceptance of what a hegemonic articulation construes as conflict – which is then accepted in a surprisingly unconflictual way. Laclau and Mouffe do not fundamentally distinguish between discursive and non-discursive practices (2001: 107), but some kind of

distinction between "antagonism" and "representation of antagonism" should be possible, precisely in order to capture the performative
effects of representations of antagonism that realize themselves as
antagonism. There is room for a distinction between "antagonism"
and "representation of antagonism" in Laclau and Mouffe's theory
since they presuppose something similar with respect to hegemony.
There they assume that hegemony is the particular representation of a
totality. If "representation of a totality" and "totality" would be the
same thing, an unbroken hegemony would ensue, which they deem
impossible. A similar distinction between "antagonism" and "representation of antagonism" should be possible, even if "representations"
affect what they represent (2001: 58), which would allow us not to
uncritically assume antagonism when such is the hegemonic frame.
When a "cultural conflict" between "Islam" and "the West" is
claimed, we not only need to critically investigate the assumptions of
exclusivity between these two terms, but also the assumption of the
actuality of a "conflict." Laclau and Mouffe's model, when applied to
such contemporary realities (they might argue: only when applied in a
bad way), runs the risk of uncritically accepting the idea of "society" as
a container of conflict, or better yet as in conflict with an extra-societal
sphere. After all, "society" never covers the entire social terrain in
Laclau and Mouffe. To sum up: although Laclau and Mouffe take a
significant step away from substantivist and identitarian conceptions
of society, which conceive society as an entity with an identity, and as a
nationalized order with a border, they on many occasions cannot
escape entertaining such a notion. Moreover, their theory of antagonism presents us with specific problems when we are to understand the
construction of "society" amidst various problematizations of immigrant integration. They forego the practical effects of "society" as a
product of social imagination. What is the practical relevance of their
denouncing it as "not a valid object of discourse"? I propose to do two
things here: first, to provide the materials for a theoretical critique of
the (quasi-)organicist imagination of society, and, second, to remain
attentive for the practical uses to which that imagination is deployed.

Luhmann's Critique of Organicism

The most consistent critique of (quasi-)organicist conceptions of society has been given by Niklas Luhmann, who critically deals with the

various sociological positions, while also incorporating much of the developments in continental philosophy and systems theory. Though it ultimately centers on a conception of a "world society," Luhmann's theory remains the most rigorously developed theory to date, and I shall use it here to illustrate the problems of conventional approaches. For Luhmann, most succinctly put, the theoretical problem of thinking of "society" in terms of a whole consisting of parts is that it always already *presupposes the whole*. Luhmann takes issue with what he calls "old European" thought. By that he refers to what I have called the mereological metaphysics of part and whole, the ontology on which the part/whole scheme presupposes a hierarchical concept of society. Indeed, according to Aristotle, where there is a whole built out of parts, there are a master and a slave, a dominant and a dominated (compare Luhmann 2000a: 326; Aristotle 2013: 1254a). The observation of parts and wholes becomes problematic once we try to observe parts and whole at the same time. One possible solution is the classical idea of the whole as more than the sum of its parts. In that case, that which the whole is "more" than its parts, its emergent properties, cannot be a part itself, since that would iterate the problem (Luhmann 2000a: 324). But if the whole is more than the sum of its parts, then how can it be considered a unity at the level of the parts as well? So far, sociological theories have not been capable of reaching a decomposition of the whole into individual parts, and to then conceptually recombine them into the whole (Luhmann 1997: 598). In other words, the emergent rest that makes the whole more than the sum of its parts is the blind spot of mereological metaphysics. The whole gains the status of necessary supplement, an a priori that remains a black box itself.

Another solution for the problem of the doubling of reality is the demand that there be homogeneity between parts and whole (Luhmann 1984: 23; Luhmann 2006: 73–74). This is expressed in formulations of a *unitas multiplex* or of *e pluribus unum*. The assumption needed for such homogeneity is that of the meta-unity of parts and whole (Luhmann 1997: 913). This removes the qualitative difference between parts and whole. Insofar as society consists of bodies,[6] it is a meta-body itself. Thus, for Plato (2003: 368c–e), the polis is

---

[6] Indeed, this is what has usually been presupposed in part/whole metaphysics (Luhmann 1984: 20–23).

"man written large." This opens the possibility of ascribing to individuals a "correct" will (which can deviate) and a "correct" knowledge (which can fail) (Luhmann 1984: 21), since the whole is only really "whole" once its individual parts represent it. And this, in turn, means that the whole represents its parts. What this presupposes, however, is again the priority of the whole, and mereological metaphysics has been characterized by a hierarchization of parts (*maiores partes, sanior pars, valentior pars*) and whole (*unum*) (Luhmann 1997: 919; Luhmann 2005b: 302). The part/whole scheme has thus coincided with a top/ bottom scheme (Luhmann 2005b: 297–300). Hierarchization of parts entails their moralization (for instance, through ideals of citizenship), and it entails an equivocation between the one (*unum*), the good (*bonum*), and the true (*verum*). A doubling of reality therefore also occurs in the axiological sense.

The mereological ideal of homogeneity can be seen in the contemporary conception of the integration of parts as their cultural assimilation to a preexisting society, characterized by a "dominant culture." Such a homogeneity demand, however, still does not solve the problem of the qualitative difference between the whole and its parts. Problems of "re-entry," of, for instance, asking whether parts and whole together constitute a whole, illustrate the problematic nature of mereological metaphysics. In sociological theory such questions are *strategically ignored*. The same goes for the possibility of simultaneously observing the level of the parts and the level of the whole. The "theory of society," Luhmann holds, has not bothered with such questions, but has left them to theology, where they originate, along with the rest of mereological metaphysics.

Over against such notions, Luhmann posits the idea of a horizontally differentiated society, characterized by what he calls functional differentiation, in which no one social system stands at the top of a hierarchy (Luhmann 1982, 1984, 1997). All social systems, according to Luhmann, are self-reproducing (autopoietic), and they cannot even be directly influenced by other systems. The system of politics may cut funding for the system of science, which is problematic for science, but that doesn't mean that politics directly interferes with science and dictates what is true and what is false.

But functional differentiation is a modern feat. A second and more fundamental critique of the part/whole scheme is that it assumes the substantiality of parts and wholes. These have a "thing-like" character, as becomes most explicit in Durkheim's *chosisme*. Despite all emphasis on dynamics, they are static if only because part and whole can never change places (Luhmann 1973: 57). Organicist thought then always consists of efforts at demonstrating the *identity* of the two sides of the *difference* between parts and whole. In other words, what is aimed at is a way out of the problem of the attenuation between parts and whole by getting rid of their difference, for instance, by regarding parts and whole as only ever realized in tandem, or by theorizing that parts and whole actually contain each other. These are theoretical forms of having one's cake and eating it. Over against this, Luhmann posits what he calls a paradigm shift in which the identity between parts and whole is replaced by the difference between system and environment (Luhmann 1997: 60–78; 1984: 35–41; 1987; 2004: 23). The introduction of this difference, in which the emphasis is much more on the actual difference than it is in the part/whole scheme, is a crucial move that gets us beyond a lot of the problems of the part/whole scheme. System and environment are not things, they are not "substantial" in the metaphysical sense of the word. They are always systemic references. "Environment" is a reference toward what a system construes as its outside, an "other reference." Likewise, "system" is either the other reference of another system, or the self-reflection of a system which is itself only possible on the basis of the continuous distinction between system and environment.

Luhmann's theory is therefore hardly a systems theory, because what is crucial in his theory is the *difference* between system and environment (2006: 74). Rather than starting with a whole, and searching for the ordering of its parts, he starts with a difference. Both sides of the system/environment distinction exist only on the basis of the reproduction of that distinction, that is, they exist as references emerging from the operations of a system that ceases to exist once it fails to distinguish itself from an environment. Moreover, system and environment are never substances, but always systemic constructions, which are contingent since another type of reference to the system's environment could have been chosen. Simply put: the system of law distinguishes itself from its environment by reproducing operations based on a lawful/unlawful distinction (a systemic code), but there is nothing in the nature of law that prevents it from taking on another defining distinction. That this is unlikely means that one contingent selection has been immensely complexified, and this is precisely the point of Luhmann's theory. In this respect, "the environment" does not exist. "Environment," like "system," is always the system-internal construction of an environment. Theories that started from the part/ whole distinction could thematize environmental relations only as "system-to-system" relations and could not recognize that "system" and "environment" don't look the same from every systemic point of view. Different systems observe the world differently. Systems are identities through differences, identities that aren't fixed but always in process.

This brings us to the last and most important objection Luhmann raises with respect to the metaphysics of parts and whole. Luhmann states, using a concept by Gianfranco Poggi, that the sociology of parts and wholes has oriented itself by using an "intra-unit orientation" (Poggi 1965: 289ff.; Luhmann 1984: 23). That is to say that the whole was always presupposed as the container within which analysis subsequently took place. Even in its concepts of difference, the part/whole scheme was in the end restricted to the boundaries of the whole (Luhmann 1973: 174). The part/whole scheme allowed a focus on either parts or whole, on the question what the whole is more than the sum of its parts, on the question of homogeneity of parts and whole, or on the integration of parts and whole, but all of this occurs within the limits of the presupposed whole. It is an always already *internal* perspective. The system/environment distinction, on the other hand, transgresses these limits by conceptualizing the *external relations* that are crucial to the very existence of a social system. Over against "old European" identity thinking, this difference thinking recognizes that social systems, although they can be regarded as autopoietically closed, only exist on the basis of their relation to an environment. As in Jacques Derrida's philosophy of difference, any identity cannot wholly rest in itself, but is dependent in its existence on a constitutive outside, on some supplement external to itself. The metaphysics of parts and whole in fact *presupposes* the a priori existence of what it should *establish*: "society."

This also means that Luhmann turns the conventional sociological perspective around: a social system doesn't exist on the basis of a solid ground (value commitments, normative order, familiarity of the life world, or determining structures), but it has *instability as ground*. The contingency of social life is formulated in the systems-theoretical principle of "order from noise." Not stability, but instability feeds social order, and similarly communication is kept going not by consensus but by dissensus. Luhmann says: "a sufficiently stable system consists of instable elements; it owes its stability to itself, not to its elements; it builds itself out of a basis that is not at all "at hand," and in precisely that sense it is an autopoietic system" (1984: 78). Rather than streamlined consensual purity, the order from noise principle means that disturbances and noise fulfill positive functions: "the process of meaning ... lives off of disturbances and feeds off of disorder, lets itself be carried by noise" (1984: 123). Contrary to theories of structure, systems theory regards the reproduction of basic elements not in terms of a "repetition" but in light of connecting potential (*Anschlußfähigkeit*) (1984: 62). Not the continuity of life, but the connecting potential of action is ensured by autopoiesis or systemic self-reproduction (1984: 507) Luhmann states: "this theory is not concerned, as are classical theories of equilibrium, with a return to a stable situation of rest after absorption of disturbances, but with the ensuring of the unrelenting renewal of systemic elements: to put it succinctly: it is not concerned with static but with dynamic stability" (1984: 79). Uncertainty is the basis of the social system. This is doubly the case, since both system and environment exist in a doubly contingent relation (Luhmann 1977: 286). No system exists as a consequence of a fixed "dominant culture" or any other kind of "hard core." Every system is contingent, and it is what it is in relation to a contingent environment that is always more complex than the system itself. Luhmann therefore strongly objects against

the idea as if morality could have had an integrating function for society, which it no longer sufficiently fulfills. Such a view misses the conflictual and polemogenous side of morality. Analyzed in terms of the sociology of knowledge, it is itself a product of the situation it laments. (1984: 318)

The sociology and social philosophy that turns "society" into a moral space assumes consensus, stability, and equality as the basis for social organization. That is possible only on the basis of the repression or exorcism of dissensus, instability, conflict, and inequality. A theory of difference such as Luhmann's has the advantage of keeping in view the productivity of instability and dissensus. Prior to stability there is repression of instability, and prior to consensus there is repression of dissensus. That is how Luhmann can argue that conflicts are "highly integrated" social systems, precisely "because the tendency exists to

consider all action in the context of animosity." Antagonism is therefore a "first rate integrating factor and precisely because of this it is
problematic" (1984: 532). Similarly, Luhmann regards "exclusion" as
characteristic of strong integration (1993: 584). Yet whoever considers
"society" as a moral space and makes the double mistake of both
regarding "integration" as consensual presupposition or moral process
and applying it at the level of individuals is by definition blind to the
fact that specifically a conflictual social system carries sustainability,
stability, and "integration," as history amply illustrates. Insofar as
conflict is a problem, it is a problem of too much instead of too little
"integration." The problem for a complex social system, according to
Luhmann, is then to ensure sufficient "disintegration" (1993: 584).
The concept of "integration" Luhmann himself deploys is not a value-
charged concept in the sense that it is not regarded as better than or
preferable to "disintegration" (1993: 584). For Luhmann, this all leads
to a definite departing with sociological organicism. As he argues in the
context of an analysis of the art system:

> It is an illusion to think that the observer ... could ever get to see a
> "harmonious whole." As becomes visible in the futility of efforts to come
> to conceptual clarification, "harmony" is an emergency formula. Nor does
> the organism metaphor ("organic unity" according to Kant and Coleridge)
> qualify. A judgement of unity only occurs ... through the play of differ-
> ences." (1995: 120)

Difference thus replaces identitarian conceptions of society for Luhmann. Yet in the everyday imagination of "society" in the context of
immigrant integration, national societies are usually depicted as closed,
identitarian containers that are faced with outsiders that have nonetheless arrived. Such a conception of society has long been useful in
social theory as well.

The Productive Paradoxes of Society

It appears that the productivity of the notion of society as a whole
consisting of parts is related to the paradox that is at the core of its
metaphysics: the fact that "parts" and "whole" are both the same and
different. What characterizes the history of sociology is both the presupposition of "society" and an effort at diagnosing its precarious state
of health. This provided sociology with an object, a coordinating

concept of collectivity, whose existence could not be doubted (except by people exorcized from the sociological canon such as Tarde), but which is at the same time problematic enough to provide the science of sociology with enough work in terms of diagnosis and even ameliorism. This is possible on the basis of what can be called the *first productive paradox of society*. It entails the idea of a *society that can be united but not ordered, but that can also be ordered yet not united*. In accordance with this paradox, society can be identified as a delimited unity recognizable as such amidst other phenomena in the world, even when this phenomenon is lacking in order. On the other hand, it is possible to observe some sort of order or regularity, which can be described as "society," which is nonetheless wanting in unity. Order and unity have thus been used as if they were separate phenomena. As if the possibility of identifying a "society" does not presuppose the existence of some delimited object, some identity that carries enough unity in order for it to be identified, and as if this observable thing *were something other than a certain observable order or regularity*. The first productive paradox of society is thus productive in the sense that, even when order is missing, "society" is observable and at hand, open for ordering proposals. And, on the other hand, even when an order exists but unity and clear-cut (cultural, economic) unity is missing, a "society" is at hand, open for unifying proposals. This bifurcation between "order" and "unity" has led to a *doubling of reality* that has to do with the doubling inherent in the part/whole scheme: as Luhmann puts it, reality is described twice, once as parts and once as whole (1984: 20; 1997: 918). And so whoever questions society's order, still presupposes some identifiable entity, bounded and unified enough for a certain order to be recognized as a distinct phenomenon. On the other hand, whoever wonders how unified society really is can only do so by pointing at a certain order and asking what its identifying characteristic is. In practice, Luhmann states, this has led to the use of two distinct observational modes: "Is something observed in its unity, then it is a whole. If the same (!) is observed in its plurality, then it is described at the level of its parts" (2000a: 325).

In reality, this doubling of reality makes the mistake of describing a certain "order" as distinct from that which enables this order to be identified, and of thinking of "unity" as something distinct from a certain order. The "order" that might be observed as some kind of pattern or regularity was not taken at face value, but was planted within a larger, more encompassing frame of "society." It was not taken as an observable order, but as an order that was always already an order *within* society. The immanence of order and unity, just like the Wittgensteinian immanence of rule and regularity (Wittgenstein 1984: 350), is what the part/whole scheme here bypasses. For a long time, this bypassing had productive results for social science. For the first paradox of society could then be rendered plausible by adding a second. This *second productive paradox of society* entails the idea that *society is itself by not yet being itself.* That is to say that a *temporalization* takes place, which allows for the assumption of an order whose unity will be realized in the future, or of a unity to be ordered in the future. This temporalization, albeit in the form of a paradox separating a factual from an ideal and counterfactual society, in effect deparadoxizes the first productive paradox of society. That is to say that the doubling of reality is rendered productive only when the two doubles can be temporalized and do not need to be confronted with simultaneously. In fact, both paradoxes balance each other, for the second paradox needs the first in order to be plausible. In order for there to be a society that is only fully realized in the future, the idea of a unity to be ordered in the future, or of an order to be unified in the future, is supportive. In the end, a productive kind of switching occurs here that renders the modern sociological edifice of "society" plausible.

Diagnosis: Social Hypochondria

The situation in which that plausibility withers away can be seen as characterized by a form of *social hypochondria*. This involves a continuous, routinized, and in part professionalized reflection *of* society and its well-being *by* society that today has its most far-reaching consequences in immigrant integration imaginaries. "Integration" has become the master concept identifying all who in one way or another appear "unadjusted to society." The unemployed, the poor, the young, the elderly, those who do not use computers, those convicted of crimes, and those in mental institutions, to name a few categories, are subject to "(re)integration in society." This society, then, has become something of a social hypochondriac: constantly touching itself, looking for spaces of lacking "integration," a social body that is obsessed with its own health and with possible incursions from its environment. The metaphor of a social hypochondriac fully exploits – to the point of explosion – the organicist remains in the prevailing imagination of society. For if society is still, however tacitly, considered by analogy to a body, if society thus indeed lives, then it must necessarily die, and the imagination of its mortality can never be far away but is likely to be repressed.

More abstractly, this comes down to the idea that every social order is a contingent ordering achievement that will be surpassed by another order. Each order produces images of its condition, as well as negations of its contingency and its possible demise or mortality. In general, social orders fare well by a negation of their two constitutive moments: their beginning and their end. The contingent foundation or "beginning" of a social order can be negated, for instance, by replacing it with a counterfactual beginning, such as a social contract. Such beginnings, because they are necessarily contingent, are vulnerable when fundamental reflection is geared toward them. That is why Pascal (1976: 64) noted that "one must forget the beginning." Calling into question the "beginning of society" or the foundation of social order gives rise to problems of legitimation. So the contract theories of the seventeenth and eighteenth century presupposed a contract but took the signing of the contract or covenant to be a counterfactual event. The founding event of the collectivity never took place. Similarly, societies have come up with ways to negate the death of the social body. The "end of society," for instance, could be seen not as an end but as an end goal, as it was in Christian eschatological thought or in Enlightenment visions of Progress. Many of such conceptions are rooted in the idea of society as a social body, composed of parts, and healthy as a whole when its parts are properly attuned and well ordered. Most social scientists today do not subscribe to explicit notions of a social body. After Comte and Spencer, and especially after the eugenic theories developed in the nineteenth century, so the argument usually goes, social science gradually emancipated from organicist and social Darwinian visions of society. Among the founders of sociology, Durkheim was one of the latest to subscribe to some explicit concept of a social body, but Parsonian functionalism was already a step further away from that. Its subsequent development and demise ended the organicist flavor of sociological theory. I argue that that may be a conclusion too quickly drawn. The roots of political, philosophical, and sociological reflection on society lie in an ancient and thoroughly organicist framework that, even if tacitly, still informs current conceptions of society.

Society is still regarded, as in Plato's *Politeia* and *Thaetetus*, as a whole consisting of parts, it is still seen as a unity that is bounded and individually identifiable, and there are continuing worries about its imminent disintegration, which Plato termed *dysnomia*. And with the loss of an encompassing plausibility of the religious and modern master narratives that allowed for the negation of the end through its transformation into an end goal, society has lost its prime ways of negating its contingency and therefore its likely end. The end can no longer be plausibly held to be an end goal, a fulfillment at the *dies irae* or a Utopia reached through Progress. In the era after the widespread credibility of teleological master narratives, then, one of the most effective ways remaining to fend off reflection on the end of society appears to be the obsessive reflection on its possible ills, its diseases or defects.

Social hypochondria, as an obsession with the social body's possible diseases is a way of negating the death of the social body, or in other words, of negating the *contingency* of the existing social order, at a time when that contingency cannot be brushed away by grand visions of transcendence and teleological end goals in the form of mass utopias (Buck-Morrs 2000: ix–x). Social hypochondria is thus in one sense a consequence of a lack of such transcendent teleological end station of society. It is the self-observation of society in times of reflexive modernity, with its chronic revision of everything that happens. So the idea of social hypochondria is not meant as another version of the "end of ideology" thesis. But it does signify a condition in which each incarnation of the transcendent, be it in the form of religion, culture, the nation, or simply the essence of society, is at stake as contingent and as lacking in encompassing plausibility.

Social hypochondria is therefore also not another way of describing the effects of a "postmodern condition," which merely signals the weak condition of the social body that, implicitly, underlies most conceptions of society. Rather, it is a way in which collective self-observations are produced in a time of functional differentiation, which is a radicalization of Max Weber's observation of a differentiation of "value spheres." As Luhmann has argued, a functionally differentiated social system has no center from which it is held together or from which it can be observed as a whole. In effect, he says, "society has no address." Politically speaking, one could think here of the problem of *articulation* of the Good that, as Charles Taylor (1989) has noted, any liberal system necessarily has. Today, when liberalism, in either republican, communitarian, or libertarian incarnations, appears as the only option in the West, that lack of articulation means that no encompassing goal or direction is present, although it is significant that "growth" is an exception. Such lack of encompassing plausibility is a consequence of the complexity of modernity, since it, as Calhoun says, "has meant in significant part the breakup – or the reduction to near-irrelevance – of most all-encompassing identity schemes" (Calhoun 1995: 195). Likewise, no observation of the whole of society has encompassing plausibility – only the problematization of its unity, the diagnosis of its problems, appears to be able to mobilize such plausibility. Social hypochondria functions as a simplifying mechanism. It is a style of discourse that allows for a readymade identification along simplex inside/outside lines. It in a sense transforms us to the situation of the Nuer, which Calhoun (1995: 196) recalls, who "had a minimally disputed set of shared rhetorics for both self-identification and recognition of others." To draw this parallel is surely to underestimate the contestedness of contemporary boundaries of "society." But then these boundaries often entail ascribed *and* appropriated identifications, and they are enforced through power hierarchies, for instance, in Dutch politics, in which "non-Western allochthons" most readily gain access to higher office and high publicity when they are critical of "their communities" or critique their former religion and call for greater efforts at "integration" (such as former secretary of state and current mayor of Rotterdam Achmed Aboutaleb, Amsterdam local politician Achmed Marcouch, or former MP Ayaan Hirsi Ali).

In the counterfactual imagination of a "society" that is secular[7] despite Muslim presence, unscathed despite crime, and homogeneous despite difference, "society" becomes an ideal that is strived for in the very presupposition that what is at stake is the *defense* of an already existing society.[8] Social hypochondria is thus *productive* in a specific sense. It gives performative plausibility to the idea of a bounded, national society. In problematizing the "integration" of those considered

---

[7] "Secular" is meant here in the sense of "non-church-going," which is how it is operationalized in research (see Chapter 3) and generally discussed in public (see Chapter 5).

[8] This is, of course, reminiscent of Michel Foucault's (1997a) analysis of the creation of the object of society in the eighteenth century through racial discourses of war.

"outside society," social hypochondria renders society itself observable. "Society" gains the possibility of identifying itself by identifying – in various social systems (e.g., social science, policy, politics) and through various social programs (e.g., culture, religion, citizenship) – those who can at least be seen *not* to be a part of it. In a sense, then, tacit assumptions of organic wholeness produce something akin to these assumptions. What they produce, a social imaginary of "society," surely exists on an ontological plane that differs from the *reality claims* that they entail (a bounded society consisting of individually integrated subjects). However, the self-referentiality of social life means that such paradoxes can be made productive.

Society is imagined as an identitarian body, but the endangeredness and the mortality of that body can no longer be considered as solved in the future either by eschatological uplifting or by secular progress. And so the only way to fend off from explicit imagination the possible end of society consists in the continuous and exclusive focus on the problems, the pathologies, the ills of society. Social hypochondria thus first and foremost appears in the guise of a self-diagnostic in terms of the "integration" of what is tacitly presupposed still to be an organic whole, a social body with a boundedness that is both cultural and moral. The idea of a temporalization and of an idealization of society in the future has lost much of its appeal in the second half of the twentieth century. If, today, we have an entire industry specialized in problematizing society, in specifying the risks it faces and the threats it is under, that is the case because the problematization of social pathologies is a potent way of keeping alive the imagination of society as a closed, ordered, unified body. Even where such assumptions are never explicitly expressed, prevailing uses of "society" share in the longstanding (quasi-)organicist imagination discussed here.

The point is then not to discard the notion of society because of either its theoretical uselessness, its practical uselessness in an age of globalization, or its political nefariousness. The point is, rather, to acknowledge the productive ways in which the imagination of society enacts power differentials by hierarchizing populations, by dividing them, by establishing asymmetries, by attributing membership of "society" only to those occupying dominant positions, and by problematizing as "unintegrated" those who do not. The organicist remainders in the imagination of society are, thus, extremely potent tools in the politics of immigrant integration and of citizenship, and in the ways culture, religion, and sexuality are made public. Precisely the fact that the conventional imagination of society does not conform to the latest insights in social theory – that difference is a more consistent starting point than identity – provides that concept with powerful performative effects. The next chapters scrutinize the programs along which integration imaginaries are spun, and the effects this has on the imagination of society.

3 | Measuring Society: Moral Monitoring and the Social Science of "Immigrant Integration"

The Very Idea of Measuring Immigrant Integration: From Colonialism to the Present

Governing imaginaries are intricately tied to certain knowledges. As a recent EU and OECD report called *Indicators of Immigrant Integration 2015* emphasizes: "Information on the integration of immigrants and their children is key for a proper policy debate" (OECD and EU 2015: 15). And yet no direct link between the two can be established if the assumption is that knowledge has "instrumental" uses in policy. As Christina Boswell (2009: 7) has argued, research is important in policy, but it is so not in instrumental ways but in two more symbolic ways. In *The Political Uses of Expert Knowledge: Immigration Policy and Social Research*, Boswell distinguishes between two such symbolic uses. The first concerns the legitimizing function of research in policy. Policy gets to be considered more legitimate if it seen to be based on forms of expert knowledge. The second is what she calls a substantiating function of research and knowledge in policy. It concerns ways in which, in contested policy areas, expert knowledge helps policy bodies or political parties solidify and substantiate their policy preferences. When applied to the ways in which expertise around immigrant integration in Europe is used, it becomes clear that instrumental uses are indeed hard to find. One reason for this is that it is rather unclear what the immediate instrumental implications are of numbers that say that certain ethnic groups do so and so on integration scales. Another reason is that such quantitative knowledge often tends to have symbolic uses. In the context of this book, it is more accurate to say that it has imaginary uses. Both symbolic uses distinguished by Boswell are relevant in the case of immigrant integration expertise. Policy and political discourse get legitimated by reference to the latest numbers, which may be presented as a grave cause for concern, and through this they function as a platform from which to initiate certain types of discourse, thereby actualizing a certain immigrant integration imaginary. At the same time, policies are substantiated by numbers, as the numbers specify certain *locations of problematization*. Numbers hierarchize ethnic groups, they pinpoint geographical asymmetries, and they single out institutional contexts relevant to immigrant integration.

So, bearing in mind the legitimizing and substantiating functions of expertise described by Boswell, it is fair to say that social science is a professional discourse that carries a certain symbolic weight. It is for that reason that Max Weber preached "value freedom" (*Wertungsfreiheit*, as an absence of "(e)valuation" in research). For a similar reason, Pierre Bourdieu (1982) has argued that it is crucial to scrutinize the scientific discourses contributing to the perpetuation of social constructions of various problems, groups, and categories. It is relevant to consider what he has called the "reality effects" of such professional discourses. In the case of a social scientific discourse on integration in the Netherlands, those reality effects pertain to the definition of social problems, such as "immigrant integration." They pertain to the construction of "groups," such as "ethnic groups," which, as I illustrate below, never refers to native Dutch. And they involve categorizations, such as "insufficiently integrated," "allochthonous," and "autochthonous" in the Netherlands and Belgium, or "migration background" versus "nonmigration background and" "foreigner" versus "nonforeigner" in Germany, and so on, extending into a wide array of national classifications that achieve the same thing: they articulate the boundaries of a national society. But even beyond that, social scientific integration discourse contributes to the fixation of the primordial object of social science itself: "society." It shares in a popular discourse, which pervades both policy and the political sphere, as well as media discourse on immigrant integration, in which the notion of persons residing "outside society" is common. My argument is that in Western Europe today, "integration" is an observational form that has far-reaching consequences for the way "society" is construed throughout such contexts. In 1988 a Norwegian White Paper argued that immigrants' rights to their "culture" could not mean the liberty to "stay completely out of Norwegian society" (quoted in Hagelund 2002: 407). The same notion of "society" and its "outside" is operative in the German problematization of "parallel societies" (*Parallelgesellschaften*), but also in the policy goals set in 2013, which equate "integration" with "social participation."[1] It is, for instance, active in the speech in which former British prime minister David Cameron famously denounced multiculturalism and in which "our values" are seen as characteristic of a "society" to which "they," in their "segregated communities," don't "want to belong." Similar conceptions of "society" and its "outside" have been active in Dutch policy discourse for two decades now. Rather than being neutral terms, such concepts have performative effects by giving a particular conception of "society" plausibility. More importantly, they give that conception a moral efficacy that has the effect of reproducing the difference between "members of society" and "nonintegrated immigrants," which is the very difference well-meaning and humanistically couched efforts at "integration" aim to remove. Much like the way James Scott discusses the practices of rendering social life "legible" in *Seeing like a State* (1998), I argue that the very idea of "integration," and its social scientific measurement, contribute to stabilizing a concept of "national society" that is intricately tied to policy efforts. This has been argued previously by Adrian Favell, who writes:

> Who or what is integrating whom and with what? This is by no means an obvious question, unless we consider, as many social scientists do, the *state* and *a society* as the unproblematic, unchallenged backdrops to these debates and processes. When political actors and policy intellectuals talk about "integration," they are inevitably thinking about integration into one, single, indivisible (national) "state," and one, simple, unitary (national) society. But it is precisely the assumptions behind these terms that need to be examined. Political language is performative: to invoke these conceptions is to attempt *create* the phenomenon of which they are speaking. (Favell 2001b: 351)

Given this performativity of integration imaginaries, the measurement of immigrant integration is, today, one prominent regime of surveillance and societal imagination. It is preceded by others, for instance, those monitoring the conditions of the poor through the institutions of the welfare state, at its height of legitimacy in the late 1970s, and by colonial efforts at measuring the "morals" of Europeans in the East Indies. Especially the latter parallel is interesting in

---

[1] www.bundesregierung.de/Webs/Breg/DE/Bundesregierung/Beauftragtefuer Integration/beauftragte-fuer-integration.html (accessed March 14, 2013).

that, as in so many Western European countries, the very recent colonial past of the Netherlands is never part of the mainstream public discussion surrounding immigrant integration. And yet the post–World War II era, with the colonial war in Indonesia and the redesign of the Dutch kingdom in 1953 – Van Reekum (2014: 86) speaks of the Dutch "empire" – had led to various forms of migration that should have drawn attention to the deep link between colonialism and migration. Today, colonialism and imperialism are not considered legitimate connections or associations in discussions of the demands that can and should be placed on immigrants. And yet, as Dienke Hondius has argued (2011), it was the end of the colonial era that ushered in a brief period in which migration became feasible for many from outside Europe. And so, the granting of freedoms to former slaves and colonialized people meant the introduction of restrictions to their mobility. The absence of such issues from the dominant public imagination no doubt has to do with the self-definition of the Netherlands as "post-racist," but it is important to be attentive to the one-sidedness of that self-definition (Romeyn 2014). It also has to do with the fact that discussion of immigrant integration is overwhelmingly conducted by white men – myself included – but that in itself is illustrative of the strong continuity between the colonial past and the (postcolonial) present.

Dutch colonial history is saturated with constructions of cultural and racial alterity. Crucially, the Dutch colonial administration was not directly interested in civilizing offences toward indigenous populations, certainly less so than their French counterparts. So questions of cultural assimilation did not immediately come up with respect to indigenous peoples. Rather, they pertained to those of mixed blood and to those colonial administrators and workers who had lived overseas for long stretches of time. The scrutiny of morals, in brief, pertained to those considered to be, in some sense or another, "Europeans." And the focus of knowledge practices was to ascertain the degree to which such people actually entertained European morals, that is, the degree to which they could be considered "real Europeans." Having said that, there were a variety of which in which difference and alterity were produced. As Frances Gouda has argued (1995), in the education of Indonesian girls in Java and Bali in the first half of the twentieth century, an image of "tradition" arose in which Indonesian women were considered as

closer to nature. This was accompanied by notions of native cultures that were part of an orientalist admiration. The end result
was, as Gouda argues, that "by dressing up ethnic traditions
according to European tastes and sensibilities in Western cultural
attire, Dutch colonial residents neatly collected and intellectually
appropriated Javanese or Balinese cultures in order to arrange them
in a taxonomy that rendered them more manageable to the
Dutch colonial regime" (Gouda 1995: 81). Such taxonomies were
strengthened by evolutionary ideas according to which natives came
to be seen as childlike, medieval, and animal-like (122). Most of
the time, though, such images did not involve forms of knowledge
advanced by actual measurement. That this did occur among inhabitants of the colonies deemed in some sense "European" is illustrated by Ann Stoler in her historical analysis of Dutch colonial
administration of the Dutch East Indies. Especially "poor whites"
and people of mixed blood were scrutinized in the extent to which
they were truly "Dutch" or, in some cases, "French," and, at the
same time, "European." She describes the court case of a French
man in Indochina seeking to prove that his *métis* son was really
"French" by arguing that his son's sense of belonging and his
cultural competences proved his Frenchness. Similarly, Stoler
describes the fact that citizenship rights – meaning: being legally
"European" – entailed the "complete suitability for European society" (quoted in Stoler 2002: 17). Today, what Stoler calls "moral
measurements" are an intricate part of a process of societal self-
identification in Western Europe.

I therefore propose to analyze the social scientific measurement of
"integration" as one social way of rendering "society" imaginable
by identifying what does not belong to it. The work of definition of
"society" is shifted toward the "outside society," and "society"
becomes preoccupied with fending off outside incursions that
threaten its wholeness and integrity. Yet it is in this problematization that "society" gains plausibility, boundaries, order, stability,
and cohesion. Rather than mystifying difference and exteriority,
I shall focus here on the way such difference is actively produced
in something very mundane: the measurement of integration by
government bureaucrats and positivist sociologists, running statistical analyses from their computers on surveys constructed out of
scales of Likert items.

The social science of immigrant integration is one site of the production of the social imagination of "society." But, as Luhmann also insists (1990: 79), such imagination presupposes certain distinctions. Imagining or observing through the lens of "integration" means observing populations in terms of a distinction of well integrated/not well integrated. Observational forms allow observations by attributing one or the other value to what is observed. For instance: in attributing an action to oneself, one marks "self" or a "self/other" distinction. My aim is to uncover how that works in the case of immigrant integration, and what its consequences are for the way various discursive programs, such as modernity, religion, or citizenship, are construed. I thus take "integration" to mean not a process of adjustment of immigrants to their "host society," but rather as a form of the imagination, a means used to observe and to render a certain object observable. This form is two-sided, and like any form in Luhmann's conception it involves an inside and an outside. The object rendered imaginable by a focus on integration is "society." Observing with the help of the distinction integrated/not integrated, which in the practice of observation is a scale (and for this reason it can be measured), enables the delineation and fixation of "society."

A prominent site where "society" becomes actualized today, I argue, is the "blind spot" of the observational form of integration. It is fundamentally unobservable with the observational form of integration, but the very observing through the distinction "well integrated"/"not well integrated" continually delimits "society" as the unscathed whole where such observations do not and cannot apply. I shall argue, therefore, that "integration" is a form that renders society imaginable by *not marking* it. "Society" remains the *permanently unmarked space* of "integration" as an imaginary form. That is to say that neither the "integrated" nor the "nonintegrated" is construed as part of what "society" is. Rather, "society" is that which is not imaginable in terms of "integration." It is that for which "integration" is simply not an issue. And only he or she is constructed as a "member of society" who is not observed in terms of his or her "integration." That is to say that *also* those who are "well integrated" remain "outside society." The fact that the unmarked is unproblematic and is equated with "society" constitutes a strong continuity with the history of colonialism, where colonial rulers were "neutral" but those of mixed blood or of questionable morals due to their long immersion in the non-neutral colonial realm were potentially problematic.

Integration thus allows distinctions on two levels. On a first level, it allows the distinction between well-integrated and lesser integrated groups and individuals. On a second level, it permanently reproduces a distinction between "society" and all those observed in terms of their "integration." That observation takes place in many settings, and the setting I discuss in this chapter is that of the social scientific measurement of immigrant integration. It is in this form of *moral monitoring*, which is a crucial part of what Niklas Luhmann has called contemporary society's "compulsive need for self-assessment" (Luhmann 2000a: 21) that the very idea of "society" gains scientific credibility.

Defining "Immigrant Integration"

It is, first of all, important to get a feel of the way "immigrant integration" is conceived in the contemporary social science of its measurement. It is a typical core concept in the social sciences, first, in that it is hardly ever defined. In theoretical sociology, the concept has its roots in organicist theories such as those of Spencer and Durkheim. Classical sociology, to a certain extent preoccupied with what Parsons dubbed "the Hobbesian problem of order," in a sense founded society on a paradox. While the differentiation of modern society posed profound difficulties in terms of morality and cohesion for someone like Durkheim, the answer to such problems lay precisely in the idea of integration through differentiation. Such a solution is propounded also by Spencer, and it is a typical form of organicist thought, focused on the organic wholeness of society. One can then procure the whole by treating its parts as individually distinct and valuable for the whole precisely in their distinctness.

The concept of integration has henceforth never quite shed its organicist or at least its functionalist connotations. It figures prominently in Parsons, who applies it at the level of the action system and sees integration as the proper alignment of the four functional prerequisites his theory proposes. And it appears in authors that have engaged critically with Parsons's work, such as Giddens, Lockwood, and

Habermas. Lockwood and Habermas propose a distinction between "system integration" and "social integration." "Social integration" for Lockwood refers to the solidarity between individuals, while "system integration" refers to the relationship between parts and whole (1992: 399). This chimes with Habermas's distinction between system and life world. But this distinction is problematic, for one, because it doubles and theoretically confuses "society," as Habermas speaks of "society" both as the ensemble of system and life world and as the sphere of possible communicative action that takes shape within the life world (1989: 149–167). In American sociology, one conceptualization that comes close to the measurement discussed in this chapter stems from Chicago School work on social integration as a form of mixing versus distance. Also, the work of Emory Bogardus (1925) and his scale of "social distance" appears timely when current measurements of integration are observed. Indeed, American sociology is highly influential at least for Dutch work on immigrant integration, and here it is especially assimilation research that is taken as a source of inspiration. Lastly, the "contact indices" used in the measurement, discussed in detail below, are reminiscent of the U.S. history of racial integration research, and in the tradition of the attention to "interracial contacts" in Myrdal's book *An American Dilemma: The Negro Problem and Modern Democracy* (1944: 650–657).

Concepts of integration thus vary distinctly. Yet Armin Nassehi has discussed the concept of integration as spanning social theory from Durkheim, via Parsons to Habermas and Alexander. All these approaches, he argues, in the end can only thematize "society" in common sense terms, that is, as a collectivity with an address. In all these theories, however different, he says, the problem of integration is in one way or another equal to the constitution of an object signified by "society." The theoretical function of "integration," he says, is to mold unity out of difference, and hence to establish a secure referent of "society" (Nassehi 2006: 329).

Although it is striking that the current sociology of immigrant integration appears cut off from explicit theorizations of integration, it nonetheless shares in this "theoretical function" of the concept. Current approaches to "integration" have been critiqued with respect to their concept of integration due to (often implicit) representations of order and harmony present in such theories. Helmut Willke goes so far as to speak of a "normalized ignorance" (Willke 1993: 245). But in a sense, that is one indication that classical theoretical presuppositions are in the end very much incorporated in the sociology of integration. While the concept was introduced in the context of immigration because it was thought to overcome the negative connotations of concepts of assimilation (Kruyt and Niessen 1997), it has never been fully theoretically severed from assimilationist presuppositions. Where concepts of integration differ, for instance, from the Parsonian concept is in the level at which they are applied. For Parsons, it was the action system that was either well integrated or not. For most sociology of immigrant integration, it is, since the 1980s, the individual that is either well integrated into society or not. This is a crucial difference to which I shall return. But visions of order and harmony have remained in current conceptualizations of integration. These imply that "society" is a preexisting whole, that there are *potential parts* of that whole in the environment of society, and that these, if they turn out to be well integrated, gain the status of actual parts of society.

Relatively unsurprising, therefore, is the fluid transition between policy definitions and scientific conceptions of integration. When, in a book by two of the most influential Dutch researchers in the field of integration research, the definition of integration is discussed, it is evaded by the remark that "in the literature on citizenship, assimilation, integration and incorporation, a number of spheres, domains, dimensions, fields, or whatever these categories may be called, are commonly discerned" (Vermeulen and Penninx 2000: 4). As a proxy for defining the concept, three strategies are taken. The first is the focus on domains, dimensions, or spheres of integration (Peters 1993; Engbersen and Gabriëls 1995). The second consists of a normative description resembling political and policy definitions. The third, which is always present in research, consists of an enumeration of indicators of integration. In essence, then, after an initial untheorized and often normative statement, the *definition* of integration is replaced by an account of its *operationalization*. Such operationalization usually takes the form of a prior distinction between "socio-structural integration" and "socio-cultural integration." While the former can be normatively described as "full participation in societal institutions," the latter may, for instance, refer to "the social contacts members and organizations of minorities keep up with the broader society and the cultural adjustments to that society" (Vermeulen and Penninx 1994, in Engbersen and Gabriëls 1995: 19). A typical way of "defining" the concept of integration is the following:

> Before I start reviewing the literature, it is fruitful to be clear about what is meant by the concepts being used. Economic integration (or incorporation) indicates the degree of economic equality between immigrants and natives. ... It is assumed that the economic integration of immigrants is stronger, the higher their participation rates, employment levels, occupational status and income. Socio-cultural integration actually refers to two closely related aspects of integration: social integration (the extent to which immigrants interact socially with natives), and cultural integration (the degree to which cultural values and patterns are shared among immigrants and natives). ... Cultural integration is assumed to be higher when immigrants are proficient in the host language and speak that language frequently, when they identify themselves as natives, when immigrants" religiosity is more similar to that of natives, and when cultural values and attitudes are shared. ... Immigrants are more socially integrated in the host country when interethnic contacts, friendships, and marriages are frequent. (Van Tubergen 2004: 23–24)

The indicators used to measure integration by this researcher are language abilities, religious participation and affiliation, labor market status, level of education, and occupational status. Apart from transforming the definitional work into the circumscribing of "indicators," the idea of being clear about what concepts mean before reviewing literature is indicative of a preconception of what "integration" means. It is clear that it has reference to individuals as yet "outside society" but possibly moving in the direction of that society. These individuals are furthermore "ethnically" or "culturally" marked, as not all immigrants are scrutinized. As the subtitle of a document by The Netherlands Institute for Social Research (SCP) on its SIM-survey illustrates, the exclusive focus is on highly specific "minority groups": "Account of the design and execution of a survey among Turks, Moroccans, Surinamese, Antillians and an autochthonous comparative group" (SCP 2007a). This chimes well with the policy distinction between "Western allochthons" and "non-Western allochthons." The former consists, for instance, of Germans, Belgians, and Americans, but also of Japanese and Indonesians (a distinction to which I shall return in Chapter 4). The latter consists mainly of those whose integration is measured. But if the definition of integration becomes apparent through the measurement methods, it is fruitful to scrutinize that measurement, which can first of all be described in its organizational context.

Regimes of Measurement in Western Europe

Some Western European regimes of measurement of integration are aimed at visualizing immigrants, while others are predominantly aimed at rendering them invisible. The Dutch regime is an example of the former. When immigrant integration was first measured on an official basis and with a national scope, more than thirty years ago (Bijl and Verweij 2012: 245), the Dutch were the arguably first to do so in Western Europe. Denmark is one of few countries to have experimented with the measurement of "socio-cultural integration," and in Germany, cultural issues were also foregrounded in the 1980s (Bommes 1996). Nowhere has that measurement been as formalized as in the Netherlands. Before going into the architecture of the Dutch regime of measurement, it is important to briefly ponder the question why that is so. Two factors would appear to have played a role here. One is the "national regime of immigrant integration." A second is the bureaucratic regime of the Netherlands. These factors combined have made the Netherlands a "forerunner" in categorizing its immigrant population (and more) under the heading of "integration."

In many Western European countries, a close connection between integration policy and integration science exists (Favell 2001b). Homologies between science and policy are one argument for the idea that there exist national regimes of measurement. Such taxonomical regimes render the nation visible in specific ways. What they do and do not include is decisive in the content of the collective imaginary. There are, likewise, many categorizations of national models of immigrant integration. For instance, there are, supposedly, a Dutch multiculturalism and a French republicanism. The problem with such categorizations is that they espouse a methodological nationalism (Wimmer and Glick Schiller 2002, 2003; Glick Schiller, Çagdar, and Guldbrandsen 2008). In a sense, when I take the "Dutch" case as an example in this book, a similar objection might be raised. However, my interest is in the way a national society imagines itself, so to speak as a Baron von Münchhausen, pulling itself up from the morass by its own hair. Methodological nationalism is a problem when comparing welfare states or labor market participation, but not when analyzing the way a national imagery is connected to an assembling concept of "society." Then, all those sites where the connection between "nation" and "society" is forged are relevant sites of analysis. And they impose their own limits to that analysis.

National "models" of immigrant integration, however, are thereby to be seen as performative constructs. The "French republican model," for instance, is hardly uncontested. Moreover, as the reports of the *Haut Conseil à l'Intégration* show (2009), the content of that model changes over time, having in recent years incorporated many more "cultural" aspects than the "open French culture" might be expected to have. For while the Dutch and French traditions, for instance, significantly differ, they lead to surprising similarities. Both countries have a vivid debate on the veil and on a possible "burqa ban," and both countries are characterized by segregation in schools and cities. Especially in the French case, where "multiculturalism" is traditionally equated with "segregation" and "ghettoization," that similarity is telling. However, it is reasonable to expect some differentiation on the basis of the difference between national polities, as well as between forms of *politesse* that are part of accounts of the nation. By the latter, I refer to the degree to which "ethnic" categorizations are tabooed for reasons pertaining to what has been called "political correctness" or, more broadly speaking, because such categorizations did not fit into existing policy frames.

Indeed, various Western European countries have tabooed the "ethnic registration" of the population. In Belgium, for instance, census data have been used to measure immigrant integration, but such data do not include "second generation immigrants," and they lack data on language, ethnicity, and religion – all "variables" deemed crucial to assessing what is called "socio-cultural integration" (Phalet and Swyngedouw 2003). In France, a republican tradition has entailed a "color blindness" that has long been a French pride, since the lack of distinction in terms of either race or ethnicity is often deemed indicative of a lack of French racism. The 2004 ban of the veil in schools is likewise a sign of the desire, in the French situation, to deny all trace of difference. But the same reluctance to categorize immigrants has led to the late rise of research of racism in France (Amiraux and Simon 2006). Thus, the social sciences in France were equally reluctant to adopt "ethnic" categorizations. French social science was, and is, moreover, divided. There are those who choose to exclusively focus on socioeconomic issues, those who prefer to study the production of difference in racism and discrimination, and there are those who vigorously defend the republican "model." Census data have not allowed the identification of "second generation immigrants," nor have they allowed properly distinguishing "immigrants" from "foreigners" and "French." Analyses of ethnic origin and cultural behavior, mostly language use and religious affiliation, have not been published by official institutes such as INSEE. The few that do exist been necessarily improvised (Simon 1999, 2003). Most famous is the study by Michèle Tribalat et al., who (in collaboration with INSEE) made ethnographic assessments of "ethnic" origins (1996).

Something similar has taken place in the United Kingdom, which is otherwise completely different in that it does include "ethnic identification" in census data and in the Labour Force Survey. Here, researchers have been pulled in different directions (Small and Solomos 2006: 250–254). And the British concept of "integration," as famously worded by Jenkins, has not given rise to sustained measurement of "cultural assimilation," even though in recent years, "Britishness" has become a hotly debated issue, and "immigrant integration" is increasingly becoming both a policy issue and a research concept in the United Kingdom (Ali and Gidley 2014). In Germany, regular surveys including ethnic origin are conducted. The SOEP survey (e.g., 2008) also includes a few questions on contacts and one on religion, but these do not amount to the Dutch level of formalization in measuring "sociocultural integration." Moreover, a problem in Germany is that the various *Länder* give differing priorities to language use; in some, German is the second language. Statistics abound in Germany, though, and they are, for instance, collected under the auspices of what was formerly the Beauftragte der Bundesregierung zur Ausländerfragen, a post that was redubbed Beauftragte für Migration, Flüchtlinge und Integration in 2005. At that time, the new Immigration Act (Zuwanderungsgesetz) gave rise to both a stricter immigration policy and a stronger focus on integration.

The Netherlands, on the other hand, has long had a pluralist view of integration, which is often mistakenly called "multicultural." In the 1960s, it was believed that immigrant "guest workers" would return. Nobody promoted their "integration," which was seen as an unwanted assimilation both by those who wished their return and by those who cherished "cultural" authenticity. When the idea of their return was finally seen as a "myth," the Netherlands opted for a model emphasizing "minority cultures." This is to be seen as part of a longer tradition in which the collective body is seen to exist as an ensemble of lower-level organic groups. Dutch history in the late nineteenth and the twentieth century is characterized by a "pillarization" along religious and ideological lines (Lijphart 1975). Its "consensus model" involved "pacification at the top" of various conflicting religious and ideological "pillars." Such a model was already waning in the late 1960s, and integration policies were never coined on its basis, but pillarization did involve the ready acknowledgment of cultural taxonomies within the Dutch population. Being without a "strong" or "thick" concept of national culture – although the lack thereof has in fact been a very strong national imagery (Van Reekum 2014) – in the 1970s, a pluralistic model based on cultural minorities was relatively uncontroversial in the Netherlands, while it was out of the question in France, or even in Belgium, the stability of which was secured by its two "autochthonous" populations of the Flemish and the Walloons.

Traditionally, statistics (the "science of the state") has been a crucial tool in the governmental ensemble because it enabled the monitoring of the population, and thereby the fixation of that population and the "society" it is attributed to (Hacking 1990). The Netherlands is known for its bureaucratic-statistical monitoring of the population, which was a main reason why, during World War II, relatively speaking by far the largest number of Western European Jews were deported from the Netherlands. As historian J. C. H. Blom says, it was "the quality, effectiveness and efficiency of the Dutch bureaucracy," with its "almost perfect registration of the civilian population" that were part of what made this possible (1989: 343–344).[2] But from the perspective of the "government of the population," which involves its statistical "speciation," it is hardly surprising that those involved in the measurement of immigrant integration deploy large-scale surveys. The Netherlands is specific in that, unlike other Western European countries, it has no census. But in the measurement of immigrant integration, this has proved an advantage. Debates about census classifications

---

[2] This is also related to the particular regime of occupation in the Netherlands, which differed, for instance, from Denmark in the stringent German control of the administration. However, it would not have been possible to deport the number of Jews had there not been preexisting census data allowing their "identification" (compare Benz, Houwink ten Cate, and Otto 1998).

have thus been avoided. While many Western European countries have shied away from "ethnic" or "religious" classification, Dutch researchers have conducted surveys among people that were "ethnically" identifiable through highly accurate local population records. This "decentralized" registration, which is "centrally" accessible by Statistics Netherlands (CBS), has put researchers in a position to come up with census-independent surveys that have been stable over time.

Finally, a certain degree of (Western) European convergence in models of immigrant integration and citizenship needs to be mentioned. Such convergence mainly exists at the level of policy, and it pertains to a shared combination of neoliberal and cultural-communitarian elements, as becomes visible in varying conceptions of "earned citizenship" in France, the Netherlands, and the United Kingdom (Van Houdt, Suvarierol, and Schinkel 2011). One tool toward that end is the Migrant Integration Policy Index (MIPEX), which monitors and "benchmarks" integration policies in the EU. MIPEX is a typical tool of national self-observation, as it "is intended as a 'mirror' that can be held up to EU member states for them to see how they are performing on migrant integration policy."[3] It is run by a consortium of twenty-five institutions and led by the British Council. Significantly, it does not measure "immigrant integration" but national policies of immigrant integration in Europe. However, its benchmarking efforts were commended by EU Commissioner Franco Frattini in 2007 as a way of evaluating and monitoring immigrant integration throughout the EU. However, precisely such EU monitoring does not involve an emphasis on "national culture" such as is present in certain national regimes of monitoring. Interestingly, many of the issues thematized as "national" in France can be heard in a similar way in Belgium or the Netherlands, and *national* discussions often involve the invocation of a supposedly *civilizational* heritage. Thus, in various countries "Islam" is construed as clashing with national cultures, but only because these cultures are "Western" or "enlightened." But for the EU, such characterizations are still problematic, as "the West" is obviously larger than the EU, and as the EU itself comprises countries whose origins in "the West" are contested. And the EU's "open method of coordination" has not been favorable to a possible EU convergence of integration regimes.

---

[3] www.integrationindex.eu/topics/2648.html (link no longer active).

A European regime of moral monitoring can thus not be said to exist as yet. The regimes that do exist differ in one important sense. So while, for instance, the French science of immigrant integration may (still) be largely concerned with rendering immigrants *invisible*, the Dutch measurement of integration renders them *visible*. But this difference in the end accomplishes something similar when the consequences for the visualization of the national society are concerned. For in both cases, immigrant integration measurement and debate is a form of moral monitoring. And in both cases, such measurement and debate *renders the national society visible* in the not naive "visual" sense that reduces the visual to binocular vision, but rather in the sense of a social imaginary that sorts realities and renders them sayable and actionable. While European assessments of immigrant integration differ, they accomplish the same. As Adrian Favell notes, "despite its somewhat old-fashioned, functionalist air, 'integration' is still the most popular way of conceptualizing the developing relationship between old European nation-states and their growing non-European, 'ethnic' immigrant populations" (2003: 13). In all cases, he argues, a bounded notion of "society" is strengthened as a consequence. When he argues that "the real problem" in survey research is "an in-built dependency on nationally-specific research technologies" (27), it should be clear that it is the combination of "nation" and "society" that is at stake in each case. National differences in similar forms of social imagination ensure the boundedness of each "society" by identifying it with a culturally defined "nation" – even when that identification takes the form of an appeal to "Western," "European," "Enlightenment," "cosmopolitan," "modern," or even "universal values."

Each national tradition of statistics involves deep-rooted notions of what a national subject is and how its position vis-à-vis society as a whole is to be conceived, for instance, through difference or assimilation. Likewise, national discourses on immigrant integration differ, also within Western Europe, and they are ambiguously related to policy differences (Koomen et al. 2013). I shall not delve into such issues here, and so I deliberately sidestep issues of methodological nationalism, as they are not central to my argument here. That argument is that, *despite such differences*, the problematization of integration can be regarded as a *technique of social imagination*. It grants plausibility to the boundedness of a society that is, sometimes more so than in other instances, considered as a "national society." In some cases it does so by rendering immigrants as invisible as possible, but in most cases, this national society is rendered visible precisely by visualizing and observing what does not properly belong to it. Often, as noted, a "national society" becomes identified by "values" or "opinions" construed as "Western." And so when I speak of "national societies" I do not mean to limit "societies" to nation-states. Rather, I wish to highlight the selectivity in the socially imagined overlap between "nation" and "society."

Minority Research Industry in the Netherlands: A Description of the Field

I shall here focus specifically on the authoritative and policy-influencing measurement of integration by semi-governmental research agencies as well as "independent" sociologists within what Essed and Nimako have termed the "Dutch minority research industry" (2006: 284). The Netherlands has a specific history of the institutionalized measuring aspects of the life of immigrants. It has done so for more than twenty years, and in this it stands alone in Western Europe. While all Western European countries problematize "immigrant integration," in the Netherlands social science has been used as a specifically professional discourse to ground such problematization. Indeed, the state-governed research institutes that measure immigrant integration have traditionally exhibited a highly modernist vision of such integration and a teleological vision of modernity. This means immigrant integration is considered a progressive process to be monitored closely in order for it to be steered by policy interventions. Hence, the role of social science in Dutch integration policy has been considerable. What becomes apparent in this measurement is the social scientific identification of the oppositional pair of "society" and "nonintegrated immigrants." This identification is achieved on the basis of an a priori definition of "society" as characterized by – in this case – "Dutch" values such as "secularism."

In the Netherlands, the social science that measures immigrant integration has a somewhat paradoxical constitution. In order to grasp the connections between academic social science and state-led measurements of immigrant integration, it is instructive to have a brief overview of the field. It consists, first of all, of two apparently contradictory research contexts. In terms of Burawoy's typology of professional, policy, critical, and public sociology, the field of integration measurement comprises a strong program of professional sociology on the one hand, and a research context that has "professional" characteristics but strong policy ties on the other. A third research context explicitly combines the first two by actively conducting policy research.

First, the field of integration measurement consists predominantly of a quantitative research school of positivist signature. Institutionally, in the last few decades this has found a home in the Interuniversity Centre for Social Science Theory and Methodology (ICS), which is a research school comprising mainly sociologists working at Utrecht University, the University of Nijmegen, and the University of Groningen. In recent years, collaborative bonds exist between ICS members and researchers at Tilburg University, which have comparable methodological and theoretical starting points. ICS has in recent years been one of two dominant research schools in the Netherlands, and in terms of funding its researchers are no doubt the most successful Dutch sociologists. Dutch research is to a large extent government financed. It is partly financed directly through universities, and partly financed through the Netherlands Organization for Scientific Research, which allocates funds on the basis of peer-review guided competition. ICS sociologists are among the most successful in those competitions. Their institutional dominance in terms of grants is matched by dominance in terms of committee membership and referee work.[4] While the Amsterdam School for Social Science Research was an interdisciplinary consortium of mostly Elias-inspired sociologists (traditionally located at the University of Amsterdam) as well as anthropologists and political scientists,[5] the ICS, while boasting "interdisciplinarity" in its research, institutionally at least consists almost exclusively of sociologists. ICS research is guided by a strong positivist conception of science that is explicitly reminiscent of early post–World War II philosophy of science. The ICS website illustrates this, and I quote somewhat

[4] One further indicator for ICS's institutional dominance is the fact that it was chosen by the Dutch national science funding institution NWO as one of nine Dutch graduate schools in its "NWO Graduate Programme."
[5] In 2010, the ASSR ceased to exist, as research schools spanning several universities were discouraged by the government, which promoted instead interuniversity competition among researchers. ICS continues to exist as a shared graduate school for Ph.D. students, while the ASSR has dissolved into a University of Amsterdam–only graduate school.

extensively to indicate the paradigmatic nature of the positivist conviction subscribed to by ICS members:

While the program addresses topics of societal significance and policy relevance, the nature of the program is knowledge driven: the program explicitly
aims at solving sociological and social science problems while contributing to
the advancement and growth of theoretical and empirical knowledge in
sociology and social science. The *research strategy* emphasizes a problem-
driven approach. Deductive theory building and the integration of theory
formation and empirical research are core elements of the research strategy.
Thus, hypotheses to be tested are systematically derived from theories with
an aim to develop general theories that allow for the integration of more
specific theories by correcting and improving them. The research strategy
thus contributes to the accumulation of coherent social science knowledge
and the reduction of the fragmentation of social science.[6]

Without doubt, it is the dominance of this paradigm in Dutch sociology that has allowed ICS researchers to dominate NWO rounds
and attract large research grants. While ICS research methodology is
informed by a version of Popperian philosophy of science, its theoretical roots lie with Coleman's rational actor sociology.[7] This leads to a
program with a strong rational actor emphasis, paired with a strong
positivistic emphasis on almost exclusively quantitative research, most
often involving large-scale survey data. Immigrant integration has been
one of several ICS researchers' foci. Immigrant integration has moreover long been a crucial research theme in the Utrecht-based European
Research Centre on Migration and Ethnic Relations (ERCOMER).

Second, the field of integration measurement consists of a body of
work produced in proximity to state policy by what could be called
"research-quango's."[8] This concerns quasi-independent research institutes such as, most prominently, SCP and the Scientific Research and
Documentation Centre of the Netherlands Ministry of Justice
(WODC). These produce authoritative and policy-setting figures and
analyses of immigrant integration in the Netherlands. The director of
SCP, also a university professor, attends weekly cabinet meetings in

---

[6] www.ics-graduateschool.nl/research/ (accessed August 17, 2015).
[7] Indicative of this is the "James Coleman Association," founded at the celebration
of the third ICS lustrum: www.ics-graduateschool.nl/james-coleman-association/
(accessed August 17, 2015).
[8] I understand QUANGO here to mean Quasi-Independent Non-Governmental
Organization.

The Hague, and the reports that the SCP produces on request of a ministerial department need political clearance before going public.[9] The Institute claims independence (it gives advice "on request and not on request"),[10] but it falls under the ministerial responsibility of the Ministry of Health, Welfare and Sport. In the drafting of its yearly work programs, however, all Dutch ministerial departments are involved. Its reports on integration, as well as those of the WODC, are basic references for politicians, policy makers, and scientists. On its website, it boasts good cooperation with all Dutch universities.

In the discussion below, I shall take the SCP's yearly reports as a prism of the measurement of integration. One important reason to do so is the striking similarity between "independent" (and mostly ICS-affiliated) integration research and SCP research. This is paradoxical to the extent that ICS research boasts policy independence. It focuses on game theory and subjectivist forms of network analysis, and, in the case of integration research, on acculturation and assimilation theories with mostly a U.S. origin. And its Popperian insistence on scientific autonomy makes clear that its characterization in terms of Burawoy's typology would be that of "professional sociology":

Appropriate *data sets* are required for the empirical testing of theories and hypotheses. Therefore the ICS dedicates much time and effort to the collection of high quality data. ... Employing such complex data sets for testing hypotheses requires, in turn, appropriate statistical models that express mathematically the main theoretical relations between the observed variables bearing on the various actors, levels, and events.[11]

It is precisely this methodological stance that explains the convergence between policy-dependent and independent research. The SCP is one element of an ensemble of governmentality such as described by Foucault (2004a). It is a state-initiated institution that monitors an enormous number of characteristics of the population, and it specifically focuses on "problematic populations." The SPVA survey (Social

[9] See the royal account of its institution: KB (Koninklijk Besluit) (1973): "Besluit houdende de instelling van een Sociaal en Cultureel Planbureau," 30 March 1973: 9.3.
[10] See www.scp.nl.
[11] www.ics-graduateschool.nl/research/ (accessed August 17, 2015).

Position and Use of Facilities by Allochthons) was the only survey for integration research until 2004, when it was superseded by the LAS survey (Life Situation Allochthon Urbanites) and the SIM survey (Survey Integration Minorities). All these surveys are based on local and national population registries of the state. They contain samples of four different "ethnic groups" and of "autochthonous Dutch," which refers to native Dutch citizens. The SIM survey is currently the key important survey in Dutch integration research. It is conducted for the SCP by a private research company, commissioned by the Ministry of Justice and devised by the SCP in collaboration with CBS. And it is the quantitative feature of its research that makes such a policy-based institution attractive to a positivist strand of research that explicitly seeks distance from the policy context. In Christina Boswell's analysis of the political uses of immigration expertise, the symbolic uses of knowledge she discerns imply a relatively loose link between policy makers and researchers (Boswell 2009: 86). In the case described here, there are strong links between those researchers with close ties to policy makers and those with loose ties to the world of policy. The end result is that the overwhelming majority of the quantitative expertise occurs within a form of "normal science" that, directly or indirectly, has strong symbolic uses in policy (in Boswell's terms, both the legitimizing and the substantiating use occur).

There is thus a substantial methodological affinity between quango research and independent research. This methodology implies a choice with definite consequences for possible outcomes, and in a definite sense it fits the ideology that guides this research. It is based on what Andrew Abbott calls the "general linear model" (2001: 37). And this methodological affinity means that a large theoretical overlap exists as well. For the operationalization of key terms, which I shall especially focus on, is necessarily shared when the same survey is used. And, finally, the SCP surveys have been the only ones big enough and available to independent researchers, so the affinity is also related to a position of monopoly. So while, as its website emphasizes repeatedly, ICS research is not "data driven," in the case of integration research the availability of large data sets surely is an important factor driving research. That there is also a strong substantial affinity becomes apparent not only from the fact that independent researchers continue to work with SCP data, but also from the fact that the SCP's main integration researcher cooperates with Utrecht-based ICS researchers in shared NWO research applications. And when, each year, most ICS Ph.D.'s don't get tenured jobs at one of the partnering universities, the SCP is one of the first places they look for a research job.

Next to research quangos and Popperian positivists, a third research context that needs to be mentioned here consists of several influential figures in the social science of integration that have had strong ties to policy. Two figures stand out, both of whom have been authors of two highly influential reports of the Dutch Scientific Council for Government Research (WRR), which produces reports for the Dutch Cabinet. First, Rinus Penninx has been very influential by combining integration research with policy advice in his work on the crucial 1979 WRR report *Ethnic Minorities*. This report gave rise to the first actual policy aimed at immigrants, called "ethnic minority policy" at the time. The report focused on the problems caused by "the immigration of large groups of different culture and/or race in an established society" (1979: vii). Penninx's preparatory study for this report (1979) has been influential in promoting the idea of "ethnic minorities," characterized by highly reified "cultures," and their gradual incorporation in society on the basis of their own cultural strengths. After having had great impact on government policies, Penninx withdrew in a more positivist mode and for years headed the Amsterdam-based Institute for Migration and Ethnic Studies (IMES), a research institute of the University of Amsterdam strongly resembling the Utrecht-based ERCOMER, in that both institutes produce regular publications on, as the IMES-website states, "the *integration* of immigrants and their descendants in host societies."[12] A second scholar of integration who has been influential in government policies is Han Entzinger. His roots lie in public administration, and after being one of the authors of another influential WRR report, called *Allochthon Policy* (1989), he went on to become director of ERCOMER until 2001. The 1989 WRR report introduced the by now near-ineradicable distinction between "allochthons" and "authochthons" in Dutch integration discourse. He was also one of the authors of the 1994 study *Home Office Policy Advice Minority Debate*, which gave rise to the policy equalization between "integration" and "citizenship." Next to ERCOMER and IMES, a third

---

[12] www.imes.uva.nl/In recent years, after Penninx stepped back as director, several members of IMES have adopted a more reflexive take on research of related issues.

institute relevant to mention here is the Rotterdam-based ISEO, which conducted integration research for the SCP.

Next to research quangos and scholars mostly situated in the positivist school of the ICS, then, three "independent" university institutes have been involved in the measurement of integration, all of them run by white native Dutch men. While researchers in the fields of culture and migration are, relatively speaking, among the most diverse in the Dutch social sciences, researchers involved in the quantification of integration may be characterized by their "whiteness" (Essed and Trienekens 2008: 53). This is only one way to interpret the long-standing entanglement of the scientific field of integration research with policy. It points at dominance in the form of what Bourdieu calls the "homology between fields." Practically speaking, this entanglement takes shape either through methodological affinity and data availability, or through direct policy-directed research. In the end, however, virtually all integration research is either directly or indirectly, though universities, state-sponsored. The social science of immigrant integration is really a state science, and as such it is the heir of what Foucault described as "social medicine." In the discussion below, I include references to work by various Dutch researchers of "integration" to illustrate the close conceptual connections between research quangos and "independent research." Some of this work is more recent, and some of it is ten years old, and this highlights a continuity, since the logic underlying it is really the same: "society" is constructed as opposed to individuals lacking in "integration."

Society as Yardstick: Measurements of "Integration" in the Netherlands

A first question for those who measure immigrant integration is: "Why do so?" When the answer is not simply "out of scientific curiosity," it is much more policy-oriented. In its 2006 book on the SIM-survey, the SCP, for instance, states:

After almost twenty years of minorities-surveys one might ask to what extent it is necessary to conduct such research – which is expensive and time-consuming. The answer is simple. Without such a source we miss important information concerning the progress and background of the integration of minority groups. (SCP 2006: 10)

I discuss the measurement of immigrant integration by means of a close reading of the SCP yearly integration reports, starting with 2003. That year is crucial because it is then that the measurement of "socio-cultural integration" was introduced. Hence, as of 2003 "integration" covers both the "structural" and the "cultural" dimension of the lives of immigrants. While the former concerns "the position minorities occupy in the social stratification" (SCP 2003: 317) and hence refers to the relative positions of individuals in the fields of employment and education, "socio-cultural integration" means something different altogether. It is described as referring to the question "to what extent minorities are part of the receiving society or that [*sic*] they instead continue to distinguish themselves from that society" (SCP 2003: 317). It needs to be said, though, that the notion of "receiving society" seems to imply that measurement only occurs in case of immigrants, which is not the case, as also the children of immigrants (often Dutch citizens) are scrutinized by measurements of "socio-cultural integration." Such definitions are in line with authoritative definitions by well-known Dutch social scientists working on the topic, such as the ones quoted above (e.g., Veenman 1995; Hagendoorn, Veenman, and Vollebergh 2003). My focus will here be on the conceptualization of "socio-cultural integration," as it most readily illustrates the construction of "society" as a selective discursive project of social imagination.

In order to regard the convergence of political and scientific definitions of "socio-cultural integration," it is illuminating that the Dutch Second Chamber of Parliament (Tweede Kamer), in its 2006 report on the issue, describes "integration" in general as follows: "integration means participation [*meedoen*] and that requires that all migrants learn the Dutch language and adopt the norms, values and forms of social conduct prevailing in our country" (Tweede Kamer 2006: 5). This chimes well with the definition of "socio-cultural integration" used by the SCP around that time. It describes such "integration" as consisting of "mastery of the Dutch language, identification with one's own group, religious experience and the degree and nature of contact with autochthons" (2007a: 17; 2007b: 163). This definition remains intact in later reports. And it is explicitly mentioned that the survey research used is able to adapt to changing debates about integration: "in recent years, for instance, the discussion on integration has increasingly shifted from structural to socio-cultural integration. A survey can accommodate this, as has happened in SIM [the survey used in 2006]"

(SCP 2006: 11). It thereby becomes clear that research is highly sensitive to mood swings in "public opinion" (and vice versa, since the newspaper article that made a harsher and assimilationist attitude *Salonfähig* in 2000, Scheffer's *The Multicultural Drama*, refers heavily to SCP publications). Conceptions of "socio-cultural integration" involve a quantifiable "distance" at which immigrants stand vis-à-vis society. In their operationalizations, therefore, all the vague generality of such definitions boils down to mainly to two factors measured. The first time the SCP reports measurements of "socio-cultural integration," it is described as "the degree to which ethnic minorities share a number of the regular norms and values of Dutch society and ... the degree of contact which they maintain with autochthonous Dutch" (SCP 2003: 142). This has remained the core of the conceptualization since, so that in 2007, the SCP could note that

in publications by the Social and Cultural Planning Office (SCP) it is by now common to operationally measure this definition, which is stated in general terms, by means of various indicators. The first (subjective) indicator is the degree to which allochthons feel Dutch or mostly connected with their ethnic group of origin. Social integration is another main indicator and refers to the degree to which allochthons and autochthons keep up contacts with each other. By ascertaining the extent to which allochthons subscribe to "modern" values, we try to gain insight in the degree of cultural integration, among which individualization and secularization. Special attention is given to the meaning of religion. (SCP 2007b: 163)

The two factors that have mostly been singled out in the measurement of "socio-cultural integration" therefore are (1) the number of "contacts" with "autochthonous" or native Dutch by "allochthons" or non-natives and (2) the degree to which "society's norms and values" are shared by immigrants. The latter is often equated to the degree of "modernity" of people's attitudes, as "Dutch society" is construed as "modern," which, first of all, means that it is "secular."

Measuring "Contacts"

In its 2009 report, the SCP refers to the variable "contacts with indigenous Dutch" as the "social component" of the "socio-cultural dimension" of "integration." It had been researching such contacts in a similar way for some years. In 2005, for instance, the SCP published the following table:

Ethnic Signature of Spare Time Contacts by Ethnic Group, Ages 15–65, 2003 and 2004/2005 (in Percentages)

	More with members of own group	Equally much with both	More with autochthones
Turks	64	26	9
Moroccans	51	34	16
Surinamese	35	43	32
Antilleans	35	32	33
(former) Yugoslavs	30	38	32
Iraqi's	42	32	26
Afghans	34	37	29
Iranians	24	37	39
Somalians	50	32	18
Autochthones (a)	3	12	85

(a) Category "more with members of own group" means in the case of autochthones: more with allochthonous groups.
Source: SCP (2005: 111).

The headline above the concluding paragraph on "contacts" then reads: "Turks associate most with members of their own group." And yet, the data used to draw this conclusion indicate that 64 percent of "Turks" associate "more with members of their own group," whereas the same goes for 85 percent of the "autochthonous" population. The problematization of the lack of contacts between "allochthons" and "autochthons" does not lead to the conclusion that "autochthons" are poorly "integrated." At most, it leads to concern regarding the "image" of "allochthons" that "autochthons" might get from such figures. Similarly, when "residential segregation," in the form of "living concentration," is discussed by SCP researchers and others as hampering the changes of "interethnic contacts," it is only "allochthons" or "non-Western migrants" who are said to be "isolated" (Van der Laan Bouma Doff 2004; Dagevos, Iedema, and Schellingerhout 2005; SCP 2009: 234).

In 2007, the SCP report published the following table, which was – more commonly – restricted to four "ethnic groups" but followed the same logic:

Ethnic Signature of Spare Time Contacts, 2006 (in Percentages)

	More with members of own group (between brackets those that never have contact with autochthons)	Equally much with both	More with autochthons
Turks	66 (35)	24	11
Moroccans	54 (30)	30	16
Surinamese	31 (14)	39	30
Antilleans	31 (17)	28	41
Autochthons	91 (52)	6	3 (a)

(a) More with allochthons.
Source: SCP (2007b: 167).

When another 2007 SCP report (2007c: 40) explicitly states that it discusses "contact" between *both* "allochthons" and "autochthons" and that the latter often fail to establish such contact, it does not question using them as a yardstick, and this type of practice continues in 2016 and, since this concerns longitudinal research, likely for years to come. This becomes apparent when the report mentions a possible counterargument against what is known as the "contact hypothesis" (the idea that "contact" improves social cohesion for instance by lessening prejudice). It states "the question raised at times is how bad it in fact is that allochthons tend to be among themselves in their free time. For there are likewise lots of social categories among autochthons that hardly interact" (SCP 2007c: 35). In other words: the category "autochthons" remains monolithic when it comes to its juxtaposition vis-à-vis "allochthons," which is standard dissectible into "Antilleans," "Moroccans," "Surinamese," and "Turks."

This type of research, which emerged in the early years of this century (which is the reason the tables I reproduce are from this era), is still common today, and it is also very frequently found in "independent" research, conducted at universities (see, for instance, Ersanilli and Koopmans 2010). A typical research description, taken from the abstract of a journal article, for instance, reads:

In this contribution we look at the social integration of the four biggest ethnic minority groups in the Netherlands (Turks, Moroccans, Surinamese and Antilleans). The operationalisation of social integration refers to the magnitude of informal contacts the ethnic groups have with autochthonous,

Dutch friends. First, we describe the degree of social integration of the four ethnic groups. Second we try to explain the differences in the degree of social integration between these groups. Crosssectional data collected in 1994 show that Antilleans have the most contacts with the Dutch, then the Surinamese, then the Turkish and finally the Moroccans who have the fewest contacts with the Dutch. (Weijters and Scheepers 2003: 144)

Indeed, it is argued by the SCP that "common in the definitions of socio-cultural integration ... is the attention for the extent to which allochthons keep up contacts with the autochthonous popula- tion" (2005: 107). Of course, "allochthons" having contacts with "autochthons" is the same as "autochthons" having contact with "allochthons," but the lack of contacts between these categories is one-sidedly attributed to "allochthons," and it accordingly has nega- tive effects on their measured "integration." It is then noted that "statistically, the chances of autochthons coming in contact with allochthons is significantly smaller than vice versa" (2007b: 167). Yet it is never remarked that "autochthons" are a category consisting only of "Dutch" ethnicity, whereas "allochthons" consists of many ethnic markers. Sometimes based on U.S. assimilation research in which contacts between members of "ethnic groups" and members of "the majority group" are researched, the latter are differentiated only when it comes to their contacts with members of other "ethnic groups" (e.g., Fong and Isajiw 2000). Yet this is not the case when it comes to the contacts of "autochthonous Dutch" with members of other groups (e.g., Dagevos, Iedema, and Schellingerhout 2005; Martinovic, Van Tubergen, and Maas 2009). In the latter case, members of various "ethnic groups" are lumped together. One can even call for more quantitative research of "social integration" *and* claim that the picture it yields means that "these contacts are described from the point of view of the allochthons" (Weijters and Scheepers 2003: 145), and one can do so without ever inquiring what their "point of view" is. Similarly, Peter Blau's work on the greater impact of contacts on smaller groups, which would problematize the assumed linearity in measurements of "con- tacts," is not used (Blau 1977). All in all, this produces an image of "Dutch society" as "autochthonous." If one is to be socioculturally integrated, one is to "come into contact" with Dutch society, which means to come into contact with "autochthonous Dutch." At times, this is referred to simply as "social integration," while "cultural integration" refers to the degree of cultural assimilation of migrants. As a recent article reports in its opening: "The extent to which immigrants engage in social interaction with natives can be labeled social integration. Social integration is just one of the aspects of immigrant integration next to structural and cultural ones, which respectively refer to the incorporation of immigrants in the job market and the adoption of values and customs of the receiving society" (Martinovic, Van Tubergen, and Maas 2009: 870). Crucially, as C. Wright Mills has noted (1959: 90), such notions of adjustment or assimilation use a biological metaphor. In fact, the social science of integration never cut loose from organicist notions of society. That becomes clear in the measurement of "modernity," which is where moral monitoring explicitly shows its ideological teeth.

Measuring "Modernity"

The statistical assessment of the degree of "modernity" of migrants and their children is the second way in which "socio-cultural integration" is measured in the Netherlands. Modernity is on the one hand seen as residing at a collective or macrolevel, specifically when "Dutch society" is dubbed "modern." On the other hand, "modernity" is individualized and, no doubt partly as a consequence of an effort at quantitative measurement, it is turned into a discrete variable measurable at an individual level. In its 2003 report, the SCP accordingly states:

In the choice of these values and norms [those at stake in "socio-cultural integration"] we adopt as yardstick a modern western world view, characterized by the ideal of individual human development, social equality (also between men and women), secularism and a democratic regulation of power. (2003: 9)

It adds that such "values" are hardly shared by all people in the "Western cultural circle," but that the Western world and the worldview of its inhabitants is nonetheless shaped by a centuries-long process of modernization, which many non-Western parts of the world have not experienced. This "hypothesis of cultural contrast," as it is called (SCP 2003: 9), lies *at the basis of the operationalization* of "socio-cultural integration," and it is therefore a hypothesis that remains untested – all differentiation on the side of "autochthons," for instance, on the basis of class position, remains part of a monolithic category that is compared with various groups of "allochthons" of a very different class background. But the most important reason that the yardstick thus obtained is never tested is that the SCP reports never mention the variation on the measured "values" within the "autochthonous" population. Degrees of "modernization" are *only* reported for those who are, throughout the analysis, *assumed* to fall short of the "modern" yardstick. This focus on "modernization" has remained, for in its 2009 report, the SCP notes:

With respect to the cultural side of the "socio-cultural position" we choose the process of modernization as focal point for the operationalization, in accordance with the direction chosen earlier (see *Report Minorities 2003; Year Reports Integration 2005 and 2007*; Dagevos 2001). Individualization, secularization and emancipation are the key concepts here. (SCP 2009: 234)

Such "key concepts" are then measured in several ways. Secularization is, throughout Dutch research on "socio-cultural integration," regarded in the rather traditional way of "nonreligiosity" – a point of view long outdated even according to its most ardent proponents in the sociology of religion. In the measurement of "secularization" as a "value," the degree to which persons report belonging to a religion is a first indicator. Second is religious participation (church or mosque visits). Third, two Likert items (on a five-point scale) were used to assess "religious choice of partner":

- It is discomforting when your daughter wishes to marry a person from a different religious faith.
- Children should go to a school that fits with the religious faith of their parents.

This type of measurement comes down to the conclusion that persons reporting to be more religious tend to be less well integrated. Groups comprising large numbers of religious persons are therefore ethnic minorities comprising less well "socio-culturally integrated members."

The general adherence to "modern views" were measured by taking the above two items together with five additional items designed to measure "emancipation" and "individualization":

- Responsibility for the money can be best given to the man.
- It is more important for boys than it is for girls to earn their own money.

– Decisions on large purchases can be best taken by the man.

– A women should stop working when she has a child.

– In important decisions, older family members should have more
influence than younger (SCP 2009: 251).

Given the fact that the emancipation of Dutch women in terms of
financial independence and working full-time lags behind nearly
every other European country, such items appear particularly one-
sided when reported only for those deemed deviating from
the "yardstick." That yardstick, which remains a "hypothesis," is
silently assumed to mean that it is "Dutch" and "modern" to grant
equal rights to women, to be completely tolerant to other religious faiths, and to never judge an individual by the group. But an
exception to the last idea is made when it comes to non-Western
religious migrants, that is, members of "groups" of "non-Western
allochthons."

Often, the "modern" character of "Dutch society" is not explicitly
mentioned, but then "socio-cultural integration" is said to amount to
the degree to which the "norms and values of Dutch society" are
adopted by migrants. These are subsequently operationalized along
the lines of "secularism," "individualism," equality between "man
and woman," the degree of subscribing to gay rights, and so on (Van
Tubergen 2004). But equally many independent researchers explicitly
refer to "modernization," for instance, by adopting a "Modernization
Index" by means of which "ethnic groups" can be hierarchically
ranked (Hagendoorn, Veenman, and Vollebergh 2003: 208–210).
Descriptive conclusions, such as "on average, immigrants have less
modern attitudes than the indigenous Dutch" (208) are then extremely
tautological when the analysis is described in terms of "the *acquaintance with the indigenous culture on modern attitudes*" (219, emphasis
added), which is discussed under the heading of "*Acquaintance with
the Indigenous Culture*" (219, emphasis in original). The tautology
becomes most explicit when it is stated that

Migrant parents pass on their normative orientations – be they more or less
individualistic, modern or adapted to Dutch society – to their children. At the
same time, education gives these children an adaptive potential. Hence, in
time the younger migrant generation will be more adapted, modern and
individualistic than its parents, but the rate of increase varies between the
groups. (2003: 13)

We have chosen to analyze attitudes toward the process of modernization in our society because "modern" attitudes indicate the degree to which minority groups are culturally oriented toward the host society. (200)

Such tautological constructions are only tempered by the striking nuance that "however, not all members of the immigrant groups can be put in the same box. Some Turks are more modern than others, and that applies equally to the other groups" (2003: 210). In reality, the very ranking of such groups on a scale derived from a supposed status quo of "indigenous Dutch culture" means that all "other groups" *are* "put in the same box" – a box constructed outside what the researchers identify as "our society" (200). For the same reason, studies of "feelings of belonging," present, as can be learned from the European Web Site on Integration (EWSI) by the European Commission,[13] throughout Europe, preconfigure their outcomes by only researching non-native respondents: any feelings of nonbelonging are only visualized among non-natives. When, to take a nonstandard example, immigrant integration was measured in Estonia in 2011, the conclusion on feelings of belonging was

Among the Estonian residents with undetermined citizenship, the feeling of belonging to the Estonian nation in a constitutional sense has strengthened. The question "The constitution provides that in Estonia, the power of state is vested in the people. Do you consider yourself as belonging to the Estonian nation in the meaning of the constitution?" was answered positively by 34% of Estonian residents with undefined citizenship in 2008 and by 52% in 2011. Among the respondents of other ethnicities who have Estonian citizenship, the attitudes have basically not changed (in 2008, 67% felt as members of the demos, now 65%). (Estonian Ministry of Culture 2011: 7)

Such statements are typical, and they recur throughout Europe: progress can be reported, and yet difference is produced. Only "residents with undetermined citizenship" and "respondents of other ethnicities" are researched, and anything below 100% becomes visible as, apparently, not quite belonging according to people's own reports! As a consequence of such built-in asymmetries, issues of cultural "loyalty" continuously appear as the self-excited product of measurements.

---

[13] Its entries under "country info" provide links to immigrant integration measurement reports in all member states: https://ec.europa.eu/migrant-integration/country-info (accessed August 17, 2015).

The Diagrammar of "Integration" and the Imagination of "Dutch Society"

There is a lot to be said about the way "culture" and "modernity" are invoked in measurements of integration. Both can be regarded as *programs*, which can be regarded as the discursive surfaces upon which "society" emerges as an entity of social imagination. Programs function as the rope lines along which the morally blank canvas of "society" is demarcated. In this chapter, I have focused primarily on the reality effects of the social scientific measurement of integration. First, analyzing such measurement allows the identification of what is, in essence, a *logic of identification*. Immanent to measurements of integration is what can be called a *diagrammar* of integration. While "culture" and "modernity" are programs that so to speak offer the discursive spaces – the subjects and the topics – of the problematization of integration, the diagrammar of integration discourse shapes the landscape of discourse within these spaces. The "processing," if one will, of programmatic topics and issues involves a diagrammatical asymmetric reference to, or problematization of, integration, ethnicity, and faulty citizenship. And this allows for the separation of society's inside and outside. Inside and outside, as the two code values of "society," are discursive attributions. They appear in an integration discourse that frequents topics and issues provided by programs such as "culture," "ethnicity," or "modernity." The diagrammar of integration discourse then refers to the way in which such topics and issues give rise to asymmetric attributions, to a taxonomy or a "speciation" of the population along the coded lines of inside/outside.

I have mostly discussed the measurement of "socio-cultural integration" here, but *exactly the same logic applies to the measurement of migrants' socioeconomic position*. This euphemism for "class position," when measured in terms of "integration," leads to the strange view that a certain class position means one resides "outside society." But why would "society" not encompass the entire range of class positions, or if one will, of socioeconomic positions? These are relative to begin with. Why would being in a disadvantaged socioeconomic position *also* mean that one really is not a member of "society"? In fact, both "culture" and "economic background" are considered as impediments to "integration":

Integration of allochthones in society refers to a process in which immigrant groups and the autochthonous population grow towards one another and fully participate in society. However, immigrants come from another country that often has a different cultural and economic background. (CBS 2014: 20)

In one stroke, then, the reciprocity in "integration" that appears to be set up here is retracted, and cultural and economic background are considered as impediments to "fully participating in society," which is apparently possible only in one way. This "society," then, lacks any pluralism or complex multiplicity. The same goes for measurements of crime, now part of integration monitors (CBS 2014). Why would committing a crime mean one is at a distance from society? It can only mean that when "society" is preconceived as a morally pure domain.

Such measurements lead to asymmetric attributions that constitute a certain diagrammar of integration. At least five diagrammatical elements can be distilled from the measurement of immigrant integration as I have discussed it here.

(1) The De-individualizing Individualization of Integration

It at once individualizes and de-individualizes "integration." "Integration" is measured not at aggregate level, but at the level of the individual. This is a shift that appears rather incongruent considering the history of the concept of integration. Etymologically, the word stems from the Latin *integer*, meaning "unscathed whole." However, it makes no more sense to say that an individual is socially "integrated" than it does to say that he or she is socially "disintegrated." While for such different sociologists as Durkheim (though, as *Le suicide* indicates, not always), Parsons, Giddens, Habermas, and Luhmann "integration" is a systemic feature, the individualization of integration allows for an *asymmetric attribution of responsibility* to those individuals in need of integration. The fundamentally relational nature of relative positions of immigrants vis-à-vis the nonimmigrant population is thereby obscured. At the same time, a de-individualization of "integration" is effectuated. For if an individual is deemed not properly integrated, then his or her *culture* or *ethnicity* is the primordial cause thereof. This is evident in the clustering of "ethnic groups" under the headings of "socio-cultural integration." Thereby, the initially individualized responsibility is smeared out over a larger group identifiable by a "culture," which in practice is reduced to a marker of "ethnicity" that comes down to an attributed nationality. This way, responsibility remains asymmetrically attributed, but this time the distinction it articulates separates "society" from "ethnic groups" consisting of culturally predisposed faulty integrated individuals.

(2) The Selective Attribution of "Modernity"

The moral monitoring that measures immigrant integration allows for a selective attribution of "modernity" and "nonmodernity." The measurement of "socio-cultural integration" takes place, for instance, by measuring the degree to which an individual holds "modern beliefs." "Dutch society" is thereby, for instance, defined as secular. One would think that the presence of one million Muslims would have one rethink that a priori notion of the character of "society" and conclude that, apparently, "society" has changed. But the social scientific measurement of "integration" makes a different move: it concludes that "society" has actually remained the same, but that there are now one million people that, to a greater or lesser degree, reside "outside society." While the modern is deemed an Enlightened Dutch society, the paradox is thereby completed of a society characterized by tolerance that is intolerant, and of a *traditionally Enlightened* society.

(3) The Dispensation of "Ethnicity"

Integration research observes through an "ethnic lens" (Glick Schiller, Çağdar, and Guldbrandsen 2008) and maintains a peculiar notion of "ethnicity." First of all, the research discussed hardly touches upon a problematization of the concept of ethnicity, let alone engages with the various literatures on the subject, ranging from cultural studies to anthropology. While ethnicity is a contested category, it is also poised with power in practice. One cannot "define" ethnicity on the basis of a person's migratory roots. First of all, ethnicity is to be regarded as an "owned" or "inhabited" identity that is actively claimed vis-à-vis other possibly contested identities. It is thus a performed category that cannot be captured by "official" classification. At the very least, it is *both* an ascribed and an inhabited category. Integration research, however, equates "ethnicity" with "nationality" and thereby objectifies and reifies it as a fixed attribute an individual cannot shed. At the same time, however, native Dutch are transformed into "nonethnic" persons. In other words, a *dispensation of ethnicity* is granted to them, and "ethnicity" becomes a marker of the "other." All that differs from "society" has to do with "ethnic" people, similar to the way one can go "ethnic shopping" or "ethnic eating." The dispensation of ethnicity is related to an ideology of "whiteness." As Hartigan notes, "white" often becomes a marker of being unmarked, it even becomes a "cultureless culture" (Hartigan 2005: 265). The dispensation of ethnicity does precisely that: it neutralizes native identity and transforms all other identities into variations, deviations from the statistical mean that is *equated with* "society." Thus, while the very idea that "Dutch" may be one ethnic identity is obscured, that identity is presented as a neutral category at the top of the identitarian hierarchy of squabbling "ethnicities."

(4) The Dispensation of Integration

Something similar takes place in terms of integration. A *dispensation of integration* exists in that native Dutch are not discussed in terms of their integration. As quoted above, their "culture" is taken as a "yardstick." When, on the other hand, that "culture" is only *assumed* or explicitly *hypothesized* to be present, this "hypothesis" is not tested (despite the positivist nature of the research in case). Rather, in order to avoid upsetting the a priori image that researchers construct of "Dutch society," native Dutch are simply left out of the equation. Their degree of "socio-cultural integration" (or of "structural integration") is measured nor mentioned. What this makes clear is that the crucial difference that the observational form of "integration" entails is not that between persons "well integrated" and persons "not well integrated," but between *those for whom "integration" is an issue at all and those for whom it is not.* The latter case concerns those granted a dispensation of integration. In their case "integration" is never and cannot ever be thematized within the diagrammar of current integration discourse. "Integration" thereby becomes a marker of what differs from "society." It becomes an observational form that renders *all that it marks* visible as not (yet) a part of "society." Society thereby becomes recognizable as the space permanently unmarked by "integration." All that it does mark, whether as well integrated or less well integrated, at the same time becomes marked as existing at a certain distance from "society." Thus, all political rhetoric, usually well-intended, of "bridges" that need to be crossed, performatively *reproduces* a distinction between "society" and an "outside society" in the very attempt to close that gap.

(5) The Genealogization of Integration

A last diagrammatical aspect of the measurement of integration concerns what I shall call the *genealogization of integration*. This projects the society/outside society differentiation into the future. "Integration" research distinguishes between first, second, and third generation "immigrants." This is, of course, paradoxical, as "second generation immigrants" have not immigrated at all. But it allows for an extrapolation into the future of a measurable population, the identification of which facilitates the identification of the mirror image of "society." It thereby secures a future reservoir of the population that can be scrutinized in terms of "integration." And this not only has the effect of a continuation of longitudinal survey research. It also sustains fixed notions of "society" over against a measurable other in the future. The concept of what can be called an "*n*th-generation migrant" mobilizes anxieties that have colonial ancestors. There is a fear that the children of migrants might not be true members of society after all, that something can go wrong even after several generations, that the essentially "un-Dutch" character proves resilient and that persons may be "unintegrated" after all. Ann Stoler describes a very similar anxiety with respect to the suspicion toward children of mixed blood in the Dutch East Indies. As she says, "underwriting colonial anxieties was the sustained fear that children of mixed parentage would always remain natives in disguise, fictive Europeans, fabricated Dutchmen, affectively bound to the sentiments and cultural affiliations of their native mothers" (Stoler 2002: 114). Likewise, today, there is cause for continued scrutiny. That scrutiny is legitimated with reference to emancipatory values of countering inequalities, and yet *there is no social-scientific reason to code such inequalities into the divisive terms of integration imaginaries*. There are only political reasons for doing so, and, clearly, social science itself is laden with politics. In the end, of course, the fact that all of this pertains to a form of social imagination means there is always truth to be found in the anxious claim that people are "fictive Europeans, fabricated Dutchmen." So are all Dutch and all Europeans.

The problem of "passing," however, well-known from studies of performativity and queer identities and already analyzed by Garfinkel (1967), applies only to "non-natives" in the nonliteral sense. This dispensation of integration, as I have called it, means that to "pass" as "Dutch" or as "European" is only up for continuous testing to those a priori considered as "different." And this adds to the credulity of the ideological foundations of the imagination of society: precisely the unmasking of the fabricated Dutchness of immigrants and the unveiling of their fictive Europeanness naturalizes both "Dutchness" and "Europeanness": *if their "fictive" enactments can be unmasked, they are, at their core, more real than imaginative fictions.* If it is possible to show, by means of rigorous knowledge practices, that some are in fact not "really" Dutch or European, then that at least assumes that there is a "real" Dutchness and Europeanness that is attainable and, in fact, assumed to exist for all those never put to the test.

The Symbolic Function of Rituals of Moral Monitoring

To conclude, I wish to briefly return to the role of social science. In the end, the yearly measurement of immigrant integration is a form of moral monitoring that can be regarded as a ritual. It is repeated yearly, it serves certain symbolic purposes, and hence its outcome is clear beforehand, although the precise numbers may vary – each year giving rise to a new distribution of hope and concern regarding the latest twists in the figures. The very institutionalization of a measurement of integration, of course, reproduces a future "integration problem," as research funding and careers depend upon continued forms of moral monitoring. But there is, of course, critique of the concept of integration in social science. That critique, however, comes mostly from anthropologists and critical race scholars who have been increasingly marginalized in public debate and academia and who can be ignored by research quangos without cost (Uitermark 2010). The Amsterdam-based IMES, for instance, was preceded by the Centre for Racism and Ethnic Studies (CRES), which existed from 1984 until 1991. Some of its main racism scholars, Philomena Essed and Teun van Dijk, have since found employment outside the Netherlands (Essed and Nimako 2006: 291–292).

In its 2009 report, the SCP explicitly deals with the problem of conceptualizing "integration." It notes how the concept is "essentially contested," and how this means it will always be normative and evaluative. Immediately following this reflexive discussion is the SCP's way of dealing with such conceptual problems: it distinguishes between two dimensions, as is often done: "Also in light of the encompassing character of the concept of 'integration,' two dimensions are often distinguished in it" (SCP 2009: 226). The two dimensions mentioned are "structural" and "socio-cultural integration." Surprisingly, in what follows the report does not at all adhere to these "often distinguished" dimensions. For the structural dimension, which is usually thought to refer, for instance, to the socioeconomic position migrants, is not even defined, let alone discussed under that title. Both educational and labor market position are discussed, and the report explicitly notes their continued relevance in light of the growing importance of "socio-cultural integration" (139), but they are not discussed under the title of "structural integration." What follows the *conceptual* distinction, which appears *after* the discussions of educational and labor market positions, is only an elaboration of the socio-cultural dimension (in the entire report, "structural" is mentioned six times, over against sixty times "socio-cultural"). Hence, on the next page, the report reads: "so the central question here is which trends are observable in the different dimensions of socio-cultural integration" (227). So the discussion is narrowed down to what was called on the previous page the "socio-cultural dimension of integration," and more specifically it is narrowed down to what are now various "dimensions" within this "dimension." These are "interethnic contacts, cultural orientations, religious identification and behavior, and mastery and use of the Dutch language" (227). In a final reflexive turn, then, the report notes how "research of socio-cultural integration may bump into critique." And in an interesting contradiction, it attempts to preempt such critique:

Perhaps the impression appears that the measurement method chosen by us implies that members of non-western groups *have* to have contacts with autochthonous Dutch or *have* to have modern beliefs. That is not the case. We need a yardstick by which to measure the differences between and within groups, but that does not imply a normative stance. ... Part of the confusion may be caused by the use of the term "socio-cultural *integration*," which undeniably has a normative bearing. For that reason we shall speak of the "socio-cultural position" of non-western migrants in this chapter. (2009: 227)

In other words, it is first admitted that the concept used for years has "an undeniably normative bearing." Then the concept is changed, *but both the measurement and the definition stay the same*, which can, of course, only mean that the normative bearing remains. The supposedly normative neutrality of the "yardstick" chosen can only be maintained because the *selection* of that "yardstick" is not problematized or even

discussed. Crucially, the possible "critique" of the SCP's way of measurement, which it dubs "confusion," would, of course, much sooner be
aimed at the presuppositions implied by certain concepts – presuppositions which surface not only in the explicit definitions of the concepts,
but also and most relevantly in the operationalizations of these concepts. It is there that the social science of integration performs a
ritualized form of moral monitoring that has a specific symbolic function. It is the "official" *machinery of social imagination* that allows for
the circumscription of "Dutch society" by way of rendering observable
those who are *not* a part of that society. That identification proceeds by
means of the various differentiating techniques that separate "society"
from those "outside society" and that make for what I have here called
a diagrammar of integration discourse.

In integration discourses, this concerns first and foremost the impos-
ition of the dual notion of "society" and of an "outside of society."
Popular and political discourse refers to various categories (such as
immigrants but also inmates) as "people outside of society." Such a
figure of speech performatively shapes the realm of "society" vis-à-vis
a societal environment that remains vague and underdefined. This
turns "society" into a pure domain devoid of social problems. For as
soon as problems are concerned, they have to do with persons "outside
society." When "integration" refers to persons "outside society," society as such has no integration problems. When crime is a problem of
people unadjusted to society, society itself knows no crime and crime
becomes a phenomenon related to people "outside society" that are to
be "reintegrated" into society. The *spatial* character of the metaphor of
an "outside society" rhetorically strengthens the plausibility of the
implied opposition. Next to this spatialized metaphor, the good will
of efforts at "integrating" those outside society can be represented in a
temporalized metaphor of a "not yet." Then, "society" is a domain
that the excluded will, in the future, come to enter, for instance, as the
positive outcome of policy efforts at integrating them in society. Space
and time rhetorically combined, it can be argued that certain "immigrants" have a more or less "long way to go."

The very discourse of integration is based on a commonsensical
differentiation between "society" and an "outside society," but that
differentiation is only discursively performed in the appeal to that
commonsensical presupposition. The social construction of "society"
is an example of performativity through symbolic forms. The notion

of "society" that is thus constructed has all the characteristics of a *prescription* rather than a *description*. It cleanses "society" from problems, which it attributes to an "outside society," which is then the object of efforts at "integration" intended with all best intentions. Sociologically, the very construction of this opposition functions as a way of defining the substance "society" by means of a *via negativa*: by conjuring up its mirror image as a constitutive outside, strewn with problems of overwhelmingly cultural nature. "Society" thereby remains a pure domain, a moral community as in Durkheim's descriptions. It is transformed into a transcendence of impeccable cultural taste and incorruptibly moral stature. Put most strongly and most provocatively, then, the symbolic function of contemporary rituals of moral monitoring consists of the *discursive ethnic cleansing* of the realm of "society."

"Integration" from Part/Whole to System/Environment

When voicing such critiques of immigrant integration, I very often get the question how otherwise to conceive of "integration." The question is asked both by policy makers and politicians and by social scientists. For these two audiences, two partly different answers can be given. My answer to the policy makers and the politicians is not to use the concept at all. It codes a variegated set of issues as problems of "integration," and it thereby commensurates wholly different practices, situations, and processes. If anything, it makes issues more vaguely defined and less immediately visible. When devising policies to counter inequality in labor or education, for instance, it helps to keep an eye on these forms of inequality without first coding them into issues of "immigrant integration." Of course, talking to policy makers and politicians is never straightforward, since they are part of practices of governing in which integration functions as a medium. It remains important to at the same time highlight the violence that entails, and in my experience policy makers are usually receptive and sympathetic to such arguments, albeit that their governing structures do not allow them to instantly change their conceptions – if only because long-term projects, including longitudinal forms of monitoring immigrant integration, tie their concerns down to certain prevailing conceptions.

The answer to social scientists is different. First, it is to take imaginaries of "immigrant integration" as an object of research, instead of assuming the realities imagined therein and taking these as research objects. Immigrant integration does *not* constitute a process whereby individuals, through some invisible force, move gradually "into" a mysterious entity called "society." Rather, it constitutes a form of social imagination along those lines. The difference is huge, even though it does not mean, as explained in Chapter 1, that integration refers to a "mere fiction of the imagination." As it stands, though, the highly political reality effects of integration imaginaries are given scientific credit and plausibility. This occurs mainly out of a mistaken and usually not explicitly realized adherence to a quasi-organicist imagination of society. The only cure for that is to move from a tacit identitarian notion of society to a notion marked by difference. Here, Niklas Luhmann's theory is helpful.

The system/environment scheme that Luhmann puts forward has as its main advantage that it doesn't presuppose what it is intended to establish. It only describes a social system in its relation to a systemic environment. Both sides of the system/environment distinction necessarily exist simultaneously, but this simultaneity lies in the insimultaneity of the simultaneous observability of both (Luhmann 1991: 44–45)! In this theory of difference, the system/environment distinction is a presupposition for observation, which means that at any time, one of its two sides can be "marked." Maintaining the *border* between system and environment means the maintenance of the system (Luhmann 1984: 35). Any theory will therefore have to indicate *from where* an "environment" is constructed (Luhmann 1993: 24). A theory of immigrant integration will therefore always have to thematize the symmetry between "inside" and "outside," rather than posit their a priori asymmetry. All discourse on a "lack of integration" that does not also subject "society" (the "inside" of the differentiation between integration and nonintegration) to an equally incisive analysis, operates from a blind spot within its observational mode. The most important blind spot of the part/whole scheme entails the "unity of their difference," that is, the fact that both are connected in one systemic form that has both an inside and an outside. This is the cause of many of the problems with empirical research of immigrant integration discussed in this chapter. The fact that a lack of interaction between "autochthons" and "allochthons" is only attributed to the latter (to the "outside" of the distinction autochthon/allochthon) is a consequence of the fact that the theories used are identity theories, not difference theories. In a sense, they can even be said to be *indifference theories.*

The same goes for the one-sided use of "ethnic," which functions as the "outside" of a distinction (nonethnic/ethnic). Its "inside" (nonethnic) is not problematized but neutralized, and made to function as the reference point from which its non-neutral ethnic other can be observed. In *Die Gesellschaft der Gesellschaft*, Luhmann discusses the consequences of departing with the part/whole scheme for the concept of integration. First, he points to the connection between "old-European thought" and the contemporary use of "integration":

The concept of integration usually remains undefined and is used ... in multiple ways. Often, empirical conditions smuggle presuppositions of consensus into its conception which remain unreflected upon. This has had as a consequence that the concept of integration is still used to formulate perspectives of unity or even expectations of solidarity, and to urge the adoption of concomitant attitudes – in old-European style! (1997: 602)

In a complex society (a concept Luhmann uses in a paradoxical way, as a last "old-European" remnant in his theory), a normative concept of integration cannot suffice (1997: 603). The hope of integration through communication of prescriptions for action can now count on "no" potentially equally as many times as it can count on "yes." The concept of integration, according to Luhmann, only makes sense when it is applied to the functional differentiation of a social system. It then refers to the reduction of degrees of freedom of subsystems, and it is an aspect of the dealing with uncertainties concerning both the outer borders of the social system and its internal borders between subsystems (Luhmann 1993: 584; 1995: 83; 1997: 603–604; 2000a: 355, 398; 2005b: 269). In Luhmann, "integration" therefore has to do with the mutual limitations that autopoietic (sub)systems place upon each other. It is not, like the conventional concept of "integration" in empirical research, restricted to the internal state of one system or whole or better yet to the state of its environment, but it has reference to system/environment relations. In order to do that, the concept has to be wrought free from the organicist context in which it refers to the connection between parts and whole. However, also in Luhmann's theory, where the concept is of secondary relevance anyway, the concept remains without much explanatory or descriptive power. Luhmann emphasizes that it does not refer to parts and wholes or on the "unity" of a social system (1997: 604). But that makes all the more clear that the concept, which is typically organicist and mereological in origin, doesn't have much more to offer.

The unity presupposed in Luhmann's theory of difference is a unity of the difference between system and environment. This distinction forms a differential unity, since we can refer to it as "this distinction" (Luhmann 1984: 41; 2000a: 11). But it is crucial that it is a *differential* unity, which means that *unity* only exists or works *as difference*. A system constitutes a unity, but that unity is to be understood as having to maintain itself through a continuous reproduction of an inside/outside differentiation (Luhmann 1973: 175). And "there is no outside ... other than as a component of the distinction between inside and outside" (Luhmann 2006: 73). C. Wright Mills's critique of the "social pathologists" of his time is illustrative of the problems of presupposing a social whole named "society" without further reflection. With respect to concepts such as "society," "the social order," "the social organization," "the mores and institutions," and "American culture":

The terms represent undifferential entities. Whatever they may indicate, it is systematically homogeneous. Uncritical use of such a term as "the" permits a writer the hidden assumption in politically crucial contexts of a homogeneous and harmonious whole. The large texture of "the society" will take care of itself, it is somehow and in the long run harmonious, it has a "strain toward consistency" running through it; or, if not this, then only co-operation of all is needed, or perhaps even a right moral feeling is taken as a solution. (Wright Mills 1969: 538)

Wright Mills connects the presupposition of such a whole with the theoretical background of organicism. He also connects it with thinking in terms of "community," which is likewise highly popular today, and with what I have here called a culturist focus. His critique of the social pathologists dates from 1943, but we can readily recognize in it the social integrationists in the social science of our day: integration exists, and therefore "society" exists, just so long as the "right moral feeling" exists.

4 | *Transformations of Racism and the Rise of Culturism*

To Speak of Racism in Western Europe

"In talk about minorities, white people often speak as dominant group members." Thus wrote Teun van Dijk more than twenty years ago (reprinted in 2002a: 308). Van Dijk is a Dutch scholar of racism who was exorcized from the Netherlands in the 1990s for arguing that racism existed as an elite discourse (Essed and Nimako 2006; Uitermark 2010). In his own words, Van Dijk was subject to "institutional marginalization":

> to conclude that the Netherlands is a racist country, and mean it too, is asking for trouble. Such a claim produces so much cognitive and emotional dissonance, especially among the Dutch elite – who see themselves as basically tolerant and progressive in ethnic affairs – that silencing or excluding the dissident is the only obvious option. (Van Dijk 2002b: 481)

When I'm writing this, much of this still holds. There is a bit more leeway for interpretations of racism, for instance, regarding the holiday figure "Sinterklaas," a white man dressed up in, among others, bishop's robes accompanied by various servants in blackface called "Black Pete" (for a recent analysis, see Wekker 2016). While black protesters against this feast have been violently arrested by white policemen in recent years, the very idea of "racism" as present in the Netherlands – while still usually critiqued or ridiculed – is at least not absent the way it has long been. When, in July 2015, the major elite newspaper *NRC Handelsblad* published a review of some books by U.S. African Americans and headlined it with the cynically and critically intended "Nigger, are you crazy?" protest came, among others, from the United States. In response, the newspaper printed some of the reactions, and it regretted having printed the headline. One of the responses, though, was by the chief editor of the other major elite newspaper, *De Volkskrant*, who – being a white man – ridiculed the very suggestion that a newspaper like *NRC Handelsblad*, which was always anti-racist, should have been racist. So while "racism exists in the Netherlands" appears to have become at least one *possible* discursive position, the denial of its existence is still standard repertoire among those who, in Van Dijk's words, talk about minorities.

To speak of racism is often identified with what integration researcher Ruud Koopmans (2005: 15) affirmatively describes as "a sense of postcolonial guilt." There exists, he believes, "an ever-present fear among authorities of being accused of racism" (ibid.). If one tries to look at such statements with some reflexivity, and with some acquaintance with the literature on racism, three things become obvious. First, in the asymmetry between authorities and minorities, the first apparently live in perpetual fear. Second, why should there not be, in some sense that needs qualification, a form of "postcolonial guilt"?[1] And third, it is clear that such denials of racism are textbook examples of, indeed, denials of racism. Van Dijk has thoroughly analyzed such denials and all the mechanisms they involve as forms of positive self-presentation and of keeping face by dominant elites. In negative judgments about immigrants, thus, disclaimers are used ("we are not racist, but ..."). Euphemisms are used ("we're not racist, we're worried"). Reversals occur frequently ("in fact, *they* are the real racists"), sometimes blaming the victim ("the ones who talk about racism are actually the racists"), and appeals to the racism of the common man occur frequently (Van Dijk 2000a).

There are strong historical parallels with Dutch colonial history here. As Dienke Hondius (2011) has shown, Dutch authorities had a long history of keeping slave trade out of sight from those living in the Netherlands. That blind eye to the contributions of the Netherlands to the global slave trade, which was dominated by the country in the first half of the seventeenth century (Blackburn 1997), continues today. Hondius illustrates how selective restrictions on the presence of blacks in the Netherlands have been in existence since the seventeenth century, and this lack of access to Europe, more broadly, she argues, "was a constant factor in its history, produced by numerous decisions, rules, laws and regulations that had the effect of keeping out the 'rest of the world'" (Hondius 2011: 390). Hondius continues to note what is crucial for my concerns here:

[1] This was pointed out to me by Marguerite van den Berg.

In retrospect, only the post-colonial migration of the twentieth century, following the independence of the former colonies in the wake of World War II and the Shoah, was a short period when access to Europe was easier for entire families and multiple generations from overseas countries in the Caribbean, Asia and Africa, because these countries had until recently been part of the European nation and their inhabitants had equal citizenship rights. These last 50 years have changed the face of Europe, but it is equally clear that post-colonial migration was restricted again soon after independence occurred. (Hondius 2011: 390)

It is fair to say that the entire historical frame of contemporary discussions of immigrant integration has been informed by these postwar years. Almost none of the preceding history emerges in the wider public imagination, despite attempts to gain recognition for the history of slavery (Wekker 2016). At most, racism is reduced to "discrimination," which constitutes a significant depoliticization. From there, it is only a small step toward the idea that discrimination, while unfortunate, is simply a fact of life, as Dutch Prime Minister Mark Rutte said in 2015:

[Discrimination] still occurs a lot in the Netherlands, and ... it really matters whether your name is Mohammed or Jan when you apply for a job. I've thought long about this, and I have come to the conclusion that I cannot solve this. The paradox is that the solution lies with Mohammed. I can't say to the Netherlands: "please don't discriminate, judge a person by character and knowledge." But when it does happen, Mohammed has a choice: either to be insulted and bail out or to keep on going. Newcomers have always had to adapt, and have always had to deal with prejudices and discrimination. You have to fight your way in.[2]

This was the Prime Minister's answer to the question what he had learned from the children he teaches an hour a week at a secondary school in The Hague. Among the many things happening in his answer (such as that most of the "Mohammeds" he is likely to meet are born in the Netherlands and are not "newcomers") it is interesting that he mentions that discrimination "still" occurs in the Netherlands. While he thus appears to believe it is a relic of a past age, he at the same time naturalizes it by saying it is something that simply happens to immigrants – he almost makes it a test of the character of immigrants to face up to it.

---

[2] www.nrcreader.nl/artikel/8412/rutte-discriminatie-los-je-zelf-maar-op (accessed August 19, 2015).

This is the post-racist imaginary common to many Western European countries today (Gilroy 1992; Essed and Goldberg 2000). It signifies a shift in the discursive repertoire of racism in that it explicitly incorporates anti-racist elements. For this reason, many argue that current harsh assimilationist attitudes toward immigrants are not to be confused with racism. The reflexive way of arguing that assimilationism is not racism is given, for instance, by George Fredrickson when he says: "if an ethnic stranger can be assimilated into the tribe or the culture in such a way that his or her origins cease to matter in any significant way, we are in the presence of an attitude that often creates conflict and misery, but not one that should be labeled racist" (2002: 7). However, as we saw in the previous chapter, assimilation is never really at stake. Rather, the emphasis on assimilation reproduces a difference between those for whom integration is an issue – however well assimilated or integrated – and those for whom it is not. Therefore, assimilationism is perhaps a misnomer; a differentialism is at stake that does seem compatible with racism. The less reflexive denial of racism in integration imaginaries holds that, since the focus is mostly on culture and not on biology, racism cannot be considered central to such imaginaries. Typical is a recent paper by two Dutch scholars who dryly discard the idea of the existence of (cultural) racism in the Netherlands. Because it is so typical of scholarship concerning minorities in Western Europe, I quote the entire abstract of their paper:

Like elsewhere in Europe, a discourse that is hostile to migrants in general and Muslims in particular has emerged in Dutch politics and media. Can we understand this Dutch migrant-hostile discourse as a kind of racism, i.e. cultural racism? The authors studied this discourse (Dutch political and media texts) and its impact on the lived experiences of Dutch Moroccan Muslims in work settings (21 interviews). They found little evidence of the concept of cultural racism as long as it maintains notions of biological or genetic hierarchy, while it becomes redundant once it abandons such notions. Alternative concepts like cultural essentialism and cultural fundamentalism are sufficient to understand this discourse as well as its impact on Moroccan Muslims' lived experiences. Cultural fundamentalism has become successful because it belongs to a different category than racism. (Siebers and Dennissen 2015: 470)

Thus one can assume the most neutral, white position there is, that of scientific objectivity, and conclude that, no, it's not racism after all! And so the tradition of finding little relevance of racism continues. This is certainly *not* my approach in this chapter. Key is to avoid affirming what Gloria Wekker (2016), partly echoing James Baldwin (1998: 293–294), calls "white innocence." What I therefore do propose to do is to look at the way "culture" has become a key program for the imagination of society. I regard culture similar to the way race functions, according to visual studies scholar W. J. T. Mitchell in *Seeing through Race*:

> race is not merely a content to be mediated, an object to be represented visually or verbally, or a thing to be depicted in a likeness or image, but . . . race is itself a medium and an iconic form – not simply something to be seen, but itself a framework for seeing through or . . . seeing *as*. (2012: 13)

More specifically, I regard culture and race as *programs along the unfolding of which society becomes imaginable as a medium of in- and exclusion*. Seeing through culture, to paraphrase Mitchell, has become one way of imagining that of which no images exist: society. Culture has become such a program, I argue, as an intricate part of the ongoing transformations of racism. I will speak of a form of *culturism* that is functionally equivalent to racism, and that is racist at its core. Rather than going along with misguided post-racist imaginaries, I use the notion of culturism to be sensitive to change and, above all, to be able *to specify and locate the racism within the logic of culturism*. In order to take seriously, in the explicit accounts often given, that many believe we live in a post-racist era – the common denial of racism argument – it is important to understand the layered character of what I will call, using Castoriadis's concept, discourses of alterity. To speak of racism and its denial, I argue, threatens to miss the intricate logic in which racism is embedded in contexts of Western European immigrant integration. I will now first highlight the rise of "culture." Then I discuss notions of "cultural racism" and "neo-racism" devised to deal with that rise, after which I will propose to analyze the intricate imbrication of racism in the dominance of culturism.

Cultural Programming and Western European State Policies of Immigrant Integration

Today, even amid a prolonged economic crisis, the canvas of Western European self-description appears painted with culture. "Culture" is everywhere in public debates surrounding integration and immigration.

And culture is so ubiquitous that for many it would seem difficult to think about immigrant integration and *not* frame the "problems" involved therein in terms of "culture." Increasingly, then, "culture" has become the site where the discursive perimeters of "society" are drawn. That is not to say that "culture" takes precedence in defining hat "society" is. In fact, a large part of what is discussed under the heading of "culture" amounts to a recoding of the economic, a recoding that destabilizes the subversive potential of issues framed in economic terms. But it does mean that "culture" has appeared as a main program for the coagulation of national societies and what is regarded as their "outside." The coding of the "religious" as "culture," for instance, in the oft-heard phrases "Islamic culture" or "Muslim culture," attests to the dominance of cultural programming. In general, "culture" involves observations based on comparison. A "cultural" phenomenon is regarded with a view to its sameness or difference to other phenomena or to other places, times, or contexts. Such comparison, however, in many cases is asymmetric. The rise of the Western concept of culture, for instance, involved a differentiation of "Culture" or "Civilization" vis-à-vis what was not "cultured" or "civilized." In the nineteenth century, it could be regarded as nationally bounded and often superior to other national cultures. And when "culture" is currently invoked as the bed rock of discussions of integration, similar asymmetries are at stake. For one, discussions of culture often involve an opposition between what is called "the dominant culture" and what is referred to as various other "cultures." It is an opposition of the one versus the many, where the many are "at a certain distance" from the one dominant culture. This nomenclature thus explicitly recognizes dominance, but it does so in two ways. First is a "statistical dominance," according to which "the dominant culture" is simply that culture shared by most people. This is risky since changes in cultural adherence or population demographics would threaten dominance. In another way, "the dominant culture" is also regarded as superior, especially where issues of gender oppression and freedom of speech are concerned. What is regarded as "dominant," then, is in fact that that is dominating, both in a numerical sense and in the sense of the cultural specifics coded as symbolic capital. This involves various paradoxes that play out in discussions of integration, and I shall highlight some of them in this chapter – for instance, those pertaining to the negation of the "cultural" character of "the dominant culture."

The focus of this chapter will be on state policies of integration. I shall be concerned with the way culture appeared as a program for the imagination of "society" in policies of immigrant integration, taking the Netherlands as my main case. The reasons for focusing on policies are twofold. First, one context of the rise of "immigrant integration" as an object of discourse consists of politics and policy at various levels. One might argue that it is the main context in that it is through policy and political debate that "integration" has become a concept that people are sufficiently familiarized with for it to be a topic both in the public sphere and in the pub (Van Dijk 2002a: 316). And, second, the state propagation of the cultural programming of discourse indicates an active involvement of the state in the definition of "society." Such involvement is not new, but it is crucial to understand how it currently takes shape, especially when the nation-state is in troubled water when the "nation" appears to lose a unity it was thought to have. The securing of a culturally identifiable and thereby governable national society is in the interest of the state, and I argue that this is likely part of why Western European states have in recent years stepped up efforts at promoting "integration." That is *not* to say that the state can achieve "integration." Such ideas would forego the state's limited role in an age of functional differentiation. Where society cannot be observed from one privileged vantage point, it certainly can't be "run" from such a point and by a complex of political, legal, and administrative systems such as the state, and especially when such states have, in many areas, ceded influence. However, the state does currently operate as a major producer of images of society. It is, especially in the northern parts of Western Europe, one of the biggest producers of integration imagery.

This has been accompanied by institutional changes. Denmark, for instance, created its Ministry of Refugee, Immigration and Integration Affairs in 2001. In Germany, a Federal Government Commissioner for Migration, Refugees and Integration has existed since 1978, but in 2005, its status was upgraded to that of Minister of State in the Federal Chancellery. As the German government website says, "this indicates the importance the German Government attaches to integration."[3] In

---

[3] www.bundesregierung.de/nn_6516/Content/EN/StatischeSeiten/Schwerpunkte/Integration/einleitungstext-integration.html (accessed August 20, 2015). Elsewhere it reads: "Angela Merkel hat gleich zu Beginn ihrer Kanzlerschaft großen Wert darauf gelegt, Integration als gesellschaftspolitisches Schlüsselthema und

Norway, two ministries deal with integration affairs. The Ministry of Labour was renamed Ministry of Labour and Social Inclusion in 2006, and in the same year, the Ministry of Children and Family Affairs was renamed "Children, Equality and Social Inclusion." In 2006 as well, a new Directorate of Integration and Diversity was established. In France, the Ministry of Immigration, Integration, National Identity and Co-Development was created in 2007. Also in 2007, Sweden created a Ministry of Integration and Gender Equality. In Belgium in 2013, a state secretary coordinates role in matters of asylum, migration, and integration. Even the names of such ministries are indicative of a specific cultural programming. In France a direct emblematic link between "integration" and "national identity" exists. In Sweden, "gender equality" and "integration" are linked. This is no coincidence, as since the late 1990s gender equality has come to be seen as characteristic of "Swedish culture," while gender inequality came to be portrayed "as characteristic of the 'culture' of 'immigrants'" (Towns 2002: 158). Also indicative is the clustering of themes. The United Kingdom does not have a separate ministry of immigrant integration, as the "regulation of aliens" was the first of new tasks added to the Home Office in 1793. One of the latest additional tasks, stemming from 2007, is "counter-terrorism."

Such associations exist in the Netherlands as well. In the Netherlands, a ministerial office was created specifically for this purpose in 1998. That means it was the first Western European country to do so. The newly created ministerial subdepartment of Immigration and Integration Affairs was relocated three times within ten years. While from its start in 1998, as a subdepartment with a Minister of Large Cities and Integration Policy, it first resided under the Ministry of Interior Affairs, it then moved to the Ministry of Justice in 2002, with the new office of Minister of Alien and Integration Affairs. Significantly, this involved a direct association between integration and crime. Within the Ministry of Justice, the office of integration affairs was organized under "International Affairs and Alien Affairs." It became clear that "integration" was seen most of all as an affair of curtailing immigration, as then Minister Verdonk explicitly stated. In 2007, the Minister

Querschnittsaufgabe für die gesamte Bundesregierung auch institutionell zu verankern." See "Das Amt der Ausländer- und Integrationsbeauftragten": www.bundesregierung.de/nn_56556/Content/DE/Artikel/IB/Artikel/ Geschichte/2009-05-28-geschichte-des-amtes.html (accessed August 20, 2015).

of Alien and Integration Affairs became the Minister of Housing, Communities and Integration, and the office was relocated again, this time organized under the Ministry of Housing, Spatial Planning and the Environment. This widened the possible scope of "integration" policy, which now came to involve the full governmental ensemble of community, neighborhood, and citizenship, while retaining links to issues of crime, if only through the connection with "neighbourhood" (a connection apparent in the close collaboration of the Minister of Housing, Communities and Integration with the Minister of Justice). Cabinet responsibility for immigrant integration subsequently moved to the Ministry of Interior Affairs and Kingdom Relations, and in 2012, it moved again, this time to the Ministry of Social Affairs and Employment, which cooperates on the issue with the Ministry of Foreign Affairs and the Ministry of Security and Justice.[4] On the one hand, this high rate of departmental relocation is indicative of the lack of clear-cut conceptualization of "integration." In fact, "integration policy" consists mostly of language and citizenship courses and of subsidies to various civil society organizations. Yet on the other hand, it is indicative both of the fact that "integration" is a signifier with a certain *expansive capacity* and of the fact that it is first and foremost an object of social imagination. That explains why an issue so hotly debated, also in the political arena, has a comparatively extremely modest policy budget. Yet precisely because the problematization of who belongs to society is in the end not a matter of policy budget but of discourse, including policy discourse, this modest budget doesn't decrease the importance of the policy texts produced and the images of cultural legitimacy conveyed in them. The spread of the use of "integration" has thereby at the same time meant the spread of the program of culture in different institutional settings. The rise to hegemony of the signifier "integration" has at the same time meant a contagiousness of "culture" as a programmatic site of observation and communication. In order to discuss the theoretical underpinnings of current conceptions of culture and the way these are related to concepts of national societies, it is instructive to first consider the rise of "culture" in integration policy discourses.

---

[4] https://ec.europa.eu/migrant-integration/country/netherlands (accessed August 20, 2015).

The Rise of Culture in Integration Policy Discourses

In a sense, "culture" has always been pivotal to integration discourse, and long before it. Any "culturalization of politics" (Žižek 2008) should be interpreted as a *re*-culturalization, since there was no time in which the politics of citizenship and the management of populations were not infused with culture. Since the late 1990s, however, various issues have become *explicitly* coded as "cultural." Along with this, stereotypical notions of policy traditions and their relation to culture have emerged, although in all cases closer scrutiny complexifies such formulas. Assimilationism in France, for instance, is considered to have always been focused on certain "republican values" as national values. And British integration policies are considered as having long been characterized by a focus on plurality. Dutch discourse on minorities, immigration, and integration has long revolved around notions of culture, albeit in varying ways. Dutch integration discourse in the last three decades, which has long been almost exclusively a policy discourse, is historically characterized by three phases. Although here, too, the danger of simplification is imminent, it is insightful to discern them here because of the shifts in explicit emphasis they embody no doubt too rigidly. They are (1) a pluralist phase, (2) a phase in which emphasis lay on structural differences and lower status in structural terms pertaining to work and education, and (3) a phase in which emphasis was/is on cultural differences. Post–World War II immigration in the Netherlands initially consisted mainly of postcolonial migration and of Indonesian repatriation. In the 1960s, "guest workers" were attracted mainly from Morocco and Turkey, and their presence was thought to be temporary. "Integration" was thought undesirable as it would hamper the return of immigrants to their countries of origin, since adaptation in the Netherlands would occur and readjustment at home would be more difficult (Entzinger 1984; Verwey-Jonker Institute 2003; Obdeijn and Schrover 2008). The "myth of return" meant that, in practice, a pluralist attitude prevailed that can be characterized as a form of culturalism. For the political left, this entailed a respectful attitude toward other cultures. For right-wing politicians, pluralism ensured avoidance of unnecessary cultural mixture or hybridization, since migrants were not really immigrants but would return.

In the 1970s, a second phase of minority discourse was ushered in with the realization that the idea of "return" was a "myth." Like

Belgium, Germany, and the Nordic countries, an awareness of being an "immigration country" came late. In Germany, for instance, though already debated by Karl-Heinz Kühn in 1979, this was not fully realized until the Süssmuth Commission in 2001 made it explicit (Meier-Braun 2002: 46–47). In the Netherlands, awareness grew in the 1980s. This phase remained culturalist with respect to the cultural identity of migrants, but it was informed by a problem awareness concerning the relatively vulnerable economic position of migrants in Dutch society – the result of deindustrialization and migratory family reunion. In the 1970s, many political parties preferred speaking in terms of "emancipation" to using the concept of "integration," which was felt by many to convey a message of cultural adaptation or assimilation (Fermin 1997). However, *Ethnic Minorities Policy*, "founded" in a sense by the sociologist Penninx in a 1979 report for the Scientific Council for Government Policy (WRR), would be the official integration policy in the 1980s, and it had definite assimilationist motives. Economic inequality, as well as differences in levels of education, (labor-market) discrimination, and racism was the focus of discourse in the 1980s. The motto of policy in the 1980s and early 1990s was: "integration with preservation of identity" (*integratie met behoud van eigen identiteit*). This formulation is one of the reasons many now speak of Dutch "multiculturalism," but this is a highly misleading interpretation of the policy aims. Although the Netherlands are often regarded as a typical case of "multiculturalism," that is not a concept that figured (at all) in Dutch policies. Multiculturalism didn't inspire these policies, nor was the substance of the multicultural version of liberal political philosophy incorporated into them. Rather, the policy based on the "preservation of cultural identity" was assimilationist (in the "misnomer" sense described above) to begin with. It assumed that the vantage point of one's "own culture" would offer a strong stepping stone toward assimilation, a process in which the stepping stone would be cast aside. As the Labor Minister of Education, Van Kemenade, said in 1982:

Although it is usually not stated very emphatically, it is crystal clear that recognition, let alone promotion of a group's own identity, values, normative orientation, behaviours and beliefs, finds its limits where these come into conflict with the values that are enshrined into Dutch society, the constitution and the law and that are part of the achievements of our society. Physical punishment, polygamy, suppression of women, forced marriages of

minors, but also the evasion of compulsory education may very well be ...
part of the indigenous identity or values ... but do not deserve to be
promoted or preserved and, indeed, must be fought. Assimilation to the
Dutch value pattern has to come first. (quoted in Uitermark 2010: 51)

Although Van Kemenade was severely critiqued in Parliament when he
proposed to place more emphasis on learning Dutch for "allochthonous" children (though they did share the label "allochthonous")
(Lucassen and Köbben 1992: 110), we find here with a crucial politician on the left basically all the stereotypes that will inform the later
culturist phase: an emphasis on the *values* that characterize *Dutch
society*, a focus on *assimilation* to those values and that society,
although it is to be kept in mind that the discursive emphasis on
assimilation *produces difference, not assimilation.* This is achieved by
a focus on a variety of *problems* having to do with the interface of
culture and the *gendered body* (which will be more extensively analyzed in Chapter 5). Moreover, from the 1980s on, immigration policies became increasingly strict (Entzinger 1984: 100–106).

During the 1990s, then, the unfortunate economic position of
certain immigrant groups (including the largest groups with Islamic
background) and the pressure on the welfare state to cut back benefits
led to the explicit idea of migration as negatively influencing Dutch
economy (Ghorashi 2003; Roodenburg, Euwals, and Rele 2003).
With the increasing explicit discursive formulation of what were
formerly policy goals only rarely – as in Van Kemenade's case –
explicitly stated, a shift toward a third phase set in, with as a key
figure the leader of the Dutch Conservative-Libertarian Party (VVD),
Frits Bolkestein, who stressed the overrepresentation of migrants not
only in low education and unemployment, but also in crime, relating
a propensity to crime to specific ethnic categories and their culture.
This phase, which I propose to call the *culturist* phase of discourse,
involved an emphasis on the need for a "tough policy" of integration,
a strict policy of immigration, and a departure from the supposed
"multiculturalism," which was now blamed as "too soft." This
entailed a new focus on one-sided individual integration in which
language and cultural adaptation were central. As Ayaan Hirsi Ali
said in 2002: "Integration is a cultural problem" (2002: 7). At this
point, "multiculturalism" emerged as a causal attribute of failed
policies and of "the integration problem" in general. Crucially,
"multiculturalism" first becomes a current concept in public

discussions of immigrant integration only *after* its supposed hegemony in policy and the public sphere. The multiculturealism that defines itself in terms of a realist awakening vis-à-vis multiculturalism in a sense secures its discursive legitimacy by inventing a history with which it claims to break. But, as former policies never were multiculturalist, this is a rhetoric of multiculturealism, in which "multiculturalism" is a mnemonic construct with performative consequences but without historical anchorage. It is a construction of history that serves present purposes in terms of the power differentials in integration discourse and, in the end, in the criteria of demarcation of "society." The culturist turn explicitly relates the negative socioeconomic indicators (including the emergence of a migrant underclass) to "culture" and to the incommensurability of culture in the plural. Cultural issues were discovered as the cause of structural inequalities, and various economic differences were coded as cultural differences. In practice, this mainly meant that religion and specifically "Islam" was causally linked to relative deprivation and crime, as was noted and critiqued by the European Commission against Racism and Intolerance (ECRI 2008). Indeed, contemporary culturism often puts "culture" and "religion" on a par, for instance, by speaking of "Islamic culture."

The discursive "discovery of culture" signifies a qualitative change setting the third phase of minority discourse apart from both earlier phases. In the first two phases, "culture" largely remained in the background of discourse. It was not problematized, but was assumed to exist in a rather essentialist fashion. In the third phase, discourse becomes culturist and cultural issues become the prime focus of integration discourse. Significantly, however, in both the earlier culturalism and the later culturism, a similar cultural essentialism prevails. So the idea of a before and an after, central to multiculturealism, is to be approached with caution. For the idea of a "before/after" or of an "old politics/new politics" divide is a continuous presence in Dutch political discourse. The pivotal figure marking the division between "before" and "after" is usually seen to be Pim Fortuyn, the maverick populist politician from Rotterdam who was shot by an environmental activist in 2002, just days before national elections in which his party (List Pim Fortuyn) gained twenty-six seats in the Second Chamber of Dutch Parliament (the Dutch House of Representatives). The 2002 elections were the first that were dominated by the issue of immigrant integration.

However, the "break" forced by Pim Fortuyn is a discursive construct in the sense that discourse reflexively produces its own memory or footing in history. By the time Fortuyn rose as a populist figure, integration discourse had been evolving in the assimilationist direction he proposed for at least a decade, including an explicit critique of "Muslim culture." The question why the Netherlands saw such a shift is often put, but equally often it is put badly. It assumes a primitive concept of causality, and it either regards the Netherlands as isolated or sees in "globalization" the Great Cause of all that's happening. Moreover, there are different questions, for instance, "Why did the political climate change the way it did?" or "How and why did a dominant integration discourse gain footing?" One of the reasons for the *political* change surely lies in the fact that prior to Pim Fortuyn, the Netherlands were in relatively calm waters governed by the "Purple Coalition," a coalition that brought together socialists and (conservative) liberals – in effect the Dutch version of "Third Way" politics. The coalition of opposites in effect meant that politics devolved into a depoliticized problem management, and indeed Wim Kok, socialist prime minister at the time, was famous for stating socialists should "shed their ideological feathers." In such a situation, as Chantal Mouffe (2005) has analyzed, the antagonistic aspect is thoroughly drained from politics, and there is room for populism as soon as a leader with charismatic appeal steps onto the stage. Pim Fortuyn was just that (Schinkel 2012).

In the culturalist phase, then, an explicit before/after awareness, signaling the failure of a pluralism that was now ex ante termed "multiculturalism" appears omnipresent. In the influential newspaper article "The Multicultural Drama" (2000), which is retrospectively seen as the breakthrough of multiculturealist awareness, publicist Paul Scheffer stated that the multiculturalist expectations of integration have been proven false and that "below the surface of public life there floats a sea of stories on the clash of cultures that are hardly if ever heard." "The Multicultural Drama" contains all the characteristics of multiculturealism: a critique of a politically correct ignorance of problems, and a call for cultural adjustment and discussion of cultural incompatibilities, specifically between "Islam" and "the West." Ron Eyerman (2008: 105) rightly analyzes Scheffer's essay as performative, and it was without doubt intended to change Dutch integration policies. Yet he sees this performativity in Scheffer's claim that there was no integration policy and his ulterior aim to change the existing policy. Eyerman furthermore thinks Dutch integration policies were characterized by multiculturalism. Yet precisely this has been the performative effect of speech acts like Scheffer's. Before multiculturalism was critiqued in the Netherlands, it was not mentioned. No policy bore the name "multiculturalism" or even closely resembled multicultural models (Taylor 1994; Modood 2007). Both its multiculturealist critiques and its sympathetic assessments see in Dutch *Ethnic Minority Policy* a pinnacle of multiculturalism, but they do so long after it was in effect. Moreover, the 1980s minority policy involved "representatives" of ethnic minorities, but these did not grant minority groups any rights nor were they actually "representative" of ethnic minority groups. They rather functioned much like alibis for the government, which, upon "consulting" representatives, could legitimately claim societal consensus, as it did in the sphere of economic policy following a mix of the Rheinland model and Dutch pillarization. Scheffer's contribution is to be seen as the breakthrough that made a rightist discourse *Salonfähig* on the political left. He basically repeated much of what Bolkestein had said a decade before him, and this is indicative of a political convergence on issues of integration – a convergence that has in fact existed most of the time since the 1950s. After 2000, left-wing political leaders have often been put in the position of having to distance themselves from a supposed multiculturalism their parties were to blame for. Often, such politicians must have known, first of all, that the left has never been in power, and, second, that they weren't "multiculturalists." But the rhetorical force of multiculturealism has led to a *politics of confession* on the left. This has been embraced by the biggest Dutch party on the left (Labor: PvdA). At the same time and in line with the call for a "new politics" that Fortuyn's ascent gave rise to, the Socialist Party chose a harsher position on integration all along, thus adding pressure on the left to embrace multiculturealism. As late as 2009, then, the leader of the Labor Party and Vice-Prime Minister Bos could state that a tough stance on "integration" was to become a focal point for his party. The politics of confession thus also involved a *politics of repetition*. And while the political center and right could pose as "having known all along" (despite having been in power for much of the supposedly "muticultural" period), the left was, and is, running in circles. On the issue of "integration," the left can do no good, as the symbolic capital of "toughness" almost automatically seems to accrue to the right.

For the last decade, the focus on "Islamic culture" has been an increasingly dominant feature of Dutch discourse on integration in the early years of the 2000s. That becomes apparent in the increased attention given to "culture" in influential policy papers and political memoranda on immigrant integration during that time (Ministry of Foreign Affairs 1994; Tweede Kamer 2005 and 2006; VROM 2007). This at once means that "integration" is regarded as specifically referring to the integration of Muslim immigrants, and that it is their "culture" – sometimes named "Turkish" or "Moroccan" and sometimes termed "Islamic" – and specifically their religion that is the focus of the current problem awareness. With the advent of politicians such as the late Pim Fortuyn and Ayaan Hirsi Ali (De Leeuw and Van Wichelen 2005), Islamic migration was explicitly seen as a "fifth column" (Fortuyn 1997, 2002a, 2002b), and warnings were issued that "the ghost of Islamic fundamentalism roams at the borders of Europe" (quoted in Van Meeteren 2010). The murder of film maker and publicist Theo van Gogh by a young and radical Islamic man (Buruma 2006; Van der Veer 2006), which also triggered Fukuyama's reaction, as well as the international attention paid to "terrorism" have further facilitated and legitimated the culturist turn in Dutch discourse on minorities and integration. Issues of religious radicalization, involving the incompatibility of Shar'ia with democracy, and issues of sexual oppression have come to the fore in policy texts, next to issues of crime and nuisance (for instance, by "Moroccan street youth"). At the same time, initiatives were deployed to "understand" the culture of the other. Thus, Dutch police started to undertake trips to Morocco to understand the Moroccan boys they encountered in Dutch cities. Not only did "crime" become a reason to understand "culture" and was a causal link between the two thereby assumed, it also meant that young boys, born in the Netherlands, were thought to be criminal because of their Moroccan culture. All the while no one has been able to explain why the parents of these boys, who, having born in Morocco, could arguably be assumed to be much more immersed in "Moroccan culture," have been systematically less criminal. In question is, of course, also *when* a social problem is individualized and/or de-individualized. When is crime classified by a collective concept, as "cultural"? It is clear that crimes committed by native Dutch are exempt from such classification – which would, of course, culturally taint the very justice system devised to deal with crime.

With respect to policy, culturism appears as assimilationism. In that respect, the Netherlands is a good representative of a broader Western European picture (Grillo 2005). Assimilationism has always been dominant in the French *laïcité* tradition (Schnapper 2003), and this has given rise to early analyses of "cultural racism" (Taguieff 1990) and "neo-racism" (Balibar 1991). But since the late 1990s, "culture" has been an especially salient topic in France, where all used to be (artificially) quite on the cultural front. Marc Augé could say in 1999, referring among other things to the issue of immigration, that "there has never been more talk of culture" in France (1999: 39). But "culture" has gained a wider Western European upsurge. While Brubaker (2001) saw a "new assimilationism" throughout Europe by 2001, the United Kingdom made an explicitly assimilationist turn in 2005, departing with its race relations–based pluralist tradition. An upsurge of "racism" had been noted in the United Kingdom in conjunction with a rising assimilationism (Back et al. 2002), involving an increasing focus on the incompatibilities between cultures (Grillo 2007). Countries such as the Netherlands, Germany, Switzerland (thematizing the 1930s notion of *Überfremdung* in a contemporary context), and the Scandinavian countries increasingly incorporated culturist elements in policy (Modood et al. 2006). Specifically the Netherlands and the Scandinavian countries became European forerunners of culturist discourse (Pred 2000; Hagelund 2002; Grillo 2003). The Netherlands was also first among Europe and an influential example for others in its mandatory civic integration tests, which emphasize Dutch language abilities and a selective knowledge of Dutch history and of "Dutch norms and values," including the acceptance of homosexuality (Joppke 2009a). Throughout Europe, the late 1990s saw the emergence of concern over the compatibility of "Islam" with Western European democracy (Modood and Werbner 1997; Soysal 1997; Zolberg and Woon 1998). Such culturist concern grew stronger in the first years of the new millennium (Foner 2005; Garton Ash 2006; Modood et al. 2006; Lentin and Titley 2011). Current Western European culturism predominantly takes the form of what Edward Said (2003) has called "orientalism." I shall mainly refer to examples from this orientalist form of culturism here. Yet there are other forms of culturism. One example concerns the 2006 proposal, briefly mentioned in Chapter 1, by a Rotterdam alderwoman to proceed with the forced abortion of single Antillean teen mothers. Early 2006, this became a news item in the Netherlands, and various politicians entered into a serious discussion about it. An MP of the Dutch conservative party (VVD), for instance, stated: "we can talk about forced sterilisation, although it is not a campaign item [in the 2006 municipal elections]."[5] A prominent member of the same party and a former minister said a day earlier she would definitely think about forced sterilisation.[6] It was thought that, due to the culture of Antilleans, single Antillean teen mothers were apparently unable to maintain a relationship and would therefore be unable to raise children. In order to prevent child abuse eugenic measures would be necessary, yet only for Antillean teen mothers. In 2009, this issue was again taken up in the form of a "discussion" in the Rotterdam municipal council, and in 2016 it again became part of a national discussion.

Such issues have gradually become intertwined with policy practices targeting specific "ethnic groups," focused, for instance, on crime among "Moroccan" and "Antillean" youth.[7] In addition, restrictions to immigration were implemented, for instance, in terms of income demands when marrying someone from outside the country. Specific urban neighborhoods, starting in Rotterdam, implemented similar income demands (120 percent of the official minimum) to bar immigrants. Initially, as the European Committee on Racism and Inequality (ECRI) recognized in its 2008 report, what later became known as the "Rotterdam Law" explicitly was intended to bar non-Western allochthons. When this proved legally untenable, the measure shifted to an income demand, which constituted a form of indirect discrimination that continues today. Meanwhile, citizenship courses incorporated much more strongly cultural demands. A "thick" identification with the nation became more explicit during the early 2000s. This resulted in the drafting of a "Historical Canon" and the institution of a Dutch "National Historical Museum." Both were called for in the 2007 Cabinet policy paper on immigrant integration. The 2011 Cabinet Paper *Integration, Bond, Citizenship*, though proclaiming "a new perspective," offers a rehash of many of the themes present in the debate since the late 1980s and early 1990s. Again, it is stated that "Cabinet explicitly distances itself from the

---

[5] Radio 1, February 18, 2006.
[6] Nova Den Haag Vandaag, February 17, 2006.
[7] Some examples are the *Integral Approach Antillians* in Rotterdam (as of 2005) and the *Moroccans Letter* by the Dutch cabinet (2008).

relativism enshrined in the concept of multiculturalism. ... Integration concerns integration into Dutch society" (Dutch Cabinet 2011: 5).

So are multiculturealists right after all? Is the turn toward assimilation a shift away from a much more tolerant multiculturalism? It hardly is. What is at stake in the denouncement of multiculturalism can be more readily interpreted as the performative production of "multiculturalism" as a negative marker that *enabled* a discursive shift toward an assimilationism that never really has "assimilation" but rather "differentiation" as its immediate objective. This does not mean that such assimilationism was not present before, since the Dutch Ethnic Minorities Policy had an assimilationist rationale. It does mean that a shift in discursive images took place. This shift gives an ex post facto plausibility to the former existence of multiculturalism, but that plausibility exists only if one buys into the critiques and confessions of "multiculturalism." Rather, multiculturealism has functioned as a discursive technique that opened up an entire new discursive space of immigrant problematization and, as its mirror effect, of national imagination. This discursive space made it possible for commentators from left to right to critique "Islam," "allochthons" or their "culture," and, most of all, "multicultural policies" for failed integration. All too often, therefore, a critique of extreme and populist politicians serves to hide the fact that the entire political spectrum has shifted: the extreme right politician Hans Janmaat was convicted for pronouncements in the 1980s that have in the meantime become conventional for Cabinet members – a fact that gives all the more plausibility to multiculturealism's claim to break with political correctness.

To sum up, the culturist imagination on "integration" has five defining characteristics:

1) It focuses on the relatively low structural status and the relatively high crime and unemployment rates of immigrants.
2) Presupposed is an essentialist view of "culture" as a stable whole of norms and values (both with respect to the "own culture" of immigrants as to the "dominant culture").
3) It operates with an individualizing focus (individual persons are or are not "integrated"; individuals are therefore mainly responsible in case of problematic integration).

4) Culture is regarded as explanatory variable for the relatively low structural status and the relatively high crime and unemployment rates of immigrants.
5) "Culture" is regarded as potentially intrinsically problematic and as incompatible to the "dominant culture." In particular here, I argue, the raced nature of this concept of culture becomes apparent.

The discursive power wielded by an integration imaginary that traverses various realms of social science, as well as the mass media and the political system, is evident in the ubiquity of culturism in politics and the public sphere, where, for instance, conservative politicians and second-wave feminists form unlikely coalitions to battle "Muslim" oppression of women. It can likewise be seen in the rise of "culture" in Western European countries with different traditions of integration. In various ways, this raises the question whether or not this amounts to a form of racism. I believe this is not unequivocally the case. In order to understand why, and before I raise suspicion of negating and thereby silently condoning racist discourses, I propose we give thought to the possibility of there being other "discourses of alterity," to use Castoriadis's concept, than racism.

Why Not Speak of "Cultural Racism"?

In Western European social science at large (not in specialized fields such as critical race studies), racism appears out of vogue. Gilroy (1992) noted as much nearly two decades ago, and the "end of anti-racism" described by him appears to have lost none of its actuality. In accordance with the homology between social scientific research agendas and policy agendas noted by Pierre Bourdieu (1975), racism has lost the relatively prominent position it had, for instance, in the 1970s and 1980s, and where it hasn't it has been depoliticized in the form of "stereotyping" or "discrimination." In analyses of migration and integration, "racism" is reduced to a passing reference at most; use of the word at conferences evokes a bored "Not that again" kind of response. At the same time, it has been found to be harder to be blatantly racist in Western Europe (Ignazi 1992). But U.S. scholarship of racism as well has undergone a reorientation. Post–civil rights thinking about racism has been troubled by the ambiguities of the new political position (Winant 2004), and it has also been stuck

conceptually between approaches that take "race" to be a more or less
objective phenomenon or at least leave room for that (Gordon 1964;
Banton 1977; Wilson 1980) and approaches that deem it entirely
illusory (Fields 1990; Appiah 1992; Gilroy 2000). Many, of course,
have taken an intermediate position (Van den Berghe 1968, 1970), and
a contemporary majority focuses on the social construction of race,
denying the genetic basis of "race" (Mead et al. 1968; Cavalli-Sforza
2000; Essed and Goldberg 2000; Omi 2001). Some hold that race is
after all a biological category (Rosenberg et al. 2002; Eberhardt 2005;
compare Carter 2007), while a recent important alternative position
has been developed by Amade M'Charek in STS, which centers on the
multiple ontologies of "race" by looking at the materialities of "race"
in practice (M'Charek 2013). Yet the position that "race" is not an
objectively existing "thing" has, according to some, given rise to a
decline in the attention given to racism (compare Miles 1993). On the
other hand, research of racism in Western Europe has increasingly
thematized racism related to culture. Most of all, it is argued that
racism is increasingly "coded as culture" (Solomos and Back 1996),
that "culture" has replaced "biology" (Mbembe 2013: 18), and that it
takes the form of a "cultural racism" (Taguieff 1990; Stolcke 1995;
Modood 1997; Castles 2000; Foner 2005).

Several influential analyses have used the term "neo-racism" to
characterize a currently salient form of racism. The concept of neo-
racism, or rather "new racism," has been introduced by Martin Barker
(1981), in an analysis of British conservatism. Similarly, Gordon
(1989) has analyzed the relationship between the new right and new
racism. New racism, in Barker's analysis, is geared first and foremost
against immigrants in the United Kingdom. Characteristic of this new
racism is the defence of a certain "way of life," the distanciation from
conventional forms of racism, and a rhetoric of common sense that
makes reference to the fair and tolerant nature of the people but also of
the righteousness of their fears of the problems of immigration (the
"Argument from Genuine Fear"). New racism, then, concerns "certain
forms of argument that, to date, had been regarded as relatively
innocent," but which are racist (Barker 1981: 10). Barker does hold
that new racism is "a theory of human nature" (21).

A later discussion by Étienne Balibar (1991) goes a step further. He
explains the features of what he conceives to be an existing neo-racism.
Balibar speaks of neo-racism, and hence frames what he observes in

terms of "racism." Yet he explicates, more than Barker does, that a certain relationship to the supposed culture of immigrants, more than a take on supposed biological characteristics, is what is at stake. Neo-racism, according to Balibar, is a more complex form of racism than "racism," since it incorporates the main counterargument against racism. That argument, largely coming from anthropology, was that there are different cultures that were different but deserving equal respect. This was what can be called a *culturalist* argument, in the sense that a specific form of cultural relativism was at its basis. In what Balibar calls neo-racism, this culturalist idea is turned topsy-turvy. Neo-racism presupposes that there are indeed different cultures and ways of life existing next to each other, and these cultures are fundamentally different in the sense that they shouldn't be mixed. In neo-racism, cultures are deemed incompatible. While racism in the conventional sense opposes the mixing of "races" – for instance, based upon eugenic theories of degeneration – neo-racism opposes the mixing of cultures. This is considered to be the main defining characteristic of neo-racism: its insistence on the incompatibility of "cultures." Neo-racism presupposes that if different cultures are to mix, trouble inevitably ensues. But because the culture from which neo-racism springs is construed as a preferred culture that threatens to be damaged by mixing with other, incompatible cultures, this form of racism has also been called "cultural racism." Cultural racism and neo-racism are surely the most relevant notions today, while "modern racism" (McConahay 1986) and "symbolic racism" (Tarman and Sears 2005) have also emerged as alternative forms.

However, although I'm not going to say that racism is not a valid category here, I do believe there are some problems with the concept of "cultural racism." First of all, there is a problematic pretension of cultural racism's newness. Yet as Ann Stoler has noted, cultural racism is hardly a recent phenomenon: "'Cultural racism' was not a recent, postmodern variation on an old theme but itself a colonial phenomenon" (2002: 17). Indeed, Frantz Fanon already noted the shift from a "vulgar, primitive racism" based on biology to a more "delicate argumentation" of what he called, in 1956, a "cultural racism" *(racisme culturel)* (Fanon 2006: 40). But perhaps what Fanon called "primitive racism" was a rather modern phenomenon, since it was based on "scientific" biology (Voegelin 1998). And no doubt one can trace the existence of "cultural racism" in Western contexts further back to, at least, Hellenic times, where definitions of "Greek" or "Roman" were similarly objects of negotiation and hierarchization. Second, "cultural racism" of course does not denote a "cultural" form of racism over against a noncultural form – every form of racism can in itself be regarded as a cultural form and product. It is rather the idea that "culture" is the new "race." Yet as a concept, "cultural racism" is a pleonasm. Third, the reflexive post-racist imagination in what is called cultural racism is somewhat missing. Racism exists covertly, and it is hidden, I argue, as the core of what can be called culturism, a rhetoric with its own discursive logic. Much racism research has shown how contemporary racisms operate "in disguise," that is, not in explicitly discursive forms but in hidden rhetorics and structural orders of hier-archy, domination, and asymmetry (Essed and Goldberg 2000). The proliferation of the discourses and imaginaries I am concerned with here has not been possible without a significant shift in their underlying normative logic. In line with Taguieff's idea (2010: 53) that there has been "a recent ideological metamorphosis of racism," I argue that such debates have justly signified a shift in "rhetorics of exclusion" (Stolcke 1995), even though I shall take issue with the very idea of "exclusion." The discursive logic of those rhetorics warrants a closer conceptual look that starts from a conception of both the logic and function of racism. I shall take Cornelius Castoriadis's claim that "the exclusion of the other has not always and everywhere – far from it – taken the form of racism" (1997: 26) as the starting point for an analysis of culturism as a functional equivalent of racism, albeit with a racist core.

So to capture both the change and the continuity, I undertake the effort to distinguish racism from what I call culturism and to show their mutual imbrication. I pursue this distinction to most effectively highlight what is at stake in integration imaginaries. Precisely because of the reflexive role played by racism, interpretations purely in terms of racism may miss important parts of the performative dynamics of such imagin-aries. Rather, I argue, it is key to disentangle culturism and racism, and to then qualify their entanglement and to *locate the racism in culturism*.

From Culturalism to Culturism

First, *culturism* is to be distinguished from *culturalism*. As Balibar rightly notes, a discourse of exclusion has emerged in Western Europe that has effectively incorporated anti-racism as a foundation for what

I prefer to call a functional equivalent of racism: culturism. Balibar notes that Lévi-Straussian anthropology delivered an important argument against racism, yet Lévi-Strauss may in fact not be the best example. For Lévi-Strauss, what matters is the acknowledgment of the common elements behind cultural differences, not the emphasis of the magnitude of differences and the lack of possibility of valuating one difference over another. While Lévi-Strauss, in *The Savage Mind*, for instance, notes how technical skill exists in non-Western civilizations where Westerners have neglected it, in *Tristes Tropiques* he is highly normative concerning the "backwardness of Islam" (1973a: ch. 39–40). It has been a rather more cultural relativist strand of anthropological theory that offered anti-racism its main arguments. The work of Boas, Sapir, Whorf, Edward Hall, and Stuart Hall has been more influential in the development of the idea that there are different cultures deserving equal respect. Franz Boas, the father of American anthropology, started out with an interest in eugenic theory (Williams 2006), but gradually moved away from biological explanations toward an analysis not of race but of racism (Boas 1910; Stocking 1974). After Boas, Ruth Benedict, Margaret Mead, and Ralph Linton continued in Boas's tradition of antiracism and cultural relativism. This amounted to a form of *culturalism*, an argument from the differences between autonomous cultures that foregoes the possibility of finding an extra-cultural or super-cultural standard by which to measure and evaluate cultural systems. Culturalism provided an important antidote against racism in the sense that it culturalized differences that were, in racist discourse, attributed to biological differences. Though the concept of culture has in sociology traditionally been superseded by that of "society," a similar culturalism can be observed there, for instance, in the work of various Chicago School sociologists (Wirth 1938; Park 1950 [1923]: 138–151).

Culturism, however, incorporates only "half" of culturalism's argument. What it takes on is the idea that different cultures exist autonomously as bounded entities (Stolcke 1995; Grillo 2003). Although anthropology can surely not be seen as a "cause" of culturist constructions of culture, as Wikan has, for instance, argued, Verena Stolcke has noted that cultural constructionist critique in anthropology, despite intending the contrary, presupposed "the separateness of cultures and their boundedness" (1995: 12). Cultural anthropology has thus in recent decades started to question its prime concept, much like

I argue there is reason to question the primacy of the sociological category of "society." In both cases, the reason is that such concepts have performative effects that are to be analyzed rather than unreflexively incorporated into social scientific analysis. In anthropology, Stolcke's intervention followed a prior discussion by Said and other scholars engaged with the analysis of Arabic peoples and the Middle East. Lila Abu Lughod, for instance, argued in 1991 that culture had started to function as race. The strategy she proposed to circumvent "the most problematic connotations of culture: homogeneity, coherence, and timelessness" involved a focus on the individual and a refusal to generalize (Abu Lughod 2006 [1991]).

Faye Harrison has argued that anthropology should be more attentive to racism, but she notes how racism has started to operate without "race" (compare Fassin 2012). But, as John Hartigan (2005: 263) has argued, one might wonder: "What is racism without race?" While Harrison speaks of an "underlying cultural logic" of racism (cited in Hartigan 2005: 264), she does not distinguish between an underlying logic of racism and a logic of a racism without race. I argue that, at least partly, the latter operates through a different logic. I also argue that in order to acknowledge this, and to be specific about the workings of domination (and not to deny the existence of racism), this warrants speaking of a "culturism," which has, as I will argue, a strong racist kernel in the more traditional sense of "racism." The recent ideological metamorphosis of racism that Taguieff speaks of has to do, according to him, with the displacement of biological inequality by an absolutization of the difference between cultures (Taguieff 2010: 53). No doubt such cultural absolutization has always been a part of racism in its more traditional understandings, but the explicit uptake of anti-racist culturism and an accompanying post-racist self-awareness is specific to contemporary forms of culturism. Whatever culturist discourse appropriates from an anthropologically informed vocabulary, it does not incorporate the argument of the impossibility of normatively evaluating cultures. When "cultures" are thought to mesh culturist logic presumes that problems occur as a result of the incompatibility of these cultures. This furthermore entails the *attribution of incommensurability* to the culture construed as the *culture of the other*. Culturism can hence be defined as *a discourse of alterity* operating on the basis of an *argument of cultural incompatibility* and by means of a *one-sided cultural attribution* and *asymmetric evaluation* of such incompatibility.

The Normative Logics of Racism and Culturism

Racism has always proven adaptive to new circumstances (Gossett 1963; Hall 1992; Essed and Goldberg 2002). Moreover, it has been argued that European racism, other than U.S. racism, was not centered on skin color but was aimed, for instance, at Irish or Jews (Smedley 1993). And as Hall (1996) has argued, "race" and culture" have always been mixed. However, culturism entails a different idea of the "innateness" of ascribed characteristics. Early European racism was perhaps predominantly biological in focus (Barsch and Hejl 2000). And a focus on racism should be crucial to social science for critical or even political reasons. But that doesn't mean one cannot see in culturism a different type of discourse from racism. For it is precisely talk of racism that has for some time now been rendered relatively politically impotent (compare Gilroy 1992). And where "race" does not figure in a dominant discourse of alterity, as it did, for instance, in early European racism, it seems crucial to understand the logic of discourses of alterity in such a way that *the existence of racism in them can be specified and qualified*.

Culturism has thus been defined as a discourse of alterity operating on the basis of an argument of cultural incompatibility. It moreover brings about a one-sided cultural attribution and asymmetric evaluation of such supposed incompatibility. In this section, this definition is further explicated through a discussion of the underlying logic of culturism, and by distinguishing it from the logic of a racist discourse of alterity. Racism is characterized by the coupling of a specific kind of normativity to assumed biological characteristics, or more fundamentally, to assumed "grounded" characteristics. The imaginary of *Blut und Boden* ("blood and soil") combines both the biological aspect and the aspect of a "ground" and is a typical form of racist imaginations. Racism presupposes an unchanging and primordial "ground" of being. This "ground" can be conceived in either a literal (territory) or in a transitive sense (biology). The normativity active here is what can thus be called a *terranormativity*: a normative logic rooted in some sort of "ground" (*terra*), be it literally the territory of birth, or the biological "ground" from which people's being and acting supposedly springs and which is collectively identified by the notion of "race." In a terranormative logic, some sort of "natural" ground is thought to determine the character and value of individuals and collectives.

Is culture not often treated as such a "ground"? I argue on this point that what is specific to culturism is that it does not directly presuppose an unchanging "natural ground" existing in (or behind/below) individuals and collectives. What hence characterizes culturism is not a form of terranormativity, but of *agranormativity*. Culturism operates on an agrarian logic of *cultivating* the biological or otherwise natural ground of man. The concept of "culture" derives from the agrarian model of cultivating the land (*terra*), which was then transposed to the social realm in "cultivating the people" (Claessens and Claessens 1979: 87; Williams 1983: 87). The notion of culturist "agranormativity" immediately indicates its relation to racist "terranormativity," and the concepts are chosen here because they simultaneously highlight the difference and the relation between these logics. Culturism involves a highly anthropologized outlook on the person as a Lockean *tabula rasa*, until "culture" shapes him or her. Yet that shaping is in culturist discourse deemed inevitable and practically unchangeable. Terranormativity presupposes a non-neutral "ground" of being. Agranormativity, equally presupposing such a "ground" of being, conceives this as initially neutral, as a ground that can and must be cultivated. Agranormativity shifts the evaluative focus toward that "cultivation."

Culturist discourse, informed by an agranormative logic, has in common with racism what Zygmunt Bauman has termed "the philosophical core of racism": that man exists before he acts, and that no action can change what he is (1989: 85). Yet in culturist discourse, the all-determining ontological stigma is not natural in kind, but cultural. Not Muslims' actions are the focus of discourse, but the "Islamic culture" ascribed to them, which is presupposed to over-code all actions and to imprint all actions with a cultural emblem of hostile otherness. Racism therefore treats the natural ground of being as actuality; culturism treats it as potentiality. Culturism hence allows for more complexity to underpin an in the end essentialist discourse, and it can hence claim to be anti-racist, all the while producing an equivalent logic of exclusion. In culturist discourse, "culture" loosely designates an "integrated whole" of "norms and values" (typical is Radcliffe-Brown 1961). Culture is, on the one hand, the "heavy" basis of "society," and every "society" is characterized by its own "culture." On the other hand, in culturist discourse "culture" is as "lite" as a lifestyle, since every culture deemed "fundamentalist" – which in

Western Europe increasingly includes every form of monotheistic religion – is regarded as a dangerous form of culture.

What happens in culturism is not merely a coding of "race" as "culture," but the bringing into practice of a different discursive focus – one that departs from explicit essentialized biological perspectives and adopts an essentialist sociological or anthropological perspective. In culturist discourse, racism can be associated with the extreme right and can hence be discredited. Yet at the same time a focus on the problematic of the culture of immigrants opens a discursive space of continued exclusion by different means. However, the logic of agranormativity is never without traces of terranormativity, and racism forms the hidden core of culturism.

The Racist Core of Culturism

While it would be too imprecise to say that culturism is merely a racism in disguise (Policar 1990; Balibar 1991; Essed 1991; Fiske 1998), racism is certainly not altogether absent in culturism. As indicated above, a distinction is in order between two general bases of racism: the *Blut* variant focuses on the inferiority of the other by blood or another biological notion; the *Boden* variant derives that inferiority from the soil on which one has been born or from another natural notion. The *Boden* variant figures prominently in various kinds of theories of climate that have existed since antiquity, and of which, in modern times, Montesquieu's is the best known. Both variants do not coincidentally have their parallels in the legal traditions concerning immigration, based either on *jus sanguinis* or on *jus soli*. To say that culturism is racism in disguise seems to too quickly dismiss the agranormative logic of culturism. For only on the basis of the above distinction between a racism based on "blood" and a racism based on "soil" can the connection between racism and culturism be made concrete. What lives on in culturism is only the "soil" version of racism. Hence it is indeed possible to say that culturism follows an agrarian logic of cultivation of a "soil" that is terranormatively presupposed.

The terranormative aspects of culturism that combine with an agranormative logic become especially visible when the hierarchization of cultures is considered. Again, the most prominent feature of culturism is that "cultures" are deemed incompatible. But how does incompatibility, or as a Dutch public philosopher (Verbrugge 2004) calls it in his "diagnosis" of Dutch culture, the "essential alienness" of the "culture" of, for instance, Muslims, lead to a hierarchized view of various cultures? Even when "cultures" are seen as incompatible, a cultural relativism or a culturalism would be possible instead of culturism. In last instance, then, that hierarchization is possible only on the basis of the silent invocation of a terranormative aspect in culturist discourse. Dutch culturism ultimately functions on the nativist premise that *here*, on *Dutch territory*, the "Dutch culture" is the *dominant culture* and that it *should remain so*. Without the last evaluative aspect, of course, a culturistically feared "Islamization" of the Netherlands would not be a problem, since in that case *a* "dominant culture" might be supposed to exist. Hierarchization of cultures involves in the last instance a "natural fallacy": that which is supposed to exist in a "dominant" way is treated as intrinsically the best *within its territorial parameters*. Incompatibilities with "other cultures" are in culturist discourse solved by means of a hierarchization of cultures in which the "dominant culture" presupposed to thrive in a specific territory is located at the "top" of the hierarchy. In that way both an explicit racism and a culturalist cultural relativism are avoided, and yet the inferiority of the others (those immersed in "nondominant cultures") is constructed.

Terranormativity, or rather the "*Boden* variant" thereof, is thus not altogether absent from culturist discourse. It functions in facilitating legitimization for the nativist claim, central to culturist discourse, that "our culture" is to be preferred, since "we were here – on this soil – earlier." This indicates at once the difference between racism and culturism. The "we were here earlier" or "we have been here longer" argument, of course, did not feature prominently in the racist discourse of colonialism. In colonialism, the "*Blut* variant" of racism was actualized, and the colonized were classed as inferior on the basis of phenotypical features presupposed as indicative of "race." In the postcolonial context, the "*Boden* variant" of racism remains potent as an argument facilitating an otherwise thoroughly culturist discourse. It is, for instance, less easily possible to form neo-Nazi organizations in Europe; yet new anti-Semitic organizations appear that no longer specifically target Jews, but Muslims, and that are specifically at odds with the "culture" of Muslims. Matti Bunzl, analyzing the shift from anti-Semitism to Islamophobia in Europe, has similarly noted how right-wing parties throughout Europe take on Jews as party members and construe them as allies in a clash between the West and Islam (Bunzl 2007).

Culturist Antiracism

Because agranormativity entails the cultivation of the cultural ground, it can stress the terranormativity and hence the racism of the culture of others. Culturist discourse thus allows one to condemn those other cultures on such grounds. In fact, this can serve as a posteriori evidence of the incompatibility of the dominant culture with those intolerant cultures. The idea that non-Westerners are more xenophobic than Westerners is not new. Marx and Engels, for instance, wrote that capitalism forces even the most ardent xenophobia of the barbarians to capitulation (1969 [1848]: 28). Culturist discourse focuses mainly on opposition between dominant "Western culture(s)" and a supposed "culture of Islam."

A Dutch journal, for instance, reported in 2006 that 60 percent of the Dutch believe that Moroccans are the most racist group (Brouwer 2006: 5). Forty-two percent found Turks to be most racist, and 56 percent found "Muslims" in general to be so. While the author of the article is critical of the mix-up between race and religion, he goes on to say that the Netherlands are a "bicultural society" in which a "cultural conflict" between "Islam" and the "Dutch society" takes place. Another example from the same decade concerns the removal of three Dutch-Turkish candidates from the electoral lists of two political parties in September 2006. The reason for this was their non-acknowledgment of the Armenian genocide of 1915–1917. This gained a lot of media attention in the Netherlands, and a picture was portrayed of a "Turkish community" in the Netherlands that would massively turn away from these political parties that traditionally could count on its vote. While a poll among Turkish Dutch showed no such thing, for weeks "the Turkish community" was construed as intolerant and as denying a genocide. A similar thing occurred in 2015, when research reputedly demonstrated that "Moroccan" and "Turkish" young men were avid supporters of ISIS terrorists. Based on this research, the Minister of the Interior sounded the alarm, but also demanded a new and more comprehensive study. This second study found that the groups in question actually showed very little support of

ISIS, but the key point is that these were, as always, considered as "population groups." To begin with, a questionnaire asking for approval of certain acts or organizations hardly ever asks to what extent respondents think the issue at hand is important. But what is more, the "population groups" that are discerned in survey research are never a consequence of that research; their existence is its *premise*. And yet it is wholly unclear theoretically how the concept "population group" or "ethnic group" acts in practice or what its ontological import is. Usually such "groups" are a priori assumptions that form the basis of research, and so any findings are automatically construed in light of "population groups," "ethnic groups," or "minority groups." The very notion of such "groups" is a clear effect of "seeing like a survey" (Law 2009). So whether research reports much or little support for ISIS, as in the 2015 case, is really irrelevant. The question is what it means to speak of such "support by ethnic groups" at all.

Even when "ethnic groups" are shown as not intolerant, racist, or supportive of terrorists, then, they are imagined as a culturally bounded "group" that could, with the next survey, well be shown to be racist. Culturist integration imaginaries also involve an explicit critique of the way discrimination and racism have been dealt with heretofore. Dutch politicians of various colors have, in recent years, repeatedly said that because of its tolerant rulings, the governmental Council for Discrimination should be abolished. Likewise, a returning debate concerns a possible change of the Constitution. Article 23 of that Constitution grants confessional schools the same government subsidy as public schools. According to conservative politicians of the liberal party (in their *Liberal Manifesto* of 2001) it was designed for Christian schools, but now that Islamic schools are appearing, it would lead to segregation as Islamic schools foster anti-modern ideas and actions. Furthermore, article 1, which prohibits all discrimination, has been offered for change. Discrimination on the basis of religion is conceived as much less serious than discrimination on the basis of "race." In other words: culturism is deemed less serious than racism.

A final example concerns the possibility of having a double nationality, which was introduced in order to further immigrant integration. When a new government was installed in early 2007, an extreme right-wing party objected to the fact that two of its appointed secretaries were in possession of double nationality and demanded they renounce their foreign citizenship. When shortly afterwards, an MP with double nationality was appointed on a Moroccan committee to further the emancipation of women in Morocco, the largest right-wing party backed the call for single citizenship out of fear that the MP in question would in effect "strengthen loyalty to Morocco" in Dutch immigrants of Moroccan descent. What is striking here is that in the Netherlands, possession of a passport has never been considered crucially indicative of national loyalty. Yet these days it is believed that for immigrants holding double nationalities, such loyalties *are* strong. For them, holding the passport of another nation is thought to severely hamper their "loyalty" toward the Netherlands, and as a consequence they are deemed to be less able to "integrate."

These are examples of the one-sided attribution of intolerant traits to immigrants. But the crucial thing is that such traits are attributed to the culture of these immigrants. When the Rotterdam municipal government said in its 2003 policy statement that "the problem is not color, but the problem does have a colour," it was referring to the cultural color, which it deems the most fundamental color (College B&W Rotterdam 2003: 12). As both racism and culturism are forms of a more fundamental phenomenon of social self-constitution through the exclusion of a constructed alterity, culturism may have a similar effect as racism does, but it operates on the basis of a different logic – one that stresses a difference between itself and racist discourse. To note this is not necessarily to fall in the trap of not recognizing a racism in disguise – a "non-racist racism," as Fiske (1998) has said, commenting on the United States. Especially where culturism does, in the end, revolve around racism at its core.

Culturist Attributions

Culture, especially in its culturist articulation, is one discursive plane upon which membership of society is discussed, contested, and most of all attributed and withheld. Whatever has to do with "culture" is to some extent "outside society." Integration policies and their increasing focus on culture have significantly contributed to the rise of the cultural program. But the very idea of integration as determined by cultural characteristics already reproduces a *difference* between "society" and, for instance, "Muslims." Thus, when Christian Joppke, one of the foremost scholars of migration and integration, comments on the attitudes of young British Muslims on homosexuality and other gender issues and speaks of the growing "rift between Muslims and the majority" (2009b: 454), he reproduces an archaic vision of "society" as something one does not belong to when one's opinions differ from the majority opinion. "Society" is in fact reduced to a community of opinion. Joppke does not draw the conclusion that, since especially young British Muslims differ in their views, this may well be indicative of a conflict *internal* to British society between a powerful majority and a symbolically denigrated minority, which would still be highly problematic in its assumptions, but less so than the idea of a "rift." More importantly, he doesn't even question the assumption that "society" exists as a given entity over against a population that is, because it is still in need of "integration," "outside society." In similar ways, Pierre-André Taguieff has pointed out that notions of tolerance, respect for others, and the right to be different can function as mechanisms of exclusion when they are tied to notions of "French society" as characterized by a common biological heritage and a culturally homogeneous basis, such as Catholicism (Taguieff 2010: 55).

That "integration," in the assimilationist meaning it has, is related to certain "cultural convictions" is a broadly shared Western European idea. It is prevalent throughout the contexts of social science, the media, policy, and politics. It has the effect of securing a *constitutive outside*, that is, of demarcating "society" by constructing a paradoxical "outside society," which never refers to another nation-state, but rather to a raced form of *cultural purgatory*. This vaguely demarcated space "outside" can be expanded or contracted, but it always highlights the limits of the morally pure canvas of "society." It is thus a blatant lack of reflexivity to assume, using a vocabulary ridden with ancient organicist connotations, that integration actually refers to persons not yet a "part of society," even though they are citizens. It is likewise a proto-sociological truism to state that a "rift" exists between "Muslims" and "society," thereby assuming "society" as a fixed and unified whole, and reducing "Muslims" to a religious identity that apparently excludes all their other identities and actions from the domain of "society."

Rhetorics of "Social Exclusion" and the Modes of Con-clusion

The gap between "society" and its cultural purgatory is variously portrayed as a "distance," a "backwardness," or a "lag." C. Wright

Mills has commented similarly on the "cultural lag" model of the "social pathologists" of his days that it "is tacitly oriented in a 'utopian' and progressive manner toward changing some areas of the culture or certain institutions so as to 'integrate' them with the state of progressive technology" (Mills 1969: 544–545). Today, that is hardly the case. The rhetoric of "bridging the gap," of "overcoming the distance" is no longer informed by grand visions of progress in which eventually all the world will come to share an advanced cultural climate. Rather, culturism is legitimized through the generous gesture of the inclusion of the other by means of cultural transformation. But precisely the necessity of assimilation, of cultivating what is construed as in first instance "essentially alien" to the "dominant culture" has the paradoxical effect of an inclusion by means of continuous exclusion. Culturism should therefore not be construed as an inclusive discourse. For it is precisely the continued emphasis on difference, on cultural incompatibility, that, on the basis of a rhetoric of inclusion, sets minorities apart. These remain observable as "ethnic" – a marker not used for those of an ethnically "neutral" dominant culture. Culturism thus performs the de-individualizing individualization discussed in the previous chapter. A specific form of acting and of being individualizes a body as "member" of a "culture," as having the accompanying "ethnicity" and as thereby being part of a "community." But at the same time culturism de-individualizes action and the body performing it by taking that body to be part of a cultural collective, a "community," which often functions as an alibi for the localization of "cultures" (Baumann 1996). Culturism hence functions as a form of management of identity. The "culture" of the other is an object for the dominant culture, a mirror image by means of which the "dominant culture" constructs and defines itself. What is cultivated in the culturist imagination is precisely the *difference* between the "culture" of the other and the "dominant culture."

There is an important strand in social theory and research that reiterates this articulation of difference. I am not solely referring here to the social science of immigrant integration. There is a much more reflexive form of social critique that nonetheless ends up reifying cultural differences. This is exemplified by the focus on "social exclusion," such as found, for instance, in Marshall but recently advocated by Margaret Somers (2008: 136–137). Somers's argument is that in order to move beyond individualizing explanations of, in her case, poverty in the United States, it is important to stress the relational nature of poverty. Therefore, she argues, it would be good to increasingly focus on *exclusion*, which retains the relational moment as central to analysis. Similar arguments can be found in Bourdieu and in work inspired by him. While the intention of this line of thought is admirable, as it is more generally in the sociology of integration, it rests on various problematic assumptions. First of all, it needs to assume, at base, a unified whole, which one can be either included in or excluded from. Second, and more importantly, it thereby reifies that whole. It assumes that that which is socially deemed "inside" is in fact the substance of belonging to society. Whereas the task of the social scientist is to be attentive to what is socially conceived as "inclusion" and "exclusion," work focusing on social exclusion incorporates commonsensical notions of exclusion. It is clear that people suffer from poverty, first of all, because of the deprivation it entails and, second, because of the relative deprivation that comes with it. But why should the social mean, or the dominant norm existing in society be equalled to society? Why does being poor mean, to a sociologist, being "excluded"? Does that not mean that a particular and socially specific idea of membership is ratified, and that received ideas of "society" and the "exclusion" from it are unreflexively incorporated in sociological analysis? Do not the poor form a crucial part of that which is called "society"? Would "society" become any better understandable by assuming that the poor, the deviant, the delinquent, the nonintegrated are not a part of it? In other words, does the focus on "social exclusion" not contribute to a certain counterfactual idealization of society as a morally pure domain? In certain ways, one could argue, it might make sense to speak of exclusion when that is not taken to mean "exclusion from society." One may, for instance, be excluded from the labor market. But in essence, the same principle applies here, for not having or finding a job is one particular mode of participation that shapes the labor market as a whole and without which – for instance, without a "reserve work force" – the labor market would not be what it was and could not be properly understood. To focus on "exclusion," then, is to ratify and legitimize the idea that "society" exists as a fixed entity. It is to accept the dominant idea of what society is and when one does not belong to it. It foregoes the fact that the constitutive outside that "society" continuously produces is an outside that is always already on the inside. It is the symbolic projection of an "outside society" and the accompanying idea of a "social exclusion" that should be critically scrutinized, not accepted as a premise of social research.

In order to depart from the concepts of inclusion and exclusion as theoretical tools, and to analyze the production of their everyday use in integration discourse, I propose to regard them as *modes of conclusion*. Con-clusion alerts us to the fact that both inclusion and exclusion are forms of being-with (*con*), or, in other words, they are relational forms. Inclusion is the positively coded mode of conclusion, while exclusion is the negatively coded mode. Exclusion, precisely because it is one mode of conclusion, is thus never to be taken literally, nor as the relational expulsion from a community of members. It is rather a socially produced form of "membership" in a more fundamental sense. It is a negatively coded form of belonging, of being related to. But this negatively coded form is nonetheless fundamentally a part of the same system that produces inclusion, for the very meaning of inclusion and exclusion derives from their being intricately connected in one and the same signifying system as modes of conclusion.

It is therefore problematic to speak of nonintegrated as "excluded from society." Such may be a dominant image in integration discourse, but the social science observing that discourse will necessarily have to deploy different theoretical concepts. A critical distance is, for instance, to be retained when detained criminals are said to eventually "return to society" by being "reintegrated" into it. For is not the prison a crucial institution *of* "society"? What theoretical insights are gained from ratifying and legitimating the commonly held belief that criminals are not a part of society and that society in fact has no problems of crime, that it houses exactly zero criminals? Criminals are not only detained in prison, but they are at the same time symbolically excorcized to a realm "outside society" – while no one denies the existence and functions of prisons in and for "society." Whatever one's opinions on such practices, it does not help social analysis at all to incorporate the conceptual logic deployed by the common sense thereof. The same goes for notions of "marginalization." When what is "marginal" is regarded as a constitutive outside, as an inside-outside, are not the "margins" in a sense at the very heart of the social body of society? Society's self-description entails ideas of "exclusion," but the description of such self-description, which is what social science does, should refrain from accepting such a *rhetoric of exclusion*. It should work with its own concepts instead.

Imagining Belonging: Allochthony and Autochthony

An important feature of Dutch integration policies is its terminological differentiation between "allochthons" and "autochthons." As Peter Geschiere (2009) has illustrated, such "chtonic" distinctions exist also in Belgium, as well as in certain French-speaking African countries. Just preceding the culturist phase in Dutch policies of integration the 1989 report *Allochthons Policy* was published by the Dutch Scientific Council for Government Policy (WRR; the official state think tank in the Netherlands). The WRR advised against the use of the notion "ethnic minority," which had been central in the second phase of integration policy (known then as "minorities policy"). They suggested replacing what they held to be a stigmatizing concept by "allochthons." This concept was contrasted with "autochthons," denoting native Dutch. This "chthonic" semantics literally has to do with the *ground* to which one belongs. "Autochthony" literally means "from this ground," while "allochthony" denotes a form of being that does not belong on "this ground." The criterion to speak of "allochthon" is to have at least one parent born outside the Netherlands from non-Dutch parents. Interestingly, then, this means that the core of the Dutch royal family consists of "allochthons."

The effect of this highly successful terminological intervention was the creation of a totalizing opposition. Whereas "minorities" was formerly not opposed to "majority," now an opposition existed between "allochthons" (lumping all "ethnicities" together) and "autochthons" (literally meaning "of this soil," which is curious given Dutch *jus sanguinis*). This opposition soon made its way into policy, and ever since, the notion of "allochthonous Dutch" appears in policy documents on integration and citizenship. This differentiation provides a ready-made nomenclature for the distinction between those belonging to "society" and those remaining "outside society." More specifically, a differentiation is made between "Western" and "non-Western allochthons." This distinction "saves" the royal family, which consists of English, German, and, most recently, Argentinian members. And perhaps surprisingly, the category "non-Western allochthons" consists not only of EU and U.S. nationals, but also of Japanese and Indonesians. Interestingly, then, (descendants of) immigrants from Indonesia, the largest Muslim country in the world, are dubbed "Western." In their case, this is related to the

Dutch colonial past. The categorization of "Indonesians" as "Western" is in a sense a postcolonial marker, indicating a "bond" that still assures the "Westernness" of Indonesia, which it has the Netherlands to thank for, unlike Malaysia, Cambodia, or the Philippines. However, this does not explain why "Surinamese" and "Antilleans," who are also (post)colonial subjects, are classified as "non-Western allochthons." Something more is relevant here. With the exception of Indonesians, the category "non-Western" in effect means "non-poor." This explains why "Japanese" are coded as "Western." In a sense the distinction is between those expected to have or to cause problems, ranging from poverty to crime, and those expected not to do so. In the end, "Turkish," "Surinamese," "Antilleans," and "Moroccans" make up the largest groups of "non-Western allochthons," and with the occasional exception of "Somalians" (in the context of genital mutilation) and a few others, they are the main objects of integration policy. "Antilleans" and "Moroccans" are especially a focus, and they are the only two groups for whom "ethnically specific" policies have existed.

What is dubbed as "non-Western" is thus a specifically cultural selection. Certain "ethnicities" are constructed as "non-Western" and as intrinsically problematic. And while "ethnic minorities" and their quasi-official spokespersons (which formerly only had the effect of legitimating policies) are no longer the addressee of policies, "ethnicity" is all over the place, and not in the sense of a constructed and "owned" identity but in a reified and ascribed sense. The Dutch *Integration Memorandum 2007–2011: Make Sure You're a Part of It!* (2007) signals the fact that "people withdraw in their own ethnic circle or their religious faith, and live so to speak with their backs to society" (VROM 2007: 12). Likewise, when "crime" is thematized in the memorandum it is in association with fundamentalism, radicalism, non-Western allochthons or minorities, or sometimes by mentioning "Antilleans" and "Moroccans." Given their "overrepresentation" in crime figures, ethnically specific policies are initiated (VROM 2007: 24). The problems are deemed most severe among "Moroccans" (which are mentioned 122 times in the 106-page memorandum). Likewise, the *Integration Memorandum 2007–2011* (2007) makes clear that the crucial difference lies between "autochthons" and "non-Western allochthons" and their relative degrees of "active participation":

Just as is expected from autochthons, allochthons are expected to do their best to conquer [sic] a place in society by learning the language, having and finishing education, gain income and take responsibility in raising their children. It is also about curiosity with respect to the ways of Dutch society and the life-world of (autochthonous) co-citizens, especially where the Dutch culture and history are concerned. By participating in society it becomes possible to increasingly identify with these. (VROM 2007: 12)

It is thus the "allochthon" population in the Netherlands that is the primary addressee of integration policy discourse. Hence the formulation above: "just as is expected from autochthons ..." At the same time, a paragraph is devoted to "radicalization," by which only a turn toward Islamic fundamentalism is denoted. This has to do with the fact that the subtext of such policy statements is a culturist discourse of integration as cultural assimilation. Self-categorizations such as "autochthonous" appear only vis-à-vis "allochthons." Otherwise, "autochthonous Dutch are simply "Dutch," a category that excludes "allochthonous Dutch" – yet this is an including exclusion for the category is meaningless without its projected outside. The necessary differential counterpart of "allochthonous" is thereby reserved for a special realm that never attains universal reach. This allows for an escape from a category bound to the other in all instances where the other is not subject of discourse. "Autochthonous" thereby becomes another concept that in fact designates or circumscribes the "allochthon," and vice versa. The stress laid on "allochthons" adjusting to "Dutch society" and its "history and culture" is even more strong in the 2011 Cabinet Paper *Integration, Bonding, Citizenship*, which repeats critiques of multiculturalism and associations with crime and terrorism and then places full responsibility with "newcomers." The emphasis on the idea that the "responsibility for integration" lies with the "newcomer" and not with government was restated in the 2013 memorandum *Integration Agenda*, which also placed strong emphasis on crime, mentioning specifically "boys and young men of Moroccan- and Antillean-Dutch background" (Dutch Cabinet 2013: 3).

What I have called the genealogization of integration is sustained by the imagination of allochthony. Allochthony is a typical product of a social imagination in that it is a fiction with material consequences. For while "allochthon" literally means "not from this ground," many children of immigrants who are born in the

Netherlands are yet identified as "allochthons." So the semantics of allochthony, though paradoxical, functions as a way of rendering future generations visible as possibly distinct – and thereby as distinct – from "society." With current policies focusing on "third generation immigrants," it is highly improbable that an "allochthon" could ever get rid of this label or, for that matter, that his or her children could live without this attribution.

Likewise, the one-sided thematization of the marker "ethnic" that has the effect of a dispensation of ethnicity and race (compare Wekker 2016) for native Dutch is facilitated by the attribution of "allochthony" to all that is "ethnic." All that is "ethnic" is possibly intrinsically problematic and is lumped together by the marker "allochthones." Something similar is at stake in the problematization of "black schools." "White schools" are schools with an autochthonous population, whereas "black schools" are schools with a relatively large population of "non-Western allochthons." "Black" is here not a racial or ethnic marker per se, but a general denomination for the "non-Western allochthon," that is, for what is relatively segregated and deemed intrinsically problematic. Allochthony/autochthony thus facilitates the identification of the demographic terrain covered by "integration." When, in 2016, it was proposed by the WRR, to possibly replace the terms, the Council immediately proposed alternatives likely to have the same effect.

Culturist Coding and the Negation of the Economy

Culturism is one program that lends credibility to the integrity of "society" as a social body. In keeping with the French meaning of the word "culturism," it is a form of *body building*. Because of this focus on a cultured form of morality, it contributes to a counterfactual description of society. Such descriptions have as an obvious advantage that they cannot be contradicted by the facts. Through the furthering of cultural programming in a policy discourse, the nation-state functions as a powerful apparatus of cultural coagulation. By equalizing "society" and "nation-state" the state's borders become mobile images of alterity. Cultural significations of otherness evoke the border in the sense of identifying those who crossed it physically but remained fundamentally, socially, on the other side. Ideas of cultural incompatibility and the determination through culture are embedded in the everyday categorizations of "allochthons," a label already reifying and objectifying. The only escape from such determination lies in "leaving one's culture." Such a voluntaristic initiation rite or primordial act of cultural assimilation is highly paradoxical. On the one hand, culture is deemed determinative of action. On the other hand, the dominant liberal culturist argument is that "one can always leave one's culture." Not leaving one's culture means, then, to be willingly determined by it, and hence all the problems related to culturally determined behavior in fact become attributable to acts of will, or rather of not wanting, of a choice not to undertake the effort to leave one's culture. This is simply one manifestation of the paradoxes of discourse in the program of culture. It is one way in which the combination of individualization and de-individualization offers diagrammatical attributions to society's "outside" whatever the substance of the matter at hand.

One important effect of the rise of the program of culture is the *depoliticization* that it entails. I draw here on an argument put forward by Wendy Brown. As she says: "depoliticization involves construing inequality, subordination, marginalization, and social conflict, which all require political analysis and political solutions, as personal and individual on the one hand, or as natural, religious, or cultural on the other." She thus describes in different terms what I have called the paradox of individualizing de-individualization. Tolerance operates as a technique of depoliticized governing, for as Brown continues:

tolerance as it is commonly used today tends to cast instances of inequality or social injury as matters of individual or group prejudice. And it tends to cast group conflict as rooted in ontologically natural hostility toward essentialized religious, ethnic, or cultural difference. That is, tolerance discourse reduces conflict to an inherent friction among identities and makes religious, ethnic, and cultural difference itself an inherent site of conflict, one that calls for and is attenuated by the practice of tolerance. (Brown 2006a: 15)

Brown thus relates essentialism and naturalization to depoliticization. I would argue that what this depoliticization most of all entails is an overcoding of the economic by the cultural. Amid arguably the greatest economic crisis since World War II, issues of culture and immigrant integration, and denouncements of "multiculturalism" keep reappearing. Excessive attention to the cultural, as Nancy Fraser has argued, pushes social justice to the background (Fraser 1995). Similarly, French sociologist Michel Wieviorka has argued for a "return of the social" in the study of immigration (2005: 60–61). The reduction of integration to a cultural matter, which can be simultaneously attributed to both individual and "external" cultural collective, eschews all responsibility on the part of "society." While there are intricate connections between efforts to curtail "illegal immigration" as a way of ensuring the integration of regular migrants, and while the Dutch crackdown on "illegal migration" started after a report noting the size of the labor black market, this does not simply involve, as Balibar (2002: 24) has said, a projection of mass fear of poverty into a "phantasmagoric space of identitary conflicts." It also has to do with a new articulation of class conflict. Migrant self-organization has been increasingly problematized in the Netherlands. Self-organizations are no longer eligible for government subsidies unless they do things to weaken ethnic identity by organizing "bridging" contacts to other ethnic categories, preferably the "non-ethnic" category of "autochthonous Dutch." But in the face of the relatively unfortunate economic position of migrants and their increased cultural problematization, such attempts at derailing existing efforts at self-organization nip potential class conflict in the bud. The problematization of assumed cultural and ethnic collective identities under which individuals are subsumed, and the simultaneous individualization of social problems, functions as a fork from which there appears no immediate escape. Political mobilization on the basis of "ethnic identity" is the worst imaginable political offence. At the same time, the problematization of economically deprived migrants and their offspring by systems of politics and policy thoroughly ethnically dispensated remains relatively undisputed.

Such economic deprivation does not resemble the existence of an "ethnic underclass," which is a concept that obscures more than it packs together in a simplifying picture. But it does obscure a crucial transformation. The emphasis on culture is indicative of an economic transition that has a strong cultural logic. This is a transition toward what can be called a *neo-liberal communitarianism* (Van Houdt and Schinkel 2010). This simultaneous focus on the individual and the collective removes emphasis on equality as class-related and furthers commitment to national culture that in various Western European countries (Sweden, Norway, the Netherlands) was "traditionally" absent. Because such countries defined their national identity by not caring much about a national identity, they serve as perhaps the most important illustrations of a transition toward "culture" that has everything to do with the local effects of a growing global economic uncertainty.

Neoliberal communitarianism, which I shall more fully discuss in Chapter 6, combines a focus on "individual responsibility" with a focus on cultural assimilation. Thus, all complaints by "allochthons" concerning, for instance, the obvious facts of the reproduction of educational and economic inequalities, are disavowed. "Allochthons" are repeatedly told, also by various successful migrants who made it to political office (such as Aboutaleb in Rotterdam and Marcouch in Amsterdam), that one should avoid falling into the "role of the victim" (*slachtofferrol*). The fact that the discursive exorcism from "society" certainly entails a form of victimization is thereby obscured. And the proto-sociological concept of a "role" of the victim assumes that victimhood is a mere act that cannot be based on serious forms of injustice.

Underneath the program of culture lies the face of the last credible collective project of Western European societies. While no longer en route to grand visions of progress, the only movement these societies aim for is economic growth. The ideal of the social body is therefore that of obesity. This last collective project, which could be called Operation Obesity, is highly ambivalent with regard to immigration. It values "diversity" as a sublimated and marketable form of difference, out of which the juridical substance, for instance, in its multicultural conception, is drained. EU countries compete for "diversity" on the market of postindustrially schooled migrants. But those migrants for whom the postindustrial society might be a stretch too far are regarded as inhibitors of national growth. They are at the same time society's "outside" and its "bottom," its "lower strata," where they are a weight to the collective body. The overcoding of their economic deprivation into plane of cultural determination and signification at once writes them out of the national march toward economic obesity and obscures the reproduction of inequality that continue to exist, despite the great advances of "second generation immigrants." The program of culture thus functions as a drawing board upon which are drawn the counterfactual contours of society. But this "society" is that which is desired by forces, not in the least those mobilized by nation-states, protecting a "status quo" that uses concepts like "integration" and images of "immigrants" as still existing "outside society" in an effort to ward off the realization that it is, and has been for some time now, no longer the status quo.

5 | Traditionally Modern: Contemporary Frameworks of Sexuality and Religion

Debating Multiculturalism: The Advent of Multiculturealism in Western Europe

In a speech at the Munich Security Conference on February 5, 2011, U.K. Prime Minister Cameron distanced himself in harsh tones from the U.K. model of "multiculturalism." This speech, ostensibly about security, Britain's role in NATO, and terrorism, focused on what Cameron described as "the root of the problem." He described this "root" as "Islamist extremism." And while distancing himself from generalizations every step of the way, Cameron zoomed in on his prime target. So with the caveats that "Islamist extremism" is not "Islam" (which is "a religion observed peacefully ... by over a billion people"), that extremism isn't religion at all but a political ideology and that a variety of factors – ranging from poverty to Western support for autocratic regimes – contribute to terrorism, Cameron explicated what he felt was "a general lesson for us all ... drawn from the British experience."[1] Islamist extremism, he concluded was fueled most of all by the failure of providing extremists with "a vision of society to which they feel they want to belong." Stronger societies and stronger identities (and presumably a stronger identity of society) are what Cameron deemed necessary. Blaming what he called "the doctrine of state multiculturalism," British policies had promoted segregation. Forgetting his earlier caveats, this had led to a self-inured "weakening of our collective identity" and to the encouragement of "Muslims to define themselves solely in terms of their religion." This generalization was a necessary link in Cameron's exposé on the "causes of terrorism," because experience has taught that many extremists had been influenced by

---

[1] "PM's speech at Munich Security Conference," February 5, 2011. Accessed at http://webarchive.nationalarchives.gov.uk/20130109092234/http://number10.gov.uk/news/pms-speech-at-munich-security-conference/ (accessed September 7, 2015).

nonextremist religious people. Cameron thus noted a process toward the formation of religious communities, as a kind of "substitute for what the wider society has failed to supply." In this speech, Cameron not only managed to link issues of "multiculturalism" and the incorporation of immigrants to problems of geopolitical security and terrorism, but he also managed to slip "Islam" into the definition of the problem by way of the causal route leading to extremism (leading to terrorism). This enabled Cameron to force a break with "state multiculturalism," involving, for instance, a change in the financing of religious organizations on the basis of the answer to the question "Do they encourage integration or separation?" He thus placed "integration" over against "multiculturalism," characterizing the latter as a "doctrine" fostering separation and segregation and a "passive toleration." This speech, framed in terms of "security" and terrorism, could well be taken from Foucault's 1977–1978 lecture series at the Collège de France, *Sécurité, territoire, population* (2004a). What is unfolded under the frame of "security" is a rearticulation of the very meaning of a "liberal society" that gives an impetus to new controls aimed at both the population as a whole ("society") and at specific subpopulations ("religious communities"). What Cameron put forward as his image of what he called a more "muscular liberalism" is the following:

A passively tolerant society says to its citizens, as long as you obey the law we will just leave you alone. It stands neutral between different values. But I believe a genuinely liberal country does much more; it believes in certain values and actively promotes them. Freedom of speech, freedom of worship, democracy, the rule of law, equal rights regardless of race, sex or sexuality. It says to its citizens, this is what defines us as a society: to belong here is to believe in these things. Now, each of us in our own countries, I believe, must be unambiguous and hard-nosed about this defence of our liberty. (Cameron 2011)

It is thus key to the liberalism put forward by Cameron that demands be made upon citizens beyond the realm of the law. Beyond what can be seen as *formal citizenship* lies the realm of *moral citizenship* in which the underwriting of certain values is crucial. In a sense, Cameron argued that it is the duty of a citizen to belong and to identify with the larger society.

It is no coincidence that the context of this speech is immigrant integration. Today, issues of immigrant integration offer the most poignant sites of articulation of national societies. Cameron's speech came at a time at which several other Western European heads of state took a similar stance in denouncing "multiculturalism." Angela Merkel, in a speech at the "Germany Day" of the Junge Union, the youth organization of her Christian democratic CDU Party on October 16, 2010, said that "multiculti [*sic*] has utterly failed." While she emphasized that "Islam is a part of Germany," the country needs a better way of dealing with immigration than the multiculturalism that existed. Merkel responded to Bavarian CSU chairman Horst Seehofer's earlier comment that "multiculturalism is dead." She understood by what she called *Multikulti* the idea, and current practice, of "living past one another." And like Cameron, Merkel emphasized the fact that "too little demands" were placed on migrants. Here too, the argument was made that "tolerance" had in fact meant a passive lack of interest. Merkel also noted the importance for immigrants of learning the German language and of their adoption of core German values. She did not go as far as Seehofer in claiming immigrants should conform to German *Leitkultur*, but in the week following her speech her Cabinet did announce stricter immigration controls, a stronger focus on German language courses, and more attention to preventing forced marriages. Similarly, Merkel mentioned swimming instruction for Muslim girls as an example of the need for a tougher stance.

Finally, Nicholas Sarkozy denounced "multiculturalism" in a TF1 interview on February 10, 2011. Sarkozy, speaking of an *échec*, said there was no doubt that "multiculturalism was a failure." As he noted: "in all democracies, we have concerned ourselves too much with the identity of those who came to us, and not with the identity of the country that took them in." Like Cameron and Merkel, he emphasized the fact that "multiculturalism" has created segregated lives: "We don't want a society in which one community lives next to another." Sarkozy stated that immigrants coming to France have to want to be part of the one, national society, or otherwise they had better not come. The interview in which Sarkozy made his comments consisted of a conversation with a panel of French citizens, in which "multiculturalism" was only one issue. When it was raised, however, it was in the context of "immigration and Islam," indicating the connection between "Islam" and that which comes from abroad. Like Cameron and Merkel, Sarkozy also emphasized what he thought was the place of Islam in France: there is "a French Islam and not just an Islam in France."

What to think of these three influential denouncements of "multi-culturalism"? Should it not be clear from the start that these three countries never did share a common approach – whether called "multi-culturalism" or something else – to what is called the "integration of immigrants"? France, in particular, had insisted on a republican trad-ition in which there would be no room for official public distinctions between "cultures," even though some have argued that the 2003 Stasi Commission on *laïcité* gave rise to certain "multicultural" measures (such as Muslim high schools) (Akan 2009). The United Kingdom comes closest to some form of "multicultural" policy, although this was never officially codified as such. Its "multiculturalism" has remained troubled by its connotations of "race," which go back to its 1976 Race Relations Act. Counter-developments were continually in place, such as the 1988 Education Reform Bill, stipulating the Christian character of school assemblies, and its contestation by reli-gious groups. What may have taken place in the United Kingdom was what the Runnymede Trust Commission (2000: 14) called a "multi-cultural drift," meaning that on a local level accommodations were made that amounted to some form of multiculturalism in practice. But even then the question is, as Anne Phillips (2007: 4) has said, what this actually meant in practice: How many Sikhs actually preferred a turban over a crash helmet when driving a motorbike? The same goes for Germany, which never had a multicultural policy. And although some have commented on a "politics of practical multiculturalism" (Löffler 2011), issues such as double nationality and equal opportunity measures never gained political majorities in Germany (Aumüller 2009). In both the United Kingdom and Germany, the local character of what is now presented as a uniform "multiculturalism" attests to the organization and incorporation of immigrants rather than to what in Germany is called *Parallelgesellschaften* ("parallel societies"). More-over, neither of these countries, nor any other Western European country, has had the kind of multiculturalism that was inscribed, for instance, in the Canadian Multiculturalism Act (1988). And when "multiculturalism" really is to cover the different policies of immigrant integration in the countries where it is currently under attack, the concept becomes hollow. It in no way resembles conceptions of multi-culturalism found, for instance, in the work of Charles Taylor, Tariq Modood, or Will Kymlicka. This is only aggravated when we consider that the three countries mentioned are really only the tip of the iceberg in current multiculturalism bashing. Similar discussions exist in Australia, Belgium, Denmark, Sweden, Norway, and the Netherlands.

So in a sense, the speeches by Cameron and Merkel and the comments by Sarkozy came late. Not only did other heads of state (such as Dutch Prime Minister Jan Peter Balkenende) precede them, but they also appear to be late contributions to their respective national debates. Already in 2004, Christian Joppke (2004) noted a shift in Western European policies from a supposed "multiculturalism" to "civic integration." Liberal critiques of "multiculturalism" were well under way in political philosophy in the 1990s, most prominently in Brian Barry's *Culture & Equality*. Similarly, in France, Mitterand's supposed "cultural relativism" was coded as "multiculturalism" by Alain Finkielkraut (1987) in the late 1980s – the only difference being that today, "multiculturalism" is seen as a leftist naiveté, whereas Finkielkraut associated its "obsession with culture" with the far right. And in Germany, discussions of "parallel societies" already existed in the second half of the 1990s (Heitmeyer 1996). But the hollowness of the concept rather attests to its discursive flexibility and productivity. Its openness to different kinds of (nationally specific) substance is exactly what gives "multiculturalism" the discursive value and the productivity it currently has. It is not so much a straw man that can be denounced, although currently this is the direction into which most political interventions appear to go. More broadly, it functions as an important parameter in immigrant integration imaginaries. It opens a space for debate, which in the 1990s could still lead to a positive embrace of positions associated with "multiculturalism," but which since the years 2000 increasingly started to function as a dystopian image, an "out-dated" and illegitimate *topos* that structures debate by serving both as a negative point of orientation and as a historical reference point. Its history is, of course, very much of the kind of an "invented tradition" (and this illustrates the political productivity of negative traditions), and its negativity also functions as a kind of censorship in discourses of immigrant integration. It does so not only in the context of politics and policy, but also in the popular imagination of many. All over Western European websites and opinion blogs, "multiculturalism" is the target of attacks. In its most extreme versions, it is, for instance, visible in A. Breivik, the Norwegian attacker who killed more than ninety people in 2011. His "manifesto" was a jeremiad against "cultural Marxism" and "multiculturalism," which he regarded as synonyms. In this 1,518-page "manifesto," published under the name "Andrew Berwick," some version of "multicultural-ism" occurs 1,164 times.[2] The dismissal of "multiculturalism" ranges from such extreme visions to the ordinary everyday realism that "multiculturalism has failed." And it runs from Christopher Caldwell's culturally conservative negation of the question "Can you have the same Europe with different people?" (Caldwell 2009: 20; note the reference to Burke's commentary on the French Revolution) to Chris-tian Joppke's sociological agreement (2009a) with Samuel Huntington's idea that Islam and extremism are one and the same, and that both are facilitated by multiculturalist policies.

The specter that most of all haunts current Western Europe, then, is what can be called *multiculturealism*. By this I understand the discur-sive figure of a supposed former "multiculturalism," which is attrib-uted to left-wing naiveté and political correctness. Whether the left was actually in power and put multiculturalist policies in place is irrelevant for the functioning of multiculturealism in current debates on immi-grant integration in Western Europe. In some countries, a more multi-culturalist model may have existed, although the very idea of "national models" of integration obscures the changes and ambiguities of such models (Bowen 2007a), as well as fact that "models" facilitate conflict and contestations over key concepts rather than presenting a consistent philosophical underpinning of policy concepts (Bertossi 2011; Van Reekum, Duyvendak, and Bertossi 2012). What is relevant is not the actual existence of some form of multiculturalism or an otherwise converging form of policy (Joppke 2007), but the converging way its denouncement ascribes a uniform and dominant reality to it, precisely in the face of differing national trajectories of accommodating non-Christian religions (Soper and Fetzer 2007). Likewise, the question whether or not multiculturealism is actually a new form of political correctness is not of primary interest here (the answer is probably: yes, it is). Crucial is its use of the trope of "realism," of seeing through politically correct and naive notions of multiculturalist living-happily-together-apart.

It is important to note here that there is also a scientific multicul-turealism. In moderate form, this consists of the bland statement that

[2] This was published as A. Berwick (2011): "2083: A European Declaration of Independence."

several societies were characterized by some form of multiculturalism. Such statements are particularly profuse with respect to the Netherlands, although most authors copy the presupposition from each other (Castles and Miler 2003: 16; Entzinger 2003; Modood 2007: 12–13; Eyerman 2008: 106; Shorto 2010). In a harsher and less detached form, this involves scholars actively promoting multiculturealism by taking stance against "multiculturalism" (Koopmans 2004; Koopmans et al. 2005; Sniderman ad Hagendoorn 2007; Joppke 2009a). Rather than ratify such assumptions, I take the supposed "multicultural past" of the Netherlands and of France, Germany, the United Kingdom, and other countries to be a political claim in immigrant integration discourse. Regardless of its "objective truth," which is subject to conceptual gerrymandering and political interpretation anyway, I take this idea to function as a discursive wedge in a variety of national contexts. In these contexts, reference to "multiculturalism" never holds when taken as an "objective" statement, but it always works productively as a point of orientation and even as a form of censorship. "Dutch multiculturalism," like most other Western European forms of multiculturalism, I therefore argue, is something of a paradox: it is a *performative effect of its denouncements*. In the Netherlands, it has been denouncements such as Scheffer's notion of a "multicultural drama" or Schnabel's idea of a "multicultural illusion" that facilitated the entry of "multiculturalism" in immigrant integration discourse. They were backed by renowned international observers such as Francis Fukuyama, who, in the context of debate on Muslim extremism claimed:

Countries like Holland and Britain need to reverse the counterproductive multiculturalist policies that sheltered radicalism. . . . In recent months, both the Dutch and British have in fact come to an overdue recognition that the old version of multiculturalism they formerly practiced was dangerous and counterproductive. (Fukuyama 2005)

So quite apart from discussions of "national models" of immigrant integration, which are highly reifying in themselves (Bertossi 2011; Duyvendak and Scholten 2011; Van Reekum, Duyvendak, and Bertossi 2012), the point is that each national context articulates multiculturealism in a different way, and yet in each national context it functions in a similarly productive way (and I use "productive" here in a nonevaluative sense of producing reality effects). That is to say that the way in which immigrant integration is seen as a problem, and the issues with which it is connected, while shared by many Western European countries, is also nationally specific in certain respects. In Sweden, for example, the problematization of "culture" was not a major issue until the 1990s. After World War II, class issues dominated public discourse. This changed when immigrant integration became a topic in the 1990s, when, as Ann Towns has said, "conceptions of the 'multi-cultural Sweden' had a major breakthrough" (2002: 167). Here, too, that breakthrough had more to do with the contestation of culture than with actually existing multicultural policies. In Norway as well, a problematization of "culture" has been on the rise since the 1990s. As, for instance, in the Netherlands, France, Belgium and Germany, it was geared mostly at the position of women. In Norway, this took the particular form of defining "Norwegian values" explicitly in terms of gender equality (Hagelund 2002). In contrast, in France the value of gender equality is but one part of a "republican" complex of values often proposed, and contested, as the royal way for the integration of immigrants. In France, "secularism" in the form of *laïcité* is a more persistent topic of debate than in Norway, in which a Lutheran State Church exists to which 75 percent of Norwegians subscribe. The national specificity of an international problematization of culture in the context of immigrant integration is one reason why Sarkozy, in the reported interview, was asked to respond to Muslims praying in the streets. Republicanism has everything to do with public visibility – and hence Sarkozy responded that "we do not want people praying in an ostentatious manner in the street." Again, whether or not multiculturalism actually existed, its denouncement functions as a medium of articulation of a particular idea(l) of the national society – in Sarkozy's case, it, for instance, served as one way to articulate the "republicanism" that France is supposedly characterized by. It denotes the problems of other cultures and the defects of domestic political opponents' ways of dealing with these problems. When "multiculturalism" is denounced, this is a nationally specific way of addressing issues of immigrant integration. Multiculturealism is therefore part and parcel of contemporary nationalism in Western countries. Like nationalism, it is an international phenomenon. Two issues in particular have stood out in terms of the attention they received in public debates about "the failure of multiculturalism": (1) sexuality and gender and (2) religion. And as such, the problematization of multiculturalism has everything to do with the articulation of modern imaginaries in which the modern is posited over against the traditional – an opposition that runs neatly parallel to the juxtaposition of "society" and "immigrants in need of integration." In this way, modernity operates as a program for the articulation of a variety of national societies. Before zooming in on the problematization of issues of sexuality and gender and religion in the Netherlands, I consider some of the connections made between these issues in Western Europe, as well as the paradox through which the program of modernity operates: on the basis of various claims to universality, it enables the imagination of particular societies.

Sexular Modernity

Rogers Brubaker has remarked that "throughout northern and western Europe, populations that had previously been identified and labeled using national-origin, religion of origin, socioeconomic, demographic, legal or racial categories – for example, as Algerians, North Africans, guest workers, immigrants, foreigners or (especially in the United Kingdom) blacks – have been increasingly identified and labeled in religious terms as Muslims" (Brubaker 2012: 2). That transformation into religious categories, I argue in this chapter, has wide-ranging consequences for the ways "immigrants" are portrayed and problematized. In Western European discourses of immigrant integration, an intricate link exists between problematizations of gender and sexuality and problematizations of religion. One example of the transformation is the 1995 intervention in Norway by Unni Wikan. In her book *Towards a New Norwegian Underclass*, the "underclass" is defined in cultural and, more specifically, religious terms. Wikan, an anthropologist whose work had a profound influence on Norwegian public and policy discourse, argued that "Muslims" as yet failed to accept gender equality and were in urgent need of doing so if they were to fit in Norwegian society (Wikan 1995). Likewise, in 2001 Sweden's government officially announced "gender equality" as part of its efforts to "exhibit Swedish culture in Europe" (quoted in Towns 2002: 157). In effect, it did so by providing a frame for the problematization of "immigrants" and for the recalibration of "Swedish society" and "immigrants." Similar issues have been raised in Belgium, where in the 1990s family pressure on Muslim girls became a topic of debate, with the consequence of inciting debate over the banning of headscarves in schools (Bracke and Fadil 2009) – a debate that con-tinues today. In France, debate on this topic led to the founding, in 2002, of "ni putes ni soumises" (neither whores nor submissives), which linked urban violence, Muslim oppression, and the rights of women, and which gained wide political support. In nearly all European coun-tries, these issues are accompanied by some form of a "veil debate," in which sexuality and religion are folded in one discursive issue.

Sexuality, broadly speaking, and religion, including secularism, can both be regarded as programs in integration discourses. They form discursive planes on which issues are debated and connected. I take them together here for two reasons. One is the fact that they constitute aspects of a more encompassing program, which can be called "mod-ernity." Thematizations of both religion and sexuality are predomin-antly framed in terms of the characteristics of "modernity" or of a "modern, secular society" vis-à-vis "traditional" values and patterns. Often, but not always, "traditional" gender relations and sexual prac-tices are related to forms of religion deemed ill-compatible with "modernity." As Judith Butler has argued, the Netherlands is probably one of the countries in which such conceptions, especially when tied to attitudes toward homosexuality, have been prevalent in a most poign-ant sense. Dutch integration policy, as Butler says, is based on the "claim that acceptance of homosexuality is the same as acceptance of modernity" (2010: 105). Such connections of secular modernity with certain sexual norms and with norms of gender equality has been aptly named "sexularism" by Joan Wallace Scott (2009). The second reason to discuss religion and sexuality in tandem here is that they follow a similar albeit reverse logic. For both intimate life and religious life are construed as forms of loyalty that bypass loyalty to the nation-state and to society. One could say that intimate life constitutes a sphere of life that is seen as "going beneath" the national society, whereas religious life is portrayed as "transcending" the national society. In both cases, the issue is that a loyalty to the national society, character-ized by neutrality and universality, is circumvented. This problematiza-tion of a *double circumvention of the universal* is a central imaginative mechanism at work in the program of modernity. It is double in that it concerns both the body and the mind. The body is accused of having loyalties to foreign bodies and to premodern sexual practices and gender relations. The mind is portrayed as having loyalties to a sphere transcending the national society, such as an *umma*, which is deemed fundamentally incompatible with the modern national society. In both cases, body and mind are connected, for the loyalty to foreign bodies, for instance, in the realm of "marriage migration" connects the body to a commitment of the mind that undermines loyalty to the national society. And vice versa, the spiritual belonging to a community transcending the national society is tied to body practices, such as the wearing of the veil, that are often related to gender relations.

To describe the functioning of the program of modernity is to describe the ways in which a variety of issues are connected in a chain of equivalence that constitutes a metaphorical tightrope upon which conceptions of "society" rest. In this chapter, that description is done by zooming in on two programs (sexuality and religion) that are intricately connected and that together make up the program of modernity. In each case, I introduce the main characteristics of the discursive program, after which I take two cases on the basis of which I describe their functioning. The first case is what is called the "import bride." The second case concerns the veil. These cases are chosen because they illustrate the coming together of the programs of sexuality and of religion in the overarching program of modernity. They both revolve around the body, and they illustrate how the traditional body is pitted against the social body of the modern national society. The body is then a prime site of inscription of norms of alterity and belonging, and of their negotiation. In both cases the national society at stake is elevated to the level of the universal. It constitutes a "neutral" sphere organized on the basis of "modern," liberal, and secular universality that is in potential conflict with particularistic conceptions of traditional gender relations and sexual practices and with notions of spiritual community and authority that are global and not tied to the national level. Judith Butler summarizes the point well when she comments on the Dutch government's framing of homosexuality: "We can see in such an instance how modernity is being defined as linked to sexual freedom, and the sexual freedom of gay people in particular is understood to exemplify a culturally advanced position, as opposed to one that would be deemed pre-modern" (2010: 105).

Something similar is at stake with conceptions of "secular modernity," which, as Butler notes as well, are "secular in a particular sense" (2010: 106). Whereas Butler thus concludes that the concept of modernity is "too general" to be of theoretical use, a sociological reading of the *uses of modernity* and of the functioning of modernity as a program in discourses of immigrant integration can highlight that the productivity of the program of modernity lies precisely in its general, fuzzy, and often paradoxical sense.

Universalizing the National Society

In portraying various immigrant cultures vis-à-vis a dominant culture, culturist discourse performs a highly productive paradox. The paradox is, of course, that membership of "society" involves a cultural adjustment, and hence "society" is characterized by "culture" as well. This paradox is resolved, first of all, in the idea that a "dominant culture" has birthrights that do not accrue to "other cultures." In this way, the dominant culture is on the one hand regarded as "a" culture, while on the other hand it is regarded as "the" culture. Second, this paradox is resolved by means of allusions to "Westernness" that, to some extent, de-particularize such "dominant cultures" as cultures that are not nation-bound but have a more universal substance. In the Netherlands, this is especially effective by means of the presupposition of "Enlightenment," which is a nationally specific way of coding "modernity," although references to "Enlightenment" appear nowadays throughout Western Europe. What is coded as "cultural" and as caused by "cultural background factors" is problematic. At the same time, "the dominant culture" is anything but problematic. This is possible on the basis of the assumption that this dominant culture is not simply any odd culture, but that it is "Culture," that is, the Culture of Enlightenment. This is not simply a culture that determines action, but one that determines through freedom. The Culture of Enlightenment is hence the culture that allows individuals to guide themselves autonomously. In that respect, it is set apart from "culture" in the plural, which determines action so to speak from the outside and thereby restricts autonomy, either by religion or by tradition. Such paradoxes allow for a shifting between the level of national culture and a larger civilizational level. A "dominant culture" is, of course, on the one hand construed as a national culture, and hence it is particular rather than universal. And yet it is not vulnerable to critique of nationalist particularism since a shift from "culture" as ethnically circumscribed to "Culture" as civilizational can be made – including the normative weight carried by "civilization" in its ethical connotations. And in one further step, such normativity is neutralized and naturalized as not simply the next primordial particularism of regional proportions, but as "liberal" or "Enlightened," as the unconstrained historical appearance of reason itself, which seems to have stage fright in other global regions. All of this is done under oblivion of that which is deemed not to conform to the "dominant culture" (such as fundamentalist forms Christianity in Western Europe). But when "Culture" is a regional civilization, this presupposes that primordially, many are not at home on this regional ground. And this idea carries all the capital of common sense, since it is "immigrants" that are thus referred to.

In intellectualized forms of current culturist discourse, one way of universalizing the liberal national society is through the invocation of an Enlightenment imaginary. Characteristic of the Enlightenment is, in the words of historian Reinhart Koselleck, the "political anonymity of reason, morals, and nature." The *politicum* of the Enlightenment is that it is apolitical and neutral (Koselleck 1959: 122). The "dominant culture" that figures so prominently in culturist discourse is accordingly conceived as the neutral place from whence "culture" is observed as determining behavior. The only cultural background of such "Enlightenment fundamentalism" is that of a "dominant culture" that is "neutral" and universal since it is enlightened. Enlightenment fundamentalism is, however, stuck with the paradox of propagating *tolerance* as one of its highest values. Tolerance, which, of course, involves tolerance toward "other cultures," has become a depoliticized technique of governing, as it has in the United States according to Wendy Brown (2006a). In the culturism of the early years of this century in the Netherlands, Enlightenment came to be regarded as characterized by tolerance over against intolerant cultures, specifically a "religious culture" such as "Islam." Voltaire's infamous battle cry "écrasez l'infame!" is brought to bear on "Islamic culture" by Dutch public intellectuals (such as Paul Cliteur, Ayaan Hirsi Ali, and Herman Philipse). As such, Enlightenment culture is imagined as tolerant, but only with respect to equally tolerant cultures. "Islam" is imagined as an intolerant culture that is hence incompatible with Enlightenment culture. It is a culture perceived as threatening the tolerance that characterizes the dominant culture. Hence the paradox exists that today: *Enlightenment has become tradition.* One might wonder what that says about the current state of the Enlightenment, but then again much leads us to think that a renewed and highly strategic reference to "the Enlightenment," after the end of ideology and the postmodernism, is really something different from "the Enlightenment" that took place in the seventeenth and eighteenth centuries.

Then again, internal paradoxes of Enlightenment were of course always present. Horkheimer and Adorno (1969: 12), for instance, called the Enlightenment "totalitarian," and Luhmann (2006: 56) has noted that Enlightenment "irrationalizes everything that gets in its way," which was reason for Foucault (1997b) to speak of the "blackmail" of the Enlightenment (compare Badiou 2005a: 78). Currently, the discursive thematization of Enlightened "tolerance," which so easily slips into a downright contradiction, leads to its association with the culturist argument from incompatibility. This quasi-ethnic Enlightenment is contrasted with the darkness of the veil, and Muslim women are portrayed as repressed and as living, in the words of an alderwoman from Rotterdam, in the "catacombs of the city." In other words: Enlightenment culture is only tolerant with respect to Enlightenment culture. In Dutch debate, this could be construed as a departure from a tradition Jonathan Israel (2001) has defined as "radical Enlightenment." But Philip Gorski (2000) already noted that paradoxes, such as Western societies becoming both more secular and more religious, can be plausible, and, according to Taylor (2007: 3) the very opposition between "secularity" and "religiosity" is problematic itself and "a secular age" is not a "post-religious" age. A paradoxical form of "Enlightenment" may thus not be an implausible imaginary after all. Enlightenment rhetoric also gives the culturist imagination a utopian element. Culturism entails bringing the other's "plot of land into culture," and thus an assimilation or integration of the other is achieved that amounts to what has been called a "whitewashing of immigrants" (Gowricharn 1998). The implicit distinction between a modern, liberal "Culture" and traditional "cultures" involves what Wendy Brown calls a "denying and disavowing of liberalism's cultural facets and its imprint by particular cultures" (2006a: 24). What can be called the "neutralization of liberalism," which is performed by liberal discourse itself, is one of the most subtle rhetorical claims embedded in liberal thought. It is a way of at the same time claiming distance from hierarchical evaluations of "cultures" and of excepting liberalism itself from the realm of culture by elevating it hierarchically above that realm. The neutralization of liberalism functions as a political ploy, but it is based on a certain disavowal of liberalism's (middle) class background. In a similar fashion, Craig Calhoun has commented on cosmopolitan claims of freedom from belonging. As he argues, "cosmopolitan liberals often fail to recognize the social conditions of their own discourse, presenting it as freedom from social belonging, rather than a special sort of belonging, a view from nowhere or everywhere rather than from particular social spaces" (Calhoun 2003: 532). Calhoun elsewhere speaks of cosmopolitanism as the "class-consciousness of the frequent traveler" (2009). In a similar way, conceptions of "liberalism" today, when deployed against notions of "traditional religion," redraw class lines along an opposition of the universal (and neutral) versus the particular (and non-neutral). This, however, again involves a highly particular reading of the Enlightenment. As Arjun Appadurai remarks, "the central feature of global culture today is the politics of the mutual effort of sameness and difference to cannibalize one another and thereby proclaim their successful hijacking of the twin Enlightenment ideas of the triumphantly universal and the resiliently particular" (1996: 43). Enlightenment fundamentalism is then one way of neutralizing liberalism, and it constitutes a part of "global culture" that, by adamantly denying its cultural character, at the same time disavows its own class character and that of its premodern, cultural antagonists.

Sexuality and Gender Equality in Integration Imaginaries

But Enlightenment fundamentalism is but one element within the culturist form of social imagination, and the neutralization of liberalism has many faces. The current strength of culturism lies in its possibility of uniting opposites: it brings together the political left and right, proponents of Enlightenment and Romantics, feminists and conservatives, Christians and secularists – all under the heading of a "modern dominant culture." Nowhere does that become more visible than in the hitherto unlikely coalitions between second-wave feminists, gay rights activists, and conservative politicians on issues of sexuality and gender equality. Such coalitions thrive on the thematization of issues considered to be "cultural": honor killings, female circumcisions and genital mutilations, forced marriages, intolerance of homosexuality, and domestic violence, all discursively associated with "Islamic culture." In the wake of a strand of feminism exemplified by Moller Okin, specifically gendered issues have increasingly become focused on the problems of "Islamic culture." As in orientalist discourse, women are regarded as the passive victims of their culture (Said 2003: 207). But this discourse has been institutionalized in policy as well: when in 2002, Minister De Geus declared that the emancipation of the Dutch woman was "completed," Muslim women were an explicit exception. That this is accompanied by various ways of addressing women that are far from emancipatory is evidenced by the fact that it is in general very easy to trace a highly differential treatment of men and women in immigrant integration policies. Women are not only predominantly regarded as potentially under threat and as lacking in emancipation, but they are, paradoxically of course, also regarded as crucial for immigrant integration because they are "mothers." They are thus predominantly and differentially framed through their potential role as parents, while men are hardly addressed as such. Mothers are considered crucial, for instance, in the prevention of culturally induced crime. A 2008 Cabinet letter to Parliament, informally entitled the "Moroccans Letter" (*Marokkanenbrief*), for instance, emphasized the problems of crime related to young Moroccan boys. It related these problems to the boys' traditional and authoritarian upbringing, only to emphasize a few lines further that often, these boys' fathers were hardly at home and sometimes parents were altogether lacking. In response, mothers are considered "key" to change, and they are seen as points of entry for policy – fathers being considered wholly impervious to change. Similarly, in Germany Angela Merkel said in 2010: "in migrant families, it most importantly comes down to the mothers, which play a dominant role in the educational success of their children" (Merkel 2010).

Parallel to this, Dutch debate about the "veil" has culminated in a burqa bill, proposed by right-wing populist Geert Wilders, was passed by Parliament in 2005 (before the Belgian ban in April 2010 and the French ban in September 2010, effective in April 2011). It proposed banning use of the *burqa* in public life, but legal obstacles initially hindered its effectuation. The right-wing Cabinet announced its effectuation in 2010, and in 2016 Parliament passed a new, more strict, bill. Meanwhile, populist members of Parliament propose a tax on the wearing of the *hijab* (as Geert Wilders said, this would be a tax comparable to environmental tax: the polluter pays) or a ban on the wearing of coats with hoods that would make Moroccan delinquents invisible to surveillance cameras when hiding under their hoods. When less populist parties respond by saying that debate should focus on actions, not on clothing, they don't escape the ratification of the fact that the groups targeted in such discussions are indeed "groups" that "cause problems."

Generally speaking, sexuality and intimate life are relevant here in two ways: (1) the supposed lack of "emancipation" among non-Western immigrants entails an intolerable suppression of women and homosexuals; (2) marriage migration constitutes a form of transnational mobility that may be construed as undermining the national unity. The first has to do with the state's monopoly of the legitimate use of violence; the second with the state's monopoly of the legitimate means of movement. I will say something about the first point here, and elaborate on the second by way of a case study of what is called "the import bride."

Intimate life, primordially in the form of sexuality, potentially *undermines* the nation-state because it is always *prior to* the nation. It points at the biological matter out of whose normative control the nation is born. The relationships between gender and the nation (Yuval-Davis 1997) and nativity and the nation (Agamben 1996) are well documented. Sexism, next to racism, has been a main nation-shaping discourse during the "springtime of nations," the nineteenth century. For the strength and integrity of the nation, a control of kinship relations has been deemed vital by states, not just in the West (Lévi-Strauss 1973b; Burguière et al. 1996; Sand 2003). This, of course, becomes especially salient when immigration is concerned. The "maladjusted" ("nonintegrated") and unregulated intimate life of immigrants can be constructed as a threat to the unity of the nation-state. In this respect it is relevant to recall Georg Simmel's point that the state, in order to maintain its unity, needs to control kinship bonds by means of their spatial determination. Social relations escaping the bounds of the state's territory remain uncontrollable for the state. Especially blood bonds exceeding the national territory have been considered highly problematic from the point of view of the nation-state (Simmel 1995 [1903]). Both the nation's unity and the state's monopoly of the legitimate means of movement are thus threatened if marriage migration is not somehow controlled and regulated. If efforts to do so are taken as a clue, intimate life proves a potent source for nation-state anxieties over national integrity coded as "integration in society." This predominantly but not exclusively becomes apparent in case of Muslim immigrants. Antilleans, in line with racist notions of the sexually overactive black man, are construed as too sexually liberated, as uncivil, hence the high numbers of crime among Dutch-Antillean youth, which are related to single motherhood, which is relatively prevalent among Dutch-Antilleans (Van San 1998). This even made the issue of obligatory abortion a legitimate point of debate, which it still is from time to time.

Diametrically opposed to the supposedly unregulated and over-sexualized intimate life of Antillean women is the construction of Muslim women as too little liberated and as over-regulated by their men, and ultimately by the Quran (compare Massad 2007). Here, the suppression of women is especially thematized, as metaphors such as "women in the catacombs of the city" (by a Rotterdam alderwoman) (see Van den Berg and Schinkel 2009) and "the caged virgin" indicate (Hirsi Ali 2006). This has come to be a center-stage issue in Dutch discourse on "integration," bringing about improbable coalitions between second-wave feminists and conservative politicians. The construction of the oppressed harem and the oppressing oriental offers all the legitimization culturist discourses need to construct, in the name of the Enlightenment, an image of its antinational other, residing "outside society." As MP Azough, of the Green Left party (whose position is considered to be the least harsh toward immigrants) said, "a liberal view towards sexuality belongs to the Netherlands" (Tweede Kamer 2005: 62). Intimate life is thus connected to the monopoly of violence of the state, since the Muslim woman is constructed as a passive victim of her husband. This is all the more reason to regulate intimate life. This happens, for instance, through parenting classes specifically targeting predominantly immigrant parents, mostly mothers.

Another point that needs to be discussed here concerns the context of Butler's remarks, quoted above. In the Dutch movie that is part of the citizenship course aspirant immigrants have to take in their country of origin prior to coming to the Netherlands, images are shown of two men kissing. These images are indicative of a way of identifying the Dutch national society with a tolerance and acceptance of homosexuality. This equalization between tolerance and Dutch society leads to the instrumental use of gay and, more generally, women's rights "in order to shore up particular religious and cultural preconditions that affect other sorts of exclusions" (Butler 2007: 10–11; 2010: 107). Beyond such instrumental use, which, of course, casts doubt on the actual substance of the acceptance and tolerance toward gays in the Netherlands, discourses in which gays are portrayed as the pinnacle of modernity are often thoroughly caught in heteronormativity. They universalize a highly particular sexual dualism, leading to a world view of heterosexuals and homosexuals. Bisexuals are admitted as a third category, which is understood as a "mix" of two more primordial types. Moreover, one has to choose. One cannot, as the Dutch poet Gerrit Komrij lamented, stay in the closet and "be secretly gay." Sexual identity is thus very much rendered a part of the public sphere, and it is construed as inauthentic if it remains invisible. And visibility at the same time means controllability in the sense that interventions are called for where people (immigrants are usually implied) feel uncomfortable seeing openly "homosexual behavior." Such dualism is considered enlightened over against non-Western narrow-mindedness, which is in blatant disregard of anthropological studies illustrating (as Foucault had done for the West) the absence (and only recent rise) of the identity of "homosexuality" but the prevalence of same-sex sexual contacts in highly gender-differentiated social contexts such as India and, interestingly given their problematization in Western Europe, Morocco.

What also becomes clear, for instance, in a pivotal policy document called *Just Being Gay* (*Gewoon homo zijn*) – which can also be read as *Being Gay in the Just/Right Way* – is that homosexuals are predominantly referred to as gay men. The policy paper, first of all, basically sets heterosexuality apart from all that is different: "With the term 'homosexuals,' this policy paper intends: lesbian women, homosexual men, bisexual men and women and transgender persons" (Ministry of Education, Culture & Science 2008: 5n1). Secondly, the very equation of the label "homosexuals" with categories one of which is called "homosexual" itself (gay men) is indicative of the underlying male definition of homosexuality. Likewise, it is gay men that kiss in the citizenship exam movie, which interestingly also contains images of a women showing her breasts. Something similar can be said about the Berlin monument for homosexuals who died during the Holocaust. This large stone, opposite the many stones of the Jewish Memorial, on the edge of the Berlin Tiergarten Park, contains a video of two men passionately kissing. It would appear that homosexual persons can predominantly be regarded only as persons for whom sex is of overriding importance. One can, of course, wonder how "emancipated" those societies are that, as especially the Netherlands, Denmark, Sweden, and Norway do, promote themselves as "tolerant" and "gender equal" countries, but the point is rather that a certain framing of such issues structures them according to the program of "modernity," which plausibilizes the national society over against "premodern immigrants."

The "Import Bride"

To further explore the workings of that program, specifically in its subprogram of sexuality and gender equality, I shall take the "import bride" as a case study to further explore the discursive connections between "Dutch society," the politicization of the personal life of "immigrants," and the issue of "integration."

John Torpey (1998) has emphasized that apart from a legitimate means of violence, the state is defined by a control of the legitimate means of movement. This pertains to a prominent example of state interference in the personal life of migrants: the regulation of what is called "marriage migration." This is one theme that is discursively nested within the broader imagination of integration in the Netherlands. It pertains to the transnational character of the intimate life of migrants, and hence to their perceived *loyalty* to the state as subjects of that state. It speaks to the state as a body of the control of the legitimate means of movement. For it is by means of a control of movement that loyalty is regulated. Transnationalism increasingly tends to defy this control of legitimate means of movement, and it is in this context that the connection between "integration" and transnational marriages is to be understood. What is promoted in the Netherlands is "mixed marriages," which are taken as a sign of "integration" (CBS 2008). This is an old theme in social science. Julius Drachsler, for instance, wrote in 1921 that "it is evident that the higher the proportion of inter-marriage-... the higher is the degree of assimilation with other groups" (1921: 19). Or as Simon Marcson said in 1950: "amalgamation, or the crossing of racial or ethnic traits through intermarriage promotes assimilation" (1950: 75). Furthermore, describing (and critiquing) the sociology of marriage in his days, Marcson notes:

Intermarriage, in sociological writings, has come to represent the surest index of assimilation. It is reasoned that when a group has lost its social visibility sufficiently to participate in intermarriage it is "assimilated." In this sense it is only the "social visibility" which inhibits intermarriage. The disappearance, or outgrowing of the group's social visibility, results inevitably in assimilation and intermarriage. . . . The final result would inevitably be an ethnically homogeneous society. (Marcson 1950: 75)

Such presuppositions appear to underwrite much of current discourse on transnational marriage. When the issue became politicized in the Netherlands, around 2000, it is in relation to a failing "integration" (Hooghiemstra 2003). The Dutch Scientific Council for Government Policy (WRR), which did not problematize the issue in a 1989 report, related it to "unease" over the participation of certain "groups" "in Dutch society." So-called "family building immigration" would hence be evidence of a "lack of orientation on Dutch society" (WRR 2001: 75). Less transnational movement thus means more "integration." The tightening of immigration controls, specifically those pertaining to marriage are related to this. Integration policy has, during the first three Balkenende Cabinets, in effect been immigration policy. Minister Verdonk quite openly stated that tighter regulations restricting the number of transnational marriages was a means of promoting "integration," since the burden of immigrants in the Netherlands would not be significantly increased if fewer marriage partners from abroad were permitted to enter.

Political labels can be used to tag transnational marriages. When in 2004 an increase in such marriages became visible, then MP Dijsselbloem (Labor Party) spoke of "Verdonk marriages," blaming Minister Verdonk's upcoming harsher immigration policy as the cause for the increase. However, in 2006, after the new integration law came into effect, the number of transnational marriages was significantly lower (Van der Huis 2007: 25–31; Van der Zwaard 2008). Specifically with respect to Turkish and Moroccan immigrants (the ones for whom the harsher law was intended), this trend continued up to 2008 (CBS 2008). In popular language, however, used both throughout the entire spectrum of Dutch media and in political discourse, the issue is labeled as being about "import brides." The "import bride" has become an index of the problematic integration mainly of Turks and Moroccans, that is, of those immigrants most readily recognized as "Muslims."

Migrant Love versus Loyalty to the Nation?

What I call "transnational marriage" here is in policy language called "family-shaping" immigration. The phenomenon of transnational marriage is studied by social scientists in the Netherlands under the heading of "ethnic intermarriage" or "ethnic endogamy." The standard type of research analyzes marriage with "co-ethnics" by constructing a dummy variable for "women" and a "race" variable involving, for lack of self-identification in Dutch population registries, "white" versus "non-white" (Van Tubergen and Maas 2007). This type of research shows many characteristics of the correlation between marriage and assimilation noted by researchers such as Drachsler and Marcson. Such studies do, however, bring interesting statistical data to light that allow for certain interesting features of the popular discourse on "import brides" to be highlighted. While a significant number of "autochthonous" men marry women from abroad, the issue of "import brides" has become discursively pertinent in case of Turkish and Moroccan so-called "second generation migrants" in the Netherlands finding a marriage partner, respectively, in Turkey or Morocco. In the period 1995–2004, for instance, half of all women who migrated to the Netherlands to marry married so-called "autochthonous" Dutch men (Van der Zwaard 2009: 11). Given such figures, it is interesting that the pejorative label of "import brides" is applied here. First of all, the issue at hand does not at all confine itself to "brides." Statistics indicate that it is very much also about women finding men abroad as it is the other way around (Hooghiemstra 2003; Van Huis 2007; Kalmijn and Van Tubergen 2006). So, straight away, there is a significant gendered coding of the issue.

Second, the notion of "import bride" not only bears the negative economic connotation that prefers export to import – a matter of accountancy. It also entails the mingling of the economic in general with the sphere of intimate life. It thus portrays "import brides" as part of marriages that stand under the suspicion of being "fake marriages." Fake marriages is the term used to describe marriages taking place only as a guarantee of legal entry with chances of naturalization. However, such marriages to a substantial degree involve the "import" of men, who are overrepresented among so-called "illegal immigrants" (Staring 1998; Van Meeteren et al. 2008). The "fake"-ness of the marriages involving "import brides" is due wholly to the economic association implicit in the term. It is reminiscent of seventeenth- and eighteenth-century "mercenary marriages," in which women were sold as commodities (Tague 2001). These marriages were, for instance, critiqued as part of popular English literature and drama, which emphasized the rights of women to be treated well. In effect, the emancipation this brought literary women meant a renewed (domestic) confinement, this time in what became the connection between marriage and love. The opposition between the mercenary marriage and the loving marriage dates from this time. It involves the first ever connection between love and marriage – one that has, sociologically speaking, been a success. And it coincides with an arrangement of both public and private life as restrained, orderly, clean, healthy, and with *politesse* that emerged during the Enlightenment (Smith 2007).

The issue of *loyalty* is the crucial theme in connection to "import brides." The very *act* of "importing" is indicative of a pre-Enlightenment contractual and economic view of marriage. In that sense, it indicates an *excess* on the part of migrant men: an excess of pre-Enlightenment economic reason. But it is also indicative of a *lack* to the extent that it signifies an absent loyalty to the Dutch state. The issue is apparently that for these men, apparently, Dutch women aren't good enough. Their lack of affection for Dutch women is then construed as a lack of emotional bond to the Dutch nation-state. That the issue is restricted to *men* "importing" *brides* is due to the fact that it is men who are the real danger to the unity, cohesion, and integration of "society," and it is Muslim men who supposedly suppress women in defiance of enlightened Dutch "tradition." As Baukje Prins has formulated the issue: "migrant women have problems; migrant men make problems" (2000: 34).

The Economy of Desire

The migrant male is thus constructed between the extremes of an *economic excess* and an *emotional lack*. His transnational orientation in matters of marriage and sexuality undermines the unity of the body of the nation. His lack of loyalty to that nation never becomes more explicit than in his most profound and intimate choice: that of his marriage partner. He is, in essence, accused of *having the wrong desire*. The faulty desire for a marriage partner that has the status of an "import bride" signifies his lack of desire for the social body of the nation and for the *corpus mysticum* of "Dutch society." The "allochthon" who marries "one of his own" and, at that, "from his own country," is thus committing *a nationalized form of adultery*. Having an "import bride" bespeaks of a lack of loyalty to the collective body of society, which is enlightened and morally superior (a true *corpus morale et politicum*). It is an affront not so much to Dutch women, but to the collective body. Here, the logic of the two bodies, documented by Kantorowicz and by Mary Douglas, implicitly structures the construction of an adulterous male whose marriage of economic excess evidences a lack of loyalty, even a betrayal, to the body of society in which. If, as Douglas says, "the body is a microcosm of society" (1996: 80), the choice for an import bride is a form of adultery to the body social.

The discursive thematization of the issue of "import brides" dates, as noted, from the early years of the 2000s, when it became evident that so-called "second generation" migrants engaged in transnational marriages in great numbers. This had been expected from their parents, who, starting out as "guest workers" in the 1950s and 1960s, had their wives come over in the late 1970s and early 1980s. And generally, "first generation migrants" were deemed more likely to search for a marriage partner in their country of origin. A policy response followed when it became clear, largely due to studies such as Hooghiemstra's (2003), that the "second generation" sought a marriage partner in their parent's country of origin,. As of 2004, future marriage partners are required to complete an "integration exam" (*inburgeringsexamen*) overseas after enrolling in a course that costs €5,000 or more. Their age has been raised from eighteen to twenty-one, meaning effectively that Dutch citizens can marry other Dutch as of age eighteen, but non-Dutch only after they turn twenty-one.

So interestingly, the only thing the state can do to counter the economized issue of "import brides" is *to levy a tax upon it*. As a consequence of a stricter immigration policy, the direct *price* of a non-EU marriage partner has risen to €5,000, and the *income* of the partner "importing" must be 120 percent of the minimum income. So in order to control and regulate the logic of economic excess of the "import bride," the state adds to the price and ups the economic stakes involved therein. The higher price can be paradoxically construed as an *economic test of love*. For *real love* involves *paying the price*, no matter how high. And here the economic excess becomes a signifier of a love beyond money, while marriages entered only for the sake of infiltrating the nation are sifted out by reducing their cost effectiveness. In this way a *genuine desire* for a marriage partner is uncovered, which does not impede on the desire for the social body of

"Dutch society." Both love and national loyalty are thus secured by means of an economy of desire.

Concomitant to this economy of love is a particular construction of the "bride." As noted, many transnational marriages do not involve the migration of a bride, but they are characterized almost as much by the migration of a groom. Nonetheless, the "import bride" has become the symbolic hang-up for the issue of transnational marriage. This involves a series of gendered images that are present in the Dutch imagination of integration at large. Most significantly, it involves the construction of the passive woman. In the transnational marriage, "woman" is a passive construct without a voice. A commodity without a will, and yet violated in her freedom. This mirrors the position of women in Dutch integration imaginaries at large, as discussed above. Coalitions in Dutch integration discourse between conservative polit-icians and second-wave feminists very often revolve around the issue of male domination in case of Muslim marriage. Women are construed as restricted to the home, beneath a veil enforced upon them, maltreated and oppressed in general. Likewise, the construction of the passive "import bride," mostly occurring in case of Muslim transnational marriage, has all the characteristics of an "Enlightened" effort to get under the veil. Given the idea(l) of women as mothers, that is, as mothers of potentially troublesome (quasi-)members of the nation, women play a central role in debate on integration and in state-led practices of citizenship, such as education. But they often play that role while being recoded into passive receptacles of either masculine dom-ination or state-led civic socialization. The "import bride" is socially invested with such ascribed passivity.

Secularism as Exorcism

The program of religion and/or secularism consists of thematizations of issues ascribed to religion or secularity. The basic tension unfolding a discursive plane here concerns the relationship between religion (although it is mainly but not only Islam which is thematized) and secularity. Often, the two are opposed, and the program of secularity (which is how I propose to call it from here on) frames issues with a view to potential incompatibilities. This, of course, concerns a highly political opposition, as is the case in all programs of integration ima-ginaries, as Charles Taylor, among others, has convincingly argued against the opposition of "religion" and "secularity." Contemporary thematizations of "secularity," on the other hand, start from positing some form of liberal neutrality, and continue to highlight the tensions between this purported neutrality and religion. The productivity of the program of secularism lies in its problematization of the circumvention of this neutrality and universality that religion is argued to effectuate. Religion requires loyalties that transcend the national society, and hence its problematization is a way of observing such national societies. This often happens in two ways: first of all, by circumscribing forms of religiosity sufficiently adapted (which often means: doctrinally watered down) to the liberal neutrality deemed characteristic of Western European societies, and, second, by problematizing all instances (ranging from religious oppression, freedom of speech, the relationship between religion and violence, or the ritual slaughter of animals) in which such adaptation is considered wanting. In their recent denunciations of multiculturalism, for instance, Sarkozy, Merkel, and Cameron all tried to in a sense encapsulate religion into the nation. Cameron and Merkel emphasized that Islam, in its nonextremist version (which according to Cameron is the only Islam), is part of the nation. And Sarkozy emphasized that there is only a "French Islam," and not an "Islam in France." What they problematized – and in the case of Cameron even denounced as irreligion – were "fundamentalist" and "radical" forms of religion. Clearly, in their respective views, "radical religion" has no place in a Western European society and needs to be uprooted.

In the Netherlands as well, and starting in the early 1990s, "Islam" has become the object of problematization, linking it to "integration in society" and specifically to an image of "Dutch society" as characterized both by "the Enlightenment" *and* by a "Judeo-Christian humanist heritage." Geert Wilders's PVV party has, for instance, proposed entering this as an official recognition of Dutch heritage in the Constitution. But the idea that the Dutch are characterized more by Christianity (and hence Judaism) and by humanism is not restricted to extreme right-wing populism. The Christian Democratic CDA also believes this heritage exists, and many conservative liberals (VVD) have no great problems accepting it, although all may differ on the consequences it should have in the present. The Judeo-Christian-humanist heritage is a formulation that is more generally part of to the framing of issues in the program of secularism. That is the case irrespective of whether it is agreed upon or not, because the productivity of this program (of any program of integration discourse) lies precisely in its framing of dissensus. Even when one disagrees, one still debates whether or not the Netherlands has a Judeo-Christian-humanist heritage. It is such debate, and not the substance of the positions taken therein, that renders "Islam" observable as an object of problematiation, and that hence renders "society" observable. What is interesting about this formulation of heritage is that when religion and its incompatibilities with "society" are concerned, that society's character as "enlightened" is qualified, paradoxically, with religious markers, specifically with Christianity and Judaism, and combined with humanism. Again, this is a productive paradox in that it allows the compatibilization of "friendly" religions, even establishing a connection with (secular) humanism. And at the same time it excommunicates "Islam" from "Dutch society." Hence, new integration laws (such as the integration abroad act, involving the obligation for new immigrants to take Dutch language courses in their home country) are almost solely applied to Turkish and Moroccan migrants, and debates on new immigration laws in Parliament center on "Islam" and countries promoting "Shar'ia." An opposition between "Dutch society" and "Islam" is thus constructed notwithstanding the fact that one million self-reported Muslims live in the Netherlands, and it hence portrays a counterfactual image – the dream of the Dutch "autochthonous" middle class – of "Dutch society."

Thus, religion, but mostly one specific religion, is heavily problematized along culturist lines not dissimilar to Huntington's notion of civilizational "incompatibilities." Religion in a sense *overarches* the nation-state. In the case of Islam, the *umma* is perceived to present a universal *corpus mysticum* perceived to be in direct conflict with the bounded and particularistic body of the nation-state. Indeed, the *umma* as "the Muslim community" can be said to involve an individual and a community obligation to "spread God's rule" (Esposito 2005: 28). It thus represents a form of *loyalty* that is not national but *transnational* in character (Black 2001: 13). The Quran, for instance, reads: "Thus We made you an *umma* justly balanced, that ye might be witness over the nations" (quoted in Esposito 2005: 29) – a loyalty in fact based upon the conviction that it altogether *transcends* the national. Yet while for certain strands of "fundamentalism," the *umma* does indeed involve a utopian ideal of a universal caliphate, in practice the efforts of even the most ardent of Islamic activists are ethnically, regionally, and nationally bounded (Ruthven 2004: 151). Yet not only are Muslims culturistically constructed as inherently "fundamentalist," "Islam" in general is said to be incompatible with liberal democracy and to be inherently opposed to the separation of church and state (Fortuyn 1997; Cliteur 2007). What happens bears many resemblances to the early-modern situation in which Hobbes and Boyle found themselves, as described by Shapin and Shaffer (1989). Hobbes had finally cleared the path for the Leviathan of a single earthly sovereign under God, excluding religious conscience and claims based upon transcendence from the realm of the political. He attacked Boyle for artificially (since "mechanically," i.e., through experiment) creating an invisible substance, a vacuum, and claiming reality for it. Thus would be introduced ghostlike beings into the public realm once again, Hobbes feared, thus giving renewed rise to religious strife and, the worst of all evils, civil war. The current situation is comparable in that civil war, the disintegration of the unity of the social body, is feared as a consequence of a feared introduction of the religious into the political sphere. Religion is thus seen to *undermine* the nation precisely because it claims to *transcend* it. In response, the program of secularism has the effect of exorcizing "Islam" from "society." It does so by neutralizing the transcending claims it ascribes to religion. This becomes particularly visible in debate on the veil, of which I wish to give a new interpretation here. At stake in debate on the veil, I argue, is not only the freedom of the individual and the place of religion in the public sphere. Beyond that, such debate brings about the reduction of religion to a *surface phenomenon*. The issue of the veil is part of a discursive plane that can be seen as the program of secularism in integration discourse, and the problematization of the veil is part of a *liberal neutralization* of religion. The religious body occupies such a central place in the program of secularism because it is the vehicle through which this neutralization operates. Let me elaborate on these points by taking the veil, or rather the logic underlying its problematization as a case study.

Reading the Illegible Body: Religion and the Body in the Liberal Imagination

Shortly after the murder of Theo van Gogh (a controversial filmmaker who often made derogatory comments on Muslims and Islam), Dutch

Islamophobia reached a new high point. More interesting than the extreme expressions of Islamophobia, however, are the expressions of the (raced) culturism that is always, if often latently there. One example, which I shall here take as a starting point to uncover an important aspect of the relationship between religion and the body, is the way an interviewed woman said she saw a "Muslim-looking man" waiting for the bus, fearing he had a bomb.[3] What I am interested here concerns not the substance of this anecdote but the logic that is apparent in it. I believe it exemplifies a logic underlying the program of secularism more generally, and that unearthing this logic can help us understand the liberal thematizations of religion and the body. The interviewed woman saw veiled women and commented, "Why did they wear these clothes that hide their hair and their figures? I felt they were shutting me out." Apart from the fear of terrorism evident in the interviewee's reference to a bomb, which is characteristic of the "hysteria zone" (Collins 2004) following a "traumatic" event (Eyerman 2008), these comments are indicative of a widely shared assumption concerning Islam in Europe. This is the assumption that religion is a *surface phenomenon*. First of all, one can "see," judging by the looks of a person, that this person is a "Muslim," since Muslims are "Muslim-looking." And this not only denotes an ascribed general affiliation, but an ascribed set of essential religious properties, involving a mind-set and predispositions to action. Though highly gendered, this ascribed set is at the same time generalized. Second, this surface is not at all superficial, it runs deep. It is a surface that hides the "real" surface. It can be read in such a way that a person cannot be read. The predominant secular image of Muslims amounts to the performance of an orthodox reading of the "Muslim." There is only one lecture possible: that the Muslim is purposely illegible. The Muslim hiding his or her true surface attains some of the characteristics of the liar, the devious, deceitful person. Indeed, discussion of the *burqa* ban in the Netherlands contains mentioning of terrorist dangers due to the possibility of hiding weapons or a bomb underneath. On a wholly different level, it invoked the possibility of cheating on exams, by having someone else take one's exams. How would examiners know? Postmodern

---

[3] The interview is available in English at www.theage.com.au/news/world/dutch-run-out-of-tolerance/2005/11/04/1130823401535.html (accessed September 4, 2015).

culture, as Zygmunt Bauman (1992: 194) has observed, produces "a constant supply of publicly legible self-definitions." The "body cultivation" that this entails is obsessed with the interface between body and world, and in this respect, the veil is perceived as shutting the body off instead of positively communicating out of autonomous choice.

The imaginary of a "surface" character of religion likewise became apparent after the attacks by two Muslims on the French magazine *Charlie Hebdo* in January 2015. Debate raged about "freedom of speech," and speech and words were considered harmless and inept. Contrary to what modern philosophy of language teaches, the idea prevailed that words do not act. Only illiberal believers think that words can act, and can harm, whereas only bullets can harm a body. On the other hand, however, this conception of (freedom of) speech was sanctified as absolutely central to liberalism. The *Charlie Hebdo* cartoons, thus, were of no consequence, but they were at the same time central to the exercise of liberal democracy. It becomes apparent here how liberalism is fond of surfaces: the empty form of speech is indeed crucial, but the substance of speech should be rendered irrelevant and harmless. It is fundamental that there be speech, but also that what is said is completely harmless. Any "depth" beyond the surface of speech thus becomes a dangerous aberration from the liberal view. Liberalism prefers substanceless speech, speech that cannot act, that does not harm (Schinkel 2015).

And yet, at the same time, what is demanded of bodies in public life is that they be read. The illegibility or the lack of "transparency" of the body of the "Muslim" may thus be invoked in various ways: as a reference to insincerity, as a reference to a body out of place, as a reference to a dangerous body – in general, it becomes a reference to the *illegitimacy* of the "Muslim" body. The illegitimacy of illegibility is bound up with the abundance of the spectacle as a "social relationship ... mediated by images" (Debord 1994: 2). In an age of consumption, of the continuous play of commodified signification, the illegible body is illegitimate, an "impure" body, comparable to what Mary Douglas describes as "matter out of place" (1966: 44). It is read as "out of place," not fitting in the prevailing order of signification. Again, this is paradoxical, because the body thus conceived, which is here highly gendered, *can,* of course, be read. The very performance of a surface reading that claims its own impossibility – the Muslim as "hiding" his or her true surface and as thus being illegible – *is* a reading of the body. In fact, it is a strong reading, one that enables, or amounts to, a ready-made classification. What is crucial is that this reading, which is based on a mass mediated code (consisting, for instance, of the cliché images whenever "Muslims" are in the news), signifies the *illegitimacy of the text*. The covering of the body becomes a proxy for a text that blocks the true surface of the body. This is a cover-up that is unmistakably and *essentially* a token of religion, of "Islam," and that is, at the same time, an insincere cover-up of a *true essence*. Covering the true liberal subject, who freely expresses his or her identity in the late capitalist marketplace of bodily signifiers, is a text with pretensions of transcendence. The "Muslim" is to be transformed (through an assimilation that always remains to come and is never realized) into the liberal order, in whichever form. In the "actually existing liberalism" that is promulgated in the program of secularism, the subject is to become the ideologically empty subject of liberalism, a reflexive and reflective screen whose innermost core is a freedom, a noncausal causality that is recognizable mainly by what it is not (e.g., religious in a particular way). But what equally defines the liberal subject in contemporary capitalism is its constant need to transform, the continuous reinvention of the self, revolving around an empty, "neutral" core. For the religious subject to approach this liberal subjecthood means, first of all, the shedding of the transcendental weight in order to enjoy the lightness of flexible being. One might argue that such an interpretation of the "emptiness" of liberal subjecthood conforms to the conservative critique of the liberal neutrality in politics. But the point is rather that the liberal critique of religion, expressed in the program of secularism, presents itself as empty, defined by freedom and neutrality. It finds all substance that presents itself as explicitly religious too heavy to bear in the public sphere – just like it sanctifies the empty form of speech but forbids the idea that speech can act or inflict harm.

This particular construction of liberalism informs the program of secularism, which means it needn't be actively endorsed by those participating in discourse, while it does frame issues and forces taking a stance toward it. The body of the "Muslim" plays a particularly important role here, because it becomes a proxy for the text of the Quran, or at least for a secular construction thereof. The body signifies in a language readily recognizable as "illegible" and therefore undeserving of recognition. In the form of, for instance, the veil, the Qur'an is read as covering the body of the "Muslim" and thereby as covering the liberal subjecthood that is the disavowed core of the person. Throughout, therefore, the claim that the body in question lacks transparency, communication, legibility is self-refuting in the reductive reading of that body as lacking in autonomy, signifying danger – in the case of women the danger of their husbands who suppress (the autonomy of) their veiled wives. But this self-refutation indicates a performative reading, a reading that denies its own performance and insists that it is being hindered, blocked by a lack of transparency, confronted with an illegible object. All the while, this indicates the normative judgment passed on the body of the "Muslim." His or her body communicates the wrong kind of communication, its enunciation belongs to the wrong order of discourse, its surface is the wrong kind of surface. Not in the least, this is based on an aged theory of communication that holds that the "sender" communicates to a passive "receiver." The observer of the body simply encodes, he or she does not code nor contribute to the construction of a "communication." The passivity of the observer stands in stark contrast to the activity of the "sender." As in the capitalism of commodified self-expression, the subject (in the capitalist logic of signification: the consumer) is the signifying center of expressive energy. Agency consists of actively offering oneself for reading practices, and of thereby expressing one's inner self, an expression that is a performance that turns its reading into a passive reception of what the performance projects. Likewise, when the "Muslim" body is read as illegible, the observer can claim a natural passivity, deducing only what is there, a surface for all to see. But this passivity of the observer only strengthens the "objectivity" of his or her observation: it is the body of the other that clearly communicates that it does not communicate. It makes transparent its own lack of transparency.

That is why the "modern" reading of the body of the "Muslim" has orthodox characteristics: it claims objectivity, it is the result of a quasi-scientific empirical observation of an otherwise passive observer. Underneath this reading therefore lie the oppositions "modern/secular," "legitimate/illegitimate," and "neutral/not neutral." And finally, this reading claims the surface character of religion and thereby denies the "deep" aspect of religion, the fact that, for its practitioners, it can have an encompassing meaning that transcends the horizontal plane of liberal and consumerist signification (compare Tillich 1959: 11; 1961: 9–10; Taylor 2007: 5). Precisely in acknowledging that religion may claim transcending power, that it involves vertical vectors that escape secular horizontal orders of signification (for the moment foregoing the issue of the secular yet problematic opposition between secularism and religion), religion is tied to the surface and denied meaning beyond surface signification, beyond insincere seduction. It is thus the very reading of the body of the "Muslim," a reading that may signify all kinds of orientalist fears, that neutralizes Islam and disavows its possible meanings beyond the surface of the body. One might say that what is conceived as "liberal" is at once "neutral" and "universal." The contemporary Western European invocation of liberalism in matters of religion in a sense involves an attempt at *neutralizing the universal* (and at the same time this amounts to an attempt to neutralize the universe, as heated discussions concerning the teaching of creationist theories in schools illustrate). And at the same time, the program of secularism exorcizes "Islam" from the realm of "society." The question of "the veil" or "the headscarf" is thus a dispute over the true surface of the body. It is, moreover, both a way of denying religion any legitimate deeper meaning than that of a surface appearance, and a way of sacralizing the true surface of the liberal body. And both have the consequence of erecting an opposition between "Islam" and "society."

The discourse concerning the liberal body vis-à-vis "Islam" has a wider range than the veil. The body in a sense functions as a site of contested inscriptions. "Religion" may be inscribed in the body, both in an ascribed sense and in an owned sense, as a way of emphasizing religious affinity (and more) in a hostile environment. John Bowen (2007b) has, for instance, illustrated how French girls wear the veil out of identification and protest against a hostile environment. Such bodies may become contested, and they may thereby become discursively coded as "suppressed" and "oppressed," as not being molded by an autonomy that has residence somewhere inside the body. In that case, the liberal subject is, so to speak, under "house arrest." The body then becomes the "dungeon of the soul," as it was in a Platonic Christian tradition and, in its modern conception, in Descartes. As noted, the subjective "owning" of this position is precisely one way of resistance against such inscriptions of the body. There is a lot to tell about the everyday subversive uses of the body in a culture of supposedly complete bodily emancipation, but here I will remain focused on those discursive constructions that figure in a broader context in which membership of society is what is ultimately at stake. In the contemporary problematizations of the body in the context of religion, at stake are both the *ownership of the body* and the *substance of public space*. The ownership of the body is at stake because the body is posited as either acting freely (yet in perfect coordination with supposedly modern, neutral, liberal demands), or as a passive site of action by a hierarchy of oppressors, starting with man and ending with tradition and religion.

While there are voices of resistance against such constructions of the body, the dominant public voices fit the subject position constructed in the liberal discourse. Women who gain attention in the public sphere are predominantly (formerly) oppressed women who have experienced an enlightening experience, a freedom experience. Ayaan Hirsi-Ali is the best example of such an intervention in the public discussion, but there are many like her (see, for instance, Verhofstadt 2006). The migrant woman, then, (who often is not a migrant in the literal sense) is best heard when she fits the role of the oppressed woman turned freedom fighter. It is on the subject of women's emancipation from "Islam" that these voices are heard, not on how to deal with the global economic crisis, nor on the everyday administrative issues that politics is full of. The migrant woman is therefore best heard when she speaks of her oppression. For many, such as Ayaan Hirsi Ali, such oppression is indeed a lived reality from which she has broken free. But while this makes the subjective basis of Hirsi Ali's essentializing categories understandable, this surely doesn't mean they are to be taken at face value.

Conclusion: From Autoimmunity to Purity

Religion and intimate life are respectively regarded as transcending the nation-state and as undermining it. There is, in and of itself, nothing particularly "enlightened" about the discourse in which, for instance, sexuality features so prominently in many Western European countries. As Abu Lughod argues that certain attitudes toward sexuality in Muslim societies do not primarily spring from religion but are shaped in religious form to endow them with legitimacy (Abu-Lughod 1986: 144), I would argue that all manner of arguments concerning sexuality do not spring from a primary and long-standing concern with an Enlightenment heritage, but are discursively connected to that heritage so as to infuse them with the authority that Habermas calls the "zwanglose Zwang des besseren Arguments." That discursive connection, however, amounts to what in terms of Derrida (2003) can be interpreted as a logic of autoimmunity.

For Derrida, religion shares with science a certain mechanical repetitiveness. He draws upon the etymology of *religio* to point to a logic of iterability and performance that underpins the logic of science. As science and religion appear as coextensive, both are in need of a partial self-destruction, as both exist by way of negating the other. Derrida takes the notion of *immunity* to elaborate this self-destruction. Religion needs to immunize itself from techno-science and tele-reason. For the sacred space it claims cannot be produced in a repetitive move that it holds in common with tele-reason, the reason of global capitalism according to Derrida (2005). But the immunity of religion is an auto-immunity, and hence it is always destructive, since the sacred is at once produced by the iterability of faith. It is that iterability that religion shares with techno-science and tele-reason. The immunitary attack of this iterability is a form of self-destruction. Religion must protect itself against its immunity. The same goes for science, which must forget its preceding religious moment. And I would argue that much the same goes for a secularism that dogmatically paradoxizes "Enlightenment" as "tradition." It exhibits a dogmatic face where its culturist substance is concerned. This dogmatism is what it shares with the religion it critiques. In fact, the critique of religion, and specifically "Islam," is the defining feature of Western European culturism. It is not Kant, setting *limits* to Enlightenment, but Voltaire who is the hero of this discourse. As such, Voltaire is often misrepresented saying "I don't believe what you say, but I will defend to the death your right to say it" (which Voltaire did *not* say, but by means of which his thought was summarized in *The Friends of Voltaire* [1906] written by Evelyn Beatrice Hall under the pseudonym of S. G. Tallentyre). This type of Enlightenment reference is part of an *Enlightenment fundamentalism* that exhibits a dogmatism imposing limits on its own credibility. It has to operate on the basis of the paradox of intolerance in the name of tolerance.

The duality of the two bodies, the one being the passive female body of the "import bride," the other the body social of "society," infuses an autoimmunitary logic into culturist integration discourse in general. For the collective body of "society" is defined in neo-nationalist fashion, but at the same time it is portrayed as having no other direction or movement, a *telos* if one will, than "growth" in the economic sense. Thus, when it critiques the supposedly economic logic of the "import bride," it critiques a primary logic of loyalty to "society." Unsurprisingly, it is specifically the migrant underclass in which "import brides" are thematized. The critique of the "import bride" turns into a logic of autoimmunity the moment the policy response to the phenomenon of transnational marriage is shaped *purely along economic lines*. Then the economic logic becomes the primary logic securing loyalty to "Dutch society." For on the one hand, those who can no longer afford an "import bride" seek a partner elsewhere, that is, in the Netherlands. And, on the other hand, those who can afford it, obviously are smitten with real love. The policy raising the economic stakes thus has the effect of undergirding the loyalty of subjects to the Dutch nation-state and society by means of an *economy of desire*. It is the excess of the economic excess, the raising of the price and the multiplication of the economic logic into a hypereconomic logic of love and loyalty, that secures loyalty to "Dutch society."

In other words, the autoimmunitary logic, as Luhmann (1984) has insisted, is a logic of *deparadoxization*. "Society," which no longer has an "address" (Luhmann 1997: 866), can imagine itself only through the excommunication of what supposedly is external to it. The collective identity of "society" deparadoxizes itself when it critiques the logic of desire inherent in religion – as love of God – and in intimate life – as the love of the "import bride." While the national society operates on the basis of a similar logic of desire and taboo on promiscuity ("loyalty"), the logic of desire of both religion and marriage are transformed into respectively a *political* and an *economic* desire. The paradox of critiquing the logic of desire on the very basis of that same logic is negated in such a way as to transform the logic of desire for "society" into a *pure* desire, based on *pure* reason and an autonomy uninterrupted by political or economic heteronomy. That is why the *tax* upon the "import bride" is not paradoxical but deparadoxizing: it strengthens the economy of desire that is discerned in the transnational marriage. The hypereconomy of desire thus instituted solves the problem of transnational marriage, as it for the most part dramatically decreases the cost-effectiveness of "importing a bride." And those few who do engage in transnational marriage are cleansed from the suspicion of economically heteronomous desire, since the willingness to go to great lengths economically can be dubbed as a test of real love, that is, of autonomous desire – love the enlightened, Dutch way: a secular kind of love.

6 | *The Uses of Citizenship*

Immigrant Integration Imaginaries and the Uses of Citizenship

Immigrant integration is closely connected to the reconfiguration of citizenship, and citizenship therefore constitutes a topology of rights, duties, attributions, and relations at which integration imaginaries feed into modes of governing. As Friso van Houdt has said in his landmark governmentality study of Dutch citizenship, citizenship functions in a variety of ways when considered from a governmentality point of view. It is, he says, a technique of distinction between populations, a technique of attribution of rights, and a technique of mobilization and of division within populations (good/bad, active/passive and so on) (Van Houdt 2014: 63). Van Houdt therefore regards citizenship as "a relational technique of government" (63–64). It has been common in social science for a long time to consider citizenship in terms of bundles of rights, and to record its evolutionary extension. According to Marshall, the dimension of "social citizenship" in particular was incomplete by the time he wrote in the early 1960s, although he envisaged an evolutionary direction in the path of the welfare state that would eventually extend the domain of citizenship to include full social citizenship, which he at the same time saw as a precondition for full political citizenship. Immigrant integration can be regarded in such terms, as involving a gradual accruement of rights, but much more is at stake in the reconfigurations of citizenship in relation to immigrant integration. My approach here is thus strongly influenced by analyses such as Van Houdt's, working in line with Foucault's conception of governmentality. In terms of social imagination, this involves certain governing images. In the social imagination of the national society in Western Europe, citizenship is a program along which subjects and their relations to the national society are imagined. Aihwa Ong similarly considers citizenship as "a cultural process of 'subject-ification,'" by which she denotes a Foucaultian process of "self-making and being-made by power relations that produce consent through schemes of surveillance, discipline, control, and administration" (Ong 1996: 737). That means it is pertinent to consider citizenship not merely in terms of "rights and obligations," but as a process along which lines of class, race, culture, and gender get to be reimagined.

The following offers a good introduction into this problematic. Right opposite the Dutch chambers of Parliament there is a Burger King with a huge billboard on its outer wall, directly facing Parliament. It reads: "Only a GRILLED burger is a REAL burger." That would not be much of an opening for this chapter were it not for the fact that the Dutch word for "citizen" is "burger," effectively rendering the billboard text: "Only a GRILLED citizen is a REAL citizen."[1] Despite obvious dissimilarities, the Burger King and Parliament have one thing in common: they distinguish between "real burgers" and lesser ("unreal"?) "burgers." In case of Parliament, the distinction is made between "active citizens" and citizens for which no distinct term is used, but which are effectively seen as citizens manqué. This chapter deals with the uses of citizenship in the social hypochondriac definition of society. As such, I regard "citizenship," first of all, as a discursive program. Of course, citizenship is more than a matter of debate and a discursive plane. It is also a mechanism of in- and exclusion operative in nation-states. I argue that it is because citizenship is such a regulatory mechanism of states – and in fact of the international system of states – that it also functions as a discursive plane upon which definitions of belonging to a society deemed to overlap with the nation are debated and redesigned. To recap, I regard it as a *program*, that is, as a plane of images forming a surface upon which the imagination of "society" can take place. The focus in this chapter will be on recent changes in citizenship law, and especially on policy discourse concerning the proper content and scope of citizenship. In images of citizenship, modernity, culture, the nation all come together. Western European definitions of the proper citizen, which is the "active citizen," is ridden with notions of being modern. In the Netherlands, Denmark, Sweden, and Norway, for instance, "gender equality" and

---

[1] The word "burger" stems from *burgher*, which means an inhabitant of a *burcht* (a fortified settlement). See, for a sixteenth-century use of the word, Stevin (2001 [1590]). Compare Prak (1997). The German "Bürger" and the Kantian/Hegelian notion of the *bürgerliche Gesellschaft* has similar origins, much like "citizen" and "citoyen" are derived from "city" and "cité."

sexual tolerance have become emblems of the nation. A visit to these countries' official government websites makes clear that this is the case almost to the extent of national marketing slogans. Not only has "ethnicity" become a marketable good, but what Comaroff and Comaroff (2009: 122–126) call "nation branding" has appeared. A specific portrayal of gender relations is part of the *marketing of the "modern" nation*. Such images are not coincidental. They at the same time signify that the proper citizen of such nations does not subscribe to views held to be "Muslim." Hence, when new citizens are introduced to the nation through civic integration courses, issues of gender equality and sexual tolerance figure prominently, and they convey an image of the nation that is both highly counterfactual – gender equality and sexual tolerance can, in different countries, not at all be taken for granted – and highly exclusive, if only in the assumption that such values are lacking in certain "non-Western" immigrants. Citizenship thus becomes a way of defining "society" over against a realm discursively constructed as "outside society," consisting of nonactive or inactive citizens and noncitizens lacking proper "integration" – which is termed cultural adjustment through "active citizenship."

The attention toward citizenship in policy follows in the wake of renewed academic interest in citizenship. For a couple decennia now, "citizenship" has been of renewed interest for social scientists and political philosophers (Kymlicka and Norman 1994; Shafir 1998; Van Gunsteren 1998). The process of globalization has often been mentioned as a main reason for this academic popularity of the notion of citizenship (Brubaker 1989; Hall 2002). Specifically, globalization entails three phenomena justifying a renewed interest in citizenship. First, globalization proves Hannah Arendt's (1978) prediction that the modern world would increasingly be faced with stateless persons such as refugees. Second, globalization involves an increase in transnational ties, engaged in by persons whose citizenship status can be multiple, mixed, and/or incomplete. A global diaspora is moreover coupled with global media that disperse images of highly local identities throughout the world. Third, globalization entails mass migrations leading to forms of quasi-citizenship such as denizenship (Hammar 1990), as well as residence in states by persons formally citizens in other states.

In light of such developments there emerged first of all a political philosophical literature that turns on the status of stateless and argues, for instance, for inclusive forms of European citizenship or "global" or "world" citizenship (Habermas 1998; Dower 2000; Falk 2003; Benhabib 2004). Second, there is a political philosophical literature that stresses the need for the exclusivity in citizenship and the link between community or culture and citizenship.[2] Third, a social scientific literature has emerged, focusing on the status of persons and pointing at conditions under which persons give transnational shape to citizenship (Bauböck 1994; Soysal 1994; Balibar 2004) or on the gender dimensions of actual citizenship (Bussemaker 1998; Lister 1998; Yuval-Davis 1999). Fourth and last is a social scientific literature focusing on the local context and aspects of citizenship and on the functioning of communities. On the one hand, this literature is composed of a communitarian strand (Putnam et al. 1993; Etzioni 1993; Walzer 1994), while on the other hand is a literature more closely resembling what Burawoy has ideal-typically called "policy sociology." This literature is policy-oriented, and in the Netherlands it is closely tied to policies of immigrant integration. Internationally, it involves the idea of the "decline of citizenship," which is often related to immigration (Jacobson 1996). What has been relatively little been emphasized is that the very thematization of citizenship has functioned in specific ways that have not remained restricted to the sphere of formal membership. The historical development of citizenship criteria that have to do with who can be admitted as a formal member of the nation-state is but one part of the equation here. Next to the formal aspect of citizenship, I argue, is a moral aspect that is relatively independently thematized. When policy documents produced by state officials emphasize certain "values" as crucial to "active citizenship," a discursive space is opened that involves images of legitimate membership to which no formal consequences are directly attached. Nonetheless, these images have their reality effects, which are to be sought in the imagination of a bounded, national society – an object that cannot be formally pinned down. So when I focus on "citizenship" as a specific *theme*, a bundle of images related to a collective imaginary – or rather to an imaginary collective – it is the *uses of citizenship* that are the focal point.

---

[2] Significantly, this appears both in more communitarian as in more contract-based liberal theories. Compare, for instance, Walzer (1983) and Rawls (1993).

State/Society Differentiation and the Role of Citizenship

From its very beginning in ancient Greek thought, citizenship has been regarded as a mechanism of in- and exclusion of states. Citizenship in that sense is also the modern, democratic form of political member-ship. As in the by now classic notion of T. H. Marshall, it concerns a juridically described set of rights and duties, and the citizen can be regarded as a bundle of such rights and duties. By regulating entrance to the state, citizenship at once secured the borders of the nation. As the modern state/society differentiation entailed a relative overlap between "society" and the nation, citizenship automatically meant inclusion in society. Therefore, Marshall could describe "social citizen-ship" as "a claim to be accepted as full members of the society, that is, as citizens" (Marshall 1992: 8). The "citizen" can thus be automatic-ally regarded a "member of society." This overlap between nation and society was always relative and always had exceptions, ranging for a long time from women to the "abnormal." But in relative terms, especially in the later twentieth century, it was possible because society, which had been differentiated from the state, formed an ethnically relatively homogeneous whole and was "regionalized." The state thus guarded the territorial borders of society. Precisely such a "regional-ized" imagination of society threatens to lose credibility in times of globalization. Until far into the twentieth century, citizenship sufficed as a guarantor of membership of both nation-state and society, but in an age in which flows of migration have become permanent, that is no longer plausible. Earlier, political membership meant, in practice, membership of society only for those who were connected by birth to nation and state, and thereby to society (Jacobson 1996: 14–15). In what he calls "ideal theory," such a model is present, for instance, in the work of John Rawls: "a democratic society, like any political society, is to be viewed as a complete and closed social system. ... [W]e are not seen as joining society at the age of reason, as we might join an association, but as being born into a society where we will lead a complete life" (1993: 41). In social science, Franz Boas has analo-gously remarked that "fundamentally, the nation must be considered a closed society. ... The differentiation between citizen and alien is not so intense as in the closed primitive horde, but it exists" (1928: 98). Such a vision of nation-state and society is no longer unproblematic. The moment society is entered by people not tied to the nation through nativity, in the predominant Western European tradition of *jus sanguinis*, the nation can less plausibly be conceived as relatively overlapping with society. While the nation-state is, in Giorgio Agamben's formulation, "a State that makes nativity or birth (*nascita*) (i.e., naked human life) the foundation of its own sovereignty" (1996: 162), such a state is in need of new sources of sovereignty, of a new functional potential, when its nation no longer overlaps with the society from which it is differentiated. When persons of different socialization gain political membership, a rift in the seamless overlap between state and nation and thereby between state and society appears. That is to say that the modern state/society differentiation that kept both apart at a controlled distance has lost in strength. This urges analyses of citizenship and the nation-state to move beyond "methodological nationalism" (Smith 1983; Wimmer and Glick Schiller 2002). The fact that the concept of citizenship nonetheless enjoys widespread popularity within the state has to do with the salience of "citizenship" as a discursive program that provides ground for debates about membership of "society." For one thing, nation-states have not taken up social scientific calls for "global citizenship." They *have* reconfigured citizenship, especially its symbolic value and the *image* of citizenship, as a form of nation branding. They have done so especially in various discursive problematizations of citizenship that have amounted to the rise of citizenship as a program. Discussions of citizenship and the articulation of citizenship in various policy texts often, in and of themselves, have not led to legal consequences, although naturalization policies are a notable exception. Naturalization is, however, but one context of the problematization of citizenship. At various local levels, as well at the national level, "citizenship" has emerged as a way of framing belonging to society. It has delineated a zone of discussion and debate also where it has not directly given rise to legally enforceable changes. In brief, integration discourse has seen the shift from a relative focus on *formal citizenship* to an emphasis on *moral citizenship*. In effect, this means that "citizenship" in a highly moralized sense has become a marker to identify membership of society. This means that many citizens in the formal sense are discursively disenfranchised by policy discourses that place them outside the moral zone of "society" even though they are formally members of the nation-state. In order to explicate how that takes place, I first wish to clarify what the concepts of formal and moral citizenship mean.

Formal and Moral Citizenship

Since ancient times, citizenship has been regarded as having reference
to inclusion in a state. At least as old is a moralization of citizenship
according to which the *real citizen* is an *active citizen*. This is evident in
the oldest known thematization of citizenship, namely Pericles' funeral
oratory. As Thucydides recounts: "we do not say that a man who takes
no interest in politics is a man who minds his own business; we say that
he has no business here at all" (1954: 119). The same goes for Aristotle, for whom the good citizen is someone actively participating in
political affairs (2013: 1275a–1277b). For the Greek political philosophers, citizenship is an *ethos*. For Romans such as Cicero it becomes a
virtus. Such approaches, which complement a formal aspect of citizenship with a moral aspect, continue to exist throughout the history of
political thought, and they still influence thought on citizenship
(Bosniak 2006: 19). With the *Déclaration des droits de l'homme et
du citoyen* (1789), in which "man" is separated from "citizen," a
distinction between "active" (*citoyen*) and "passive" (*homme*) is
repeated. Robespierre indeed regarded citizenship a "public virtue"
(Dunn 2005: 117). Thus, a distinction can be made between *formal
citizenship* – denoting juridically codified rights and duties of citizen-
members of states – and *moral citizenship* – referring to a counterfactual ideal of citizen participation (compare Kymlicka and Norman
1994: 353; Habermas 1998). Formal citizenship has reference to both
juridical status as membership of a juridico-political order and to social
rights. I thus subsume under "formal citizenship" also that which has
been called "social citizenship" and which refers to certain social rights
(compare Fraser and Gordon 1998). Both "civic citizenship" and
"social citizenship" can thus be regarded as forms of formal
citizenship. Moral citizenship is something quite different and entails
an *extra-legal normative concept* of the good citizen. It is not merely a
factual and descriptive but also a counterfactual and prescriptive
notion. I take the formal and the moral to be two aspects of citizenship.
That is to say that this is an analytical differentiation. They do not exist
wholly independent of each other in articulations of citizenship. There
is, for instance, a moral aspect to the formal obligation of paying one's
taxes. But these aspects do get highlighted in a very selective way.
When the discursive articulations of the program of citizenship are
concerned, the moral aspect is what defines the perimeters of the

discursive terrain. The formal/moral distinction thus offers a good vantage point from which to analyze the uses of citizenship as a program enabling the diagrammatical attribution of belonging and not belonging to "society."

In the articulation of the moral aspect of citizenship "democratic citizenship" can be at stake (compare Stewart 1995), or it can be simply "active citizenship" (the Netherlands, for instance, hosts a special university chair in "active citizenship," which is closely tied to citizenship policy). "Active citizenship" has long had reference to forms of political participation. The good citizen is, then, as in Pericles and Aristotle, someone who actively engages in political life, who, for instance, votes and is active in political organizations such as a party. Such a view is in line with the republican tradition, but moral citizenship (for instance as "civic engagement") can equally be found in communitarian approaches to citizenship (Putnam 2000). The notion of "active citizenship" as political participation was thematized in the last century as "political education" in the 1920s and 1930s (Merriam 1931) and as "political socialization" in the 1950s and 1960s. Such a notion still has widespread currency in the Netherlands as in other Western European countries, but it is not what primarily concerns me here. I focus instead on the more recent *moralization of citizenship* in which citizenship has been incorporated in policies of immigrant integration. That means that, taking the Dutch situation as my case, I critically analyze the substance given in national and local citizenship policy discourse to the moral aspect of citizenship. I deliberately do not present an extensive discussion of the nation-state and issues of nationalism, for one, because contemporary Dutch nationalism has been dealt with extensively by Van Reekum (2014), but also because moral citizenship is my main interest here, and it pertains *not* to nation-state membership but to the imagination of "society" and its "insiders and outsiders."

From Formal to Moral Citizenship: The Virtualization of Citizenship in Dutch Policies of Integration

The last few decades have signaled a shift in focus from formal to moral citizenship in Dutch citizenship policies. In the early 1990s debate existed on a shift from welfare to workfare in the Netherlands in which citizenship was connected to workfare, yet such debate – while

informed by notions of a "new paternalism" (Mead 1997) – still
primarily centered on a certain notion of formal citizenship, involving
codified rights and duties. Since 1994, however, a shift from formal to
moral citizenship has taken shape in Dutch policies concerning citizenship. The main reason for this is the incorporation of "citizenship" in
policies of "integration." I therefore briefly discuss the development of
such policies in the Netherlands.

"Integration" Becomes "Citizenship"

At the start of the culturist phase in integration discourse and the
accompanying policy, "citizenship" becomes, according to Parliament,
"the leading principle for the new vision on the presence of
persons from diverse cultures in the Netherlands" (quoted in Driouichi
2007: 25) Citizenship thereby becomes a "choice" for "participation
in Dutch society" (quoted ibid.: 26). Citizenship is thus not conceived
as a status but as a choice, a *potentiality* whose actualization is the
individual's *responsibility*. What comes to the fore with the thematization of citizenship in integration discourse is, on the one hand, a
culture-centered way of thinking – practices exemplifying the "active
citizen" are practices normalized according to "the dominant culture" –
and on the other hand a loyalty-centered way of thinking – the "good
citizen has "loyalty" toward "society" (Vermeulen 2007: 54).
This became especially succinct in the 2007 discussion in Parliament
on double nationalities, discussed in Chapter 4. The issue of "loyalty"
came to the fore in political debate on integration and citizenship
around 1992 and 1993, and the Cabinet took up a position deemed
"from the nineteenth century" a few years earlier (Driouichi
2007: 124). The *equalization* between "integration" and "citizenship,"
or rather the definition of "integration" as "citizenship," dates back to
1994. Following the advice of Van der Zwan and Entzinger, two
prominent Dutch social scientists, citizenship became the central
focus of policies of integration (Ministry of Interior Affairs 1994a).
Politically, the equalization between integration and citizenship was
promoted in the Conservative Party: "the integrated immigrant
has become a *citizen*, in the widest possible sense of the word. Thus
regarded, 'integration' equals the classical notion of 'citizenship'"
(VVD 1994: 4). And the agenda-setting Cabinet paper *Contourennota
Integratiebeleid Etnische Minderheden* (*Memorandum Integration*

Policy Ethnic Minorities) (Ministry of Interior Affairs 1994b) read: "The primary goal of integration policy is … the realization of the activating citizenship of persons from ethnic minority groups." In a letter from the Minister of Alien Affairs and Integration in 2003, and in the yearly Cabinet budget paper from 2004, the equalization between "citizenship" and "integration" appears complete, and both are put on a par. In 2003, "integration" is defined as "shared citizenship" by research quangos involved in the measurement of integration who thereby explicitly remain in step with policy discourse: "Integration can be regarded as a process of acquiring citizenship and participating in society by allochthons in three societal domains" (CBS and WODC 2006: 1, 3). In 2004, the Cabinet described it as "shared citizenship of minorities and allochthons."[3] Likewise, analyses with more distance to policy put "citizenship regimes" on a par with "integration regimes" (Koopmans and Statham 2001).

The recent Cabinet paper on integration, *Integratienota 2007–2011* (*Integration Memorandum 2007–2011*) (2007), which was drafted by a new and relatively left-wing minister, has been perceived as a break with the xenophobia and harshness of recent years, but, illustrating the fundamental nature of the shifted discursive parameters of Dutch policy discourse, it brought twofold continuity: (1) "citizenship" remains the dominant accent of the government's integration policy, and (2) a neoliberal thematization of "individual" or "own responsibility," which came up during the culturist phase of integration discourse, remains. Regarding its goals, the paper said, for instance, in a paragraph entitled "Active Citizenship Is Now Needed": "societal emancipation and social integration, and within these a strong accent on citizenship" (VROM 2007: 7). The subtitle of the *Integration Memorandum*, *Make Sure You're a Part of It!* (*Zorg dat je erbij hoort!*), stresses the importance attached to "individual responsibility." Thus, the government made "an appeal to all citizens to participate in society on the basis of mutual acceptance and equality" (VROM 2007: 6). That, of course, presupposes the possibility to *not* take part of "society." And the 2011 "integration paper" by the Cabinet, *Integration, Bonding, Citizenship*, stressed "individual responsibility" possibly the most, emphasizing that "integration"

---

[3] *Miljoenennota 2004*, VI Justitie, 3–6: Asiel, migratie en integratie, beleidsart. 6.4: Integratie minderheden, p. 178.

now becomes the full responsibility of the individual, socially and financially (individuals have to pay for their citizenship courses and exams). Paradoxically, by allotting full responsibility to the individual, and by once again leaving the organization of citizenship courses to the market, it stated that the "Cabinet hereby contributes to a Dutch society that everyone ... can make into a home by actively participating in it" (Dutch Cabinet 2011: 15). The paper explicitly mentioned then British Prime Minister Cameron's notion of a "Big Society" as a source of inspiration for the route chosen.

Thus, as Van Huis and De Regt have noted, "citizenship has become an important concept in policies of integration and "inburgering" (becoming-citizen). This means that newcomers must live by certain duties, must assume responsibilities, must participate in and show active involvement in society" (Van Huis and De Regt 2005: 396). This emphasis on citizenship can, for instance, be related to the perceived "failure" of earlier policies of integration (Vermeulen 2007: 71). A "bridging function" is expected of citizenship (VROM 2007: 6). But because citizenship is mostly a case of individual responsibility (such as "raising your children well" or "making sure you're a part of it"), the bridging effort is placed solely on the side of those citizens whose citizenship is in need of improvement.

The Virtualization of Citizenship

The effects of the two processes mentioned above – the increased emphasis on "culture" and the increasing emphasis on "citizenship" – are twofold: (1) citizenship is increasingly framed as *moral citizenship* and (2) citizenship is being *virtualized*. The first means that the emphasis on citizenship focuses mainly on the moral aspect of citizenship. The second means that citizenship thereby becomes, instead of an *actuality* (a juridical status), a *virtuality* (a possible but absent actuality in diffuse and shifting moral terms). This also means that citizenship has increasingly become a *virtus*, a virtue as in the Roman humanist notion of citizenship. The "messier" and more diffuse concept of moral citizenship blurs the formal side of citizenship through the discursive framing of the idea that one is only a *real* citizen when one is an *active* citizen. The equalization between "integration" and "citizenship" entails a *virtualization of citizenship* to the extent that *the citizenship of those who are citizens in the formal sense but are construed as insufficiently integrated is reduced from actuality to virtuality.* Not all Dutch "migrants" and therefore not all those who are the object of assessments of "integration" are in possession of the formal citizenship status. There is, for instance, a difference between the juridical statuses of "citizenship" and "denizenship" among migrants (Snel and Engbersen 1999: 276). What is crucial, however, is that such notions refer to inclusion in the nation-state, while "integration" refers primarily to inclusion in "society." There is, in the Netherlands, a significant number of people who are formal citizens but who are at the same time the object of problematizations of "integration." Since "integration" equals "citizenship," the citizenship of this group is downplayed, in effect virtualized, and they are thus discursively disenfranchised.

Of course, the emphasis on moral citizenship can lead to juridical codification into aspects of formal citizenship. While as such, the moralization of citizenship would only gain a juridical codification, what mostly has happened up to the present is that the *discourse* on citizenship has run into its own limitations and formulated forms of *unenforceable force.* In Parliament, it was noted in 2005 that, beyond formal and juridically codified demands, nothing could be demanded from migrants: "we must accept the fact that there are limits to what we can enforce in the name of shared citizenship." Yet the limits to formal demands at once define the terrain of a culturist discursive force, which poses unenforceable demands. These limits in fact mark the border between state and society. The traversing of these limits by integration-cum-citizenship policies illustrates the moralization of citizenship as a diffuse hybrid between the state's force and the government's ideology on civic behavior. It is precisely the power of the state vis-à-vis the citizen whose moral citizenship is problematized that shapes the virtualization of citizenship as a form of unenforceable force. This becomes apparent in the reversal of the trajectory that immigrants in the Netherlands follow. Before the culturist phase in policies of integration it was assumed that once the immigrant had become a citizen in the formal sense he or she would in time commit himself to society and become a citizen in the moral sense as well. Currently, however, it is the other way round. As one Dutch legal scholar has noted, it is now predominantly assumed that the migrant is first to become a citizen in the moral sense and to integrate into society before he or she can become a citizen in the formal sense. In that sense, the immigrant now has to *earn* permanent residence and nationality by proving his or her acceptance of the fundamental norms of Dutch society (Vermeulen 2007: 101). A double process thus takes place. On the one hand, newly arrived immigrants are required to first gain moral citizenship in order to apply for formal citizenship status as the crowning achievement of their becoming-citizen (*inburgering*). On the other hand, many who have formal citizenship status but who purportedly lack "integration" as a consequence of their lack of "cultural adjustment" are construed as only halfway there. For them, formal citizenship status is indeed a purely formal thing, and in their case the loyalties involved in moral citizenship are the real prize.

"Active citizenship" now appears as the panacea for the two problems addressed by the *Integration Memorandum 2007–2011*: the fact that "autochthons" experience fear of Muslims, and the fact that "allochthons" feel unaccepted. Active citizenship as a form of cultural adjustment on the side of the latter solves both problems in a universal (national) language of "citizenship." In that context of collective identity construction on the "autochthon" side, the memorandum contained the plans for a "Charter Responsible Citizenship," noted that the "Dutch Canon" has been presented, and took the initiative to open a "Museum of National History" (this never materialized) (compare Van Reekum 2014). Meanwhile, similar discursive divisions become visible at the local level of citizenship policies.

The "Regionalization" of Citizenship: The Virtual Citizen on the Local Level

Citizenship has been reported to be "disaggregated" (Benhabib 2004) or "eroded" (Turner 2001). This fragmentation of aspects of citizenship now located at different levels of executive agency is accompanied by a "regionalization" of citizenship that locates citizenship at different levels along a local/global axis. The state discourse on "integration as citizenship" takes place not only on the national level analyzed above, but also on the local level of cities and municipalities that construct their own notions of the "active citizen." The local dimension of citizenship is increasingly thematized (Uitermark et al. 2005; Modood et al. 2006). A focus on the local level is specifically crucial, first of all, since citizenship is multilayered (Yuval-Davis 1999; Balibar 2004; Van Houdt 2014), and, second, since the relatively diminished importance of the state in times of globalization propels the urban arena into a site of contested citizenship (Schinkel 2009). The discursive recalibration of citizenship at the local level is thus an important part of the spread and reach of the program of citizenship. A *regionalization of citizenship* thus takes place along with the moralization of citizenship. The virtualization of citizenship therefore also occurs on the local, municipal level. This means that citizenship is not only construed as "national citizenship," but also as "local citizenship." Alternatively, "state citizenship" may be contrasted with "street citizenship" (Duyvendak and Uitermark 2006), in which a specifically local substance is given to policies focused on "good" or "active" citizenship. This involves keeping the street clean and greeting one's neighbors, as is posted on plaques in specific streets in poor neighborhoods in Rotterdam as part of the "city etiquette" project.

On the one hand, we have the idea that local citizenship is regressive in the sense that citizenship was once a local affair. "Citizens" or "citoyens" lived in the "city" or the "cité"; "burghers" (*bourgeois*) lived in the "burght" (*bourg*). The "droit de cité" provided protection from the feudal sovereign, and citizens were hence restricted to the city. When the political unit extended beyond the city, citizenship became national. That did not abolish local aspects of citizenship, that is, rights and duties aggregated on a local level, but it did prioritize national citizenship. The regionalization of citizenship can be said to occur in part as a consequence of the problematization of national citizenship, which gives salience to the local level as a way of gaining hold of the population through citizenship when the dominant conception thereof is weakened in the process of globalization. The regionalization of citizenship thus fits Roland Robertson's (1995) idea of "glocalization" that signals the renewed relevance of the local in times of globalization. In that sense, the regionalization of citizenship is the consequence of a shift in the spatial focus of integration policies. Generally, that shift is one from the national level to the level of the city, from the city to the city quarter, and from there to the street (Van Putten 2006). Compatible with the fluidity of local/national levels characteristic of "governance," an ever tighter zooming in on "the problems" has taken shape in policies of integration, and the focus on citizenship has meant an increasingly regionalized focus on local forms of citizenship. As Godfried Engbersen, a prominent Dutch sociologist and chairman of the Royal Netherlands Academy of Arts and Sciences committee on the Future of Dutch Sociology has remarked, politics emphasizes "the importance of the old integration frameworks of village, neighbourhood and family." Referring to Ulrich Beck, he dubs such politics as "zombie-politics," using obsolete notions to describe a changed social reality (Engbersen and De Haan 2006: 1). The regionalization of citizenship shows, however, that the local level is highly pertinent in laying down a discursive program that functions as a space of diagrammatical attribution of belonging to society.

As an illustration of the virtualization of citizenship at the local level of citizenship policies, I discuss two of the largest Dutch cities: Rotterdam and The Hague. Along with Amsterdam, these are two of the most diverse cities, containing more than 150 nationalities. While Dutch cities do not exhibit strong segregation along "ethnic" lines as a consequence of a regulated housing market, these cities do have quarters in which large numbers of "(non-Western) allochthons" live segregated from "autochthons." While Rotterdam has been known for its "tough stance" on issues of immigrant integration, The Hague, while housing many migrants as well, has comparatively hardly been in the news regarding such issues.

"Active Citizens" in Rotterdam

Rotterdam is a somewhat atypical case to discuss, since it is the city in which Pim Fortuyn rose to fame. This right-wing politician put "Islam" on the Dutch political and policy agenda and was murdered in 2002 by an animal rights activist. His party Leefbaar Rotterdam (Liveable Rotterdam) was the dominant party in office in Rotterdam from 2002 to 2006. In a sense, it continued certain exceptional measures initiated earlier by the Labor Party (PvdA), such as the determination of the aforementioned "Hotspot Zones," in which "Intervention Teams" (so-called since 2002) enter and search people's homes, and in which all persons can be stopped and searched – something that is provided for by law, for instance, in the United States, but that is exceptional (in the Schmittian political philosophical sense of the term; see Agamben 2002) in the Netherlands. Such measures earned Rotterdam the label of a "policy laboratory" (Noordegraaf 2008), for the city took the initiative in implementing drastic and exceptional policies that were revolutionary in the sense that they preceded legal codification and frequently explored the limits of legislation (Van den Berg et al. 2006). The city, for instance, wanted to determine areas in which no persons of a specified ethnic background could move in to live. Since this was deemed discriminatory, this policy was changed into one requiring persons moving into such a designated area to earn at least 120 percent of the minimum yearly income, a measure that was recently found to be indirectly discriminatory in the report on the Netherlands by the European Committee against Racism and Intolerance (ECRI 2008). In 2005 this policy was codified by Dutch Parliament on a national level in the "Umbrella and Exception Law," which is commonly known as the *Rotterdam Law*. Another example of "policy innovation" in Rotterdam concerns the "City Marines" that have been active there since 2002. These are higher-level executive civil servants, nine in total, with a clearance from the mayor to do whatever they deem necessary in a certain street or city area and to thereby bypass existing regulations for the implementation of new executive initiatives. A last example is the Rotterdam Safety Index, an instrument devised in 2001 to measure the safety of Rotterdam as a whole and of its neighborhoods. It is a composite quantitative construct involving an "ethnicity" variable according to which a neighborhood's safety automatically increases when less "non-Western allochthons" live there (Noordegraaf 2008). As one of the aldermen of "Liveable Rotterdam" said in a typically culturist fashion: "Color is not the problem, but the problem does have a color." By the second mention of "color" he thus referred to all that is not "ethnically colorless," that is, all that is culturally "different" and "distant" from Rotterdam and the Netherlands.

Within that context of policy innovation and multiculturealism, the city of Rotterdam put forward its "Rotterdam Citizen's Code." This document was a typical example of problematizing moral citizenship in a policy statement that, precisely because of the extra-legal and generally vague notions of moral citizenship, amounted mostly to symbolic policy. In it, the City Council "analyzes the problems and sets the norms we must live by in order to solve these problems" (Rotterdam City Council 2006: 1). The problem is thus seen as the breaking of norms, and the solution is thought to be a restating of the norms that are being broken. That implies that the problem is caused by ignorance of the norms on the part of those causing the problem. Indeed, these are, by implication, considered to remain outside the "society" that Rotterdam is, which is defined by these norms. The citizens to which the Code is addressed, then, can be said to be citizens only in the formal sense, precisely because they lack the moral citizenship involved in being a member of a society defined by norms. And paradoxically, for the City Council such is precisely the reason for formulating the Citizenship Code. The Code consists of the following items: "We Rotterdammers (citizens of Rotterdam):

1. assume responsibility for our city and for each other and do not discriminate;
2. use Dutch as our common language;
3. do not accept radicalization and extremism;
4. raise our children to be full citizens;
5. treat women equally to men and with respect;
6. treat homosexuals equally to heterosexuals and with respect;
7. treat people of (different) religious conviction and people without conviction equally and with respect." (Rotterdam City Council 2006: 1)

The idea of "active citizenship" is incorporated in the Code to the extent that its first statement is further elucidated by the idea that "We take active part in society," which is complemented by "We take part of society outside our own ethnic or religious community" (Rotterdam City Council 2006: 7). That the difference between "active participation" and the lack thereof is "cultural" in character becomes obvious in the statement that "we raise our children with sufficient attention to Dutch values, norms, culture and traditions" (Rotterdam City Council 2006: 7). It thereby becomes clear that "being proud of Rotterdam," as the Code puts it, has first and foremost to do with abiding by *Dutch* culture. In a sense, the local thematization of citizenship is but a regionalized expression of a national assemblage in which the local inserts itself. The "cultural clash" that the Code bespeaks is clearly that between "Dutch culture" (seen as "Western" and "modern") and "Muslim culture" (seen as "non-Western" and "traditional"). This becomes most apparent in items 3, 5, 6, and 7 above. The thematization of radicalization refers solely to Islamic radicalism. The thematization of gender issues, involving "women" and "homosexuals," refers to the assumed position of these "groups" among Muslims, and the thematization of religion first and foremost prescribes that *Muslims* tolerate others. This became apparent in the public debates on *Islam and Integration*, which were organized in 2005 by the Rotterdam City Council and which led to the formulation of the Citizenship Code. These debates made an explicit connection between "Islam" and the problems of "integration." Integration was thereby reduced to the problematic affair of "Western" Rotterdam with "Islam," and the city was posited right in the current of the clash of civilizations." The Code is the culturist outcome of the topics discussed during these debates – topics that were pre-fixed and that set up an a priori opposition between "society" and "Islam."

"Active Citizens" in The Hague

As mentioned, Rotterdam is a somewhat atypical example, since it experienced an upsurge of Fortuyn's extreme right party, which helped strengthen its exceptional status as a "policy laboratory" – a status that befits the city, which, with one of the world's largest harbors, takes pride in being a city that works instead of one that talks (as becomes apparent both in Erasmus University Rotterdam's slogan, "The University that Works," and in the Rotterdam football club Feyenoord's club song, "No Talk but Action"). A city much less in the avant garde of policy initiatives is The Hague. The seat of the Dutch national government, the city itself is very segregated along "autochthon/allochthon" lines, and quite silently so. It is hardly ever in the news for its policies. It is therefore interesting to see to what extent The Hague citizenship policy also discursively articulates a virtualization of citizenship.

To that end, I analyze the city's most recent policy paper on citizenship, as well as the website on which it can be found (the two sources contain different substances attributed to citizenship). In line with the shift in national policy since 1994 described above, the city of The Hague finds that

in the past few years the term "integration" has had a negative press. On hearing the word integration many people think of the new inhabitants of the city of The Hague who should adapt themselves to the existing and established society. The term citizenship however makes everything equal. This . . . paints a better picture because after all we are all citizens.[4]

---

[4] "What Is Citizenship?" (English summary by the city of The Hague), at www.dehaagseontmoeting.nl/assets/dho/upload/Gem%20Den%20Haag%20en %20het%20burgerschapsbeleid%20_Engelse%20vertaling.pdf (link no longer active).

And it adds what it means that "we are all citizens": "we all want a clean, beautiful and safe city to live in." Next, however, citizenship is reformulated from a shared form of *being* ("we are all citizens") to a shared *task*: "we have opinions that we want to express. We all want a city where we can have a good working and home life. Therefore the task of citizenship is for everyone." The idea of citizenship as a task marks a transition from citizenship as actuality to citizenship as virtuality, a moral virtue that is not necessarily present but may remain a possibility, a potential (un)realized. Hence the question posed in the (most recent) Policy Memorandum on Citizenship *Being the City Together: Citizens Make the Difference* (2006): "Citizen: something you are or something you become?" (The Hague City Council 2006: 7). The municipal government sees its role as follows: it "wants to stimulate our citizens to take responsibility for the quality of housing and community life in our city." It furthermore becomes evident that citizenship – stated here as "good citizenship" – means that you are "owner of his [the citizen's] street," "you receive education, you work or you contribute in other ways to the city. For example: by raising your children to the best of your ability, by volunteering at activities in society or by following a social training scheme" (The Hague City Council 2006: 7). "Good citizenship" also means "giving shape and color to The Hague together." In the 2006 memorandum (which the "What Is Citizenship?" text on the website accompanies), another definition of citizenship can be found:

There are many definitions of citizenship. We keep it simple. For us, citizenship means that people feel involved: their effort to contribute by themselves to the improvement of the social climate and also to take responsibility for their social environment; that is what we call citizenship. A citizen feels co-owner of his [*sic*] street and his neighborhood. The school of his children is his school; the tree in front of his house is his tree. The public space is the living room of the city where one meets one another. Where one seeks support from each other and where one shares experiences with one another. A citizen realizes that social quality is not a right nor a present, but something one must make, anew every day, with each other. (The Hague City Council 2006: 7)

The Hague thus "keeps it simple": to "citizens," "social quality" is not a "right." In this way, social rights that are part of Dutch formal citizenship are relocated under moral citizenship. Moreover, the public space is modeled after private space (the "living room"), which legitimates a paternalist discourse that seeks to turn the private into a public affair and thematizes the proper "raising of children" as "citizenship." The definition of "good citizenship" thereby effortlessly crosses public/private boundaries. Persons who are not "good citizens" in the public living room surely cannot be good citizens in the private living room. What is more: the problems in the private living room are the cause of the problems in the public living room. That is why, in the Dutch version of "new paternalism," the idea is that "real problems are behind the front door" (Tokmetzis 2007: 3) or, alternatively, in the mother's womb, either way calling for "early intervention" dubbed "prevention." Current local citizenship policies in Dutch cities is closely tied to new paternalist policy discourses and practices, and the problematization of "raising children," which is of recent date in Dutch policies since the 1970s, is to be seen in this light. Citizenship becomes a form of civility. This makes the private "living room" a public affair. Moreover, the "own responsibility" of citizens is thematized in conformity with neoliberal notions of "responsibility" (Ossewaarde 2006). It is then the local government that states, as in the subtitle of the 2006 memorandum: "citizens make the difference." The difference between formal and moral citizenship is clearly present here:

Being a citizen is a right. Whoever is active does not gain extra rights, whoever keeps aloof forfeits none. But, next to a juridical concept, citizenship is also an attitude towards life. In this memorandum we are not speaking of citizens in the sense of carriers of citizen's rights, but of citizenship as a way of life, of giving meaning to one's own existence by taking social responsibility. (The Hague City Council 2006: 7)

To this quasi-existential and moralized notion of citizenship, consequences are attached in case of failure to live up to "citizenship as an attitude towards life." The associations made concern "anti-citizenship," "rudeness" and "anti-societal behavior," in which cases "non-willing" persons are concerned. Society is a "society of the willing," and as in Rousseau's *volonté générale* the "non-willing" falls outside the contractual community. The citizen that "keeps aloof" is a citizen in the formal sense but remains "anti-societal," nonparticipating, and outside "society," which is formed in part on the surface of the program plane of "citizenship."

Programming Citizenship: Neoliberal Communitarian Governmentality in Western Europe

What becomes apparent in the virtualization of citizenship is a peculiar combination of "individual responsibility" and cultural assimilationism. A perspective that captures the occurrence of this combination in policy discourse is informed by Foucault's concept of governmentality. Foucault used this concept to describe the rationality of a form of governing based on what he called biopower. This is a form of power that tacks onto the biological life of populations. Governmentality refers to "rationalities of rule" that take the management of the population as their starting point. As Foucault – who used different notions of governmentality – writes: "governmentality" refers to "the ensemble formed by the institutions, procedures, analyses and reflections, the calculations and tactics that allow the exercise of this very specific albeit complex form of power, which has as its target population, as its principal form of knowledge political economy, and as its essential technical means apparatuses of security" (Foucault 1991: 102). Informed by the concept governmentality, Barry Hindess has likewise described citizenship as part of an international management of populations. Foucault used the concept of governmentality mainly to describe the (neo-)liberal mode of governing. Scholars in his footstep have noted the paradoxical convergence of a neoliberal focus on individual responsibility with culturally conservative views (Dean 1999; Brown 2006b; Miller and Rose 2008). This cultural conservatism can take the form of a communitarianism, which exists at various levels. It exists in the frequent invocation of "community" as both the problem and the answer to various social problems, ranging from integration to crime and safety. But it also exists at the level of the national community, where it promotes a symbolic image of spatial boundedness, and hence spatial distance and inside/outside differentiation. Here, it also induces calls for cultural assimilation to "bridge" such distances.

It is thus possible to speak of a governmental strategy of *neoliberal communitarianism* (Schinkel and Van Houdt 2010), in which citizenship becomes moralized and, in case of lack of cultural adjustment, virtualized. Neoliberal communitarianism entails what can be called a "double helix" of neoliberal elements and communitarian elements. Friso van Houdt has given an extensive analysis of the ways neoliberal communitarianism plays out not only in immigrant integration policies but also in crime policies (Van Houdt 2014). He has moreover traced its lineage back to the transformation of German ordoliberalism in the 1940s and to the communitarian critique of neoliberalism in the 1980s and 1990s (204–206). As his account shows, "individual responsibility" and the idea of a "social contract" or of "earned citizenship" are paired with notions of "community" and "cultural adjustment." This is a process that can be tracked, in each case with a different national substance, in countries such as the Netherlands, France, and the United Kingdom.

In the United Kingdom, for instance, the "new deal for citizenship" has transformed citizenship into a contract that entails three stages. Prior to acquiring full British citizenship coupled to permanent residence is what is called "probationary citizenship," in which the individual is required to "integrate fully into British society," which also means persons should "demonstrate they have earned their right to British citizenship" (Van Houdt, Suvarierol, and Schinkel 2011: 412–413). This means they meet the following requirements: "Proficiency in the English language and knowledge of life in the UK; Paying taxes, economic self-sufficiency, demonstrating genuine relationships; Obeying the law; Joining in with the British way of life (active citizenship)." Responsibility for this "new deal" lies with the individual, while the contract involves a point system for which the state keeps score.

In France, the *Contrat d'acceuil et d'intégration* is, as the name indicates, a contract as well. It involves a three-tiered emphasis on "French language," "civic formation," and "living in France." Here, too, the individual is "responsibilized," which was thought to be in line with the voluntary nature of French national membership by the Haut Conseil d'Intégration. But interestingly, the signing of the contract became obligatory in 2006. The French *Contrat* also involves the idea of earning one's citizenship. What the individual is especially required to illustrate is a *responsibility to integrate*, which means individuals are able to "find their place in French society" (Van Houdt, Suvarierol, and Schinkel 2011: 413–414).

We can see in neoliberal communitarianism another incarnation of the de-individualizing individualization. The responsibility of the individual is in policy discourse and in citizenship requirements. And the responsibility of the individual is thematized there where it in practice comes down to exhibiting "responsibility" in creating, or being active in, "community," which is here the national community. At the level of the nation, the nation can thus be continuously presupposed but at the same time called into existence. It is in the end the neoliberal subject, the "responsible individual," that is the cornerstone of the national community, as this "community" exists only in and through the "assuming of responsibility" by the individual. The *self-referentiality of the nation* lies in the fact that the nation is a community of individuals that have the freedom and responsibility to bring about that nation. And vice versa, the freedom of the individual is not possible without the cultural assimilation that ensures true membership of the national community called "society." While, in a social hypochondriac way, the national society is thus always under threat, it always at the same time emerges with a cultural robustness that forms the core of the solution to such threats.

At the level of the subject, the "double helix" of neoliberalism and cultural assimilationism indicates the assumption, inherent in citizenship discourse, that true liberal subjecthood involves a cultural conversion. True freedom and responsibility, which liberalism on the one hand poses as innate and essential to the subject, are culturally dependent and have to be learned. A liberal philosopher such as Rawls admits as much when he says that some form of political socialization into liberal subjecthood is needed. Hence, Sheldon Wolin rightly notes: "that this ... does not strike Rawls as illiberal is because the anonymous power of acculturation has been pressed into service to do the work of repression" (2004: 550). Neoliberal communitarianism is a form of governmentality, the discursive elements of which make for a program that allows the identification of "society" and its true "members." It marks the difference between members and nonmembers, which it codes in terms of integration-cum-citizenship, as a difference between liberal subjecthood and lacking subjecthood. When individual "responsibility" is the problem, including the responsibility to culturally adjust, true freedom is apparently lacking. It is these connections that can be found throughout Europe. "New Labour" in the United Kingdom and the "Third Way" politics inspired, for instance, by Giddens are a typically neoliberal communitarian rationality of government. At the same time, countries such as Germany and the Netherlands were able to combine neoliberal economic policies with both Christian Democratic and socialist-inspired notions of community. For a cultural milieu that defines itself with reference to "modernity," the neoliberal subject becomes the exponent of the nation par excellence. Historically, "citizenship" has more generally been one way to expand the nation and sublimate class conflict, for instance, with the national annexation of the proletariat in the early twentieth century (Balibar 1988: 726).

Foucault's governmentality perspective is challenging and enlightening because it allows one to look beyond sovereign models of the state. It makes clear that policy exists at various levels, and that the governing of the population is not restricted to the sphere of "the government." Given the social hypochondriac character of contemporary Western European "society," bio-power is an important tool. However, my focus is restricted mainly to the discursive domain, as I am interested in the social imaginary of "society." It is precisely the fact that moral citizenship is not codified but rather diffuse that makes moral citizenship a program for the discursive delineation of society. Moral citizenship remains discursive, but the difference between membership of the nation-state and membership of society is precisely the fact that the latter is noncodified and discursive in nature. Moreover, the paradox of unenforceable force can be solved by the invention of extra-legal policy practices such as the Rotterdam "Intervention Teams" who enter homes on the basis of "ethnic" criteria of selection and without the proper legal warrant in areas designated through special directive. Such "policy experiments" framed as "exceptional measures" and as "administrative innovation" are hailed by politicians and policy makers alike precisely because of the fact that they precede possible legal codification. Neoliberal communitarianism thus works along two paths, and they involve two forms of what has been called "responsibilization." On the one hand, the "autochthonous" subject, which is mostly assumed to be a liberal subject, is urged to assume an already existing responsibility. On the other hand, the "allochthonous" subject, which is constructed as not yet a liberal subject, is responsibilized in the sense of a cultural adjustment in which an as yet lacking "responsibility" is created for the first time. This is the responsibilization that requires civic integration courses and state-sponsored parenting classes, but also exceptional measures such as "intervention teams" that check to see how well children are raised, how clean people keep their house, how they pay their bills, and how many people live in the same house. As one member of a Rotterdam intervention team said: "we basically come for everything" (Schinkel and Van den Berg 2011).

Citizenship is thus a program that provides the space of coagulation of "society." Today, this program is shaped by neoliberal communitarianism. That is to say that the issues that are debatable in the discursive space of "citizenship" are structured according to a dual logic. Two lines run along the surface of this program, combining the individualized with the de-individualized in a double helix. This combination facilitates ready-made diagrammatical attributions to either "society" or "outside society." The regionalization or localization of citizenship illustrates the breadth and density of that program.

In his well-known text *The Politics of Recognition* (1994: 37), Charles Taylor states that it is crucial not to create a difference between "first-class" citizens and "second-class" citizens. That is certainly true from a normative perspective. But from a descriptive perspective (which I do not claim to be necessarily non-normative) such diagrammatical differentiation has its productive aspects. Though in a violent way, it provides "society" with a demarcation otherwise difficult to retain with plausibility. The virtualization of citizenship thus amounts to such a differentiation, by distinguishing "citizens" from "nonintegrated" persons that are discursively exorcized from society. In the case of Dutch policy, the rift between formal and moral citizens can be construed along these lines as a difference between citizens and national subjects. In effect, however, that leads to the discursive articulation of these "citizens" – immigrants who are citizens in the formal sense – as quasi-subjects, at once protected and feared within the nation-state. Neoliberal communitarianism thereby also connotes the balancing act of preserving a specific kind of openness and closure. Cultural assimilationism is not the backward reflex of exposure to a global scene; it is one aspect of the regulation of that exposure. Desired forms of (neoliberal) openness require specific forms of cultural openness, which is first thought to require an assimilation *into* such openness – one has to be "liberal" enough to be "open," and part of what is paradoxically called an "open society."

The very emphasis on moral citizenship in what is to a large extent state-initiated policy discourse indicates a shift in the state's orientation. In general, the state moves away from social welfare and direct interference with economic life toward new forms of control, surveillance, and monitoring. Citizenship is one venue at which the state finds a new functional potential in times of globalization. The moralization and ensuing virtualization of citizenship concerns not inclusion in the nation-state, but inclusion in the discursive domain of "society." The role of the state (at various levels) in the regulation of citizenship has shifted from controlling the formal borders of the nation-state to *controlling the borders of the "national society."* As Badiou remarks, "the State is not founded upon the social bond, which it would express, but rather upon un-binding, which it prohibits" (2005b: 109). A more diffuse and especially discursive process has thereby been initiated. For while in- and exclusion in the nation-state is a juridical matter, in- and exclusion in "society" is a discursive matter that cannot be legally codified. The first is foremost a matter of formal citizenship, the second of moral citizenship. Moral citizenship can, of course – with a time lag – be legally codified (and formal citizenship can be analyzed for moral aspects), but that does not mean that the in- and exclusion of "society" can be codified. And through the image of the "active citizen," the image of "society," of what society is and who belongs to it, looms large. The shift in focus of the state has to do with the destabilization of the modern state/society differentiation. The state, which implicitly regulated the in- and exclusion of society by regulating the in- and exclusion of the nation under conditions of homology or overlap between society and the nation, now has to operate on two fronts. It needs to regulate the in- and exclusion of the nation-state mostly by means of formal citizenship. But because, given the effects of migration, the nation and society no longer coincide, it is relevant for the state to formulate the substance of moral citizenship as adherence to a "dominant culture." Thus, as Appadurai notes, "states … are everywhere seeking to monopolize the moral resources of community, either by flatly claiming perfect coevality between nation and state, or by systematically museumizing and representing all the groups within them in a variety of heritage politics that seems remarkably uniform throughout the world" (1996: 39). In laying down the contours of a discursive program of "citizenship," the state gains a certain power of articulation in what "society" is, as it becomes a key force behind the predominant self-observation of society. The social imagination of what "society" is to a large extent runs via the national state, which depends on the ready identification of a national society both for its efficacy and for its legitimacy. But it can feed that social imagination only at the cost of differentiating the good and active citizens from the not so good and "inactive" citizens. This has the effect of a virtualization of citizenship in which the formal aspects of citizenship are downplayed relative to the moral aspects, which are found lacking especially in immigrants and their descendants – the ones disturbing the imagined match between nation and society.

7 | *Social Science: Between Moral Monitoring and Public Sociology*

Although Western European countries have had different policies of immigrant integration, many share the idea that there was actually one, that it is called "multiculturalism," and that the time has come to move past it. I have argued in this book that, often by invoking themes such as modernity, secularism, and citizenship, debates on "multiculturalism" and "immigrant integration" have by and large operated as a way of giving plausibility to images of national society. Such images are, of course, central to social science, and this raises the question what the position of social science is or should be in such debates. Clearly, many in social science have jumped on the "multiculturealist" bandwagon, proclaiming, for instance, that immigrant integration succeeds better if "multiculturalist" policies would be discarded (Wikan 2002; Koopmans et al. 2005; Sniderman and Hagendoorn 2007). Perhaps even more have operated on the basis of a tacit multicultureism, incorporating culturist categories into large-scale quantitative analyses of immigrant integration, as Chapter 3 showed. Both these options – explicit multiculturalism and implicit culturism – involve normative and often policy-oriented stances. In this final chapter, I aim to tease out the consequences of my analysis in the previous chapters for the way social science conducts its business. I have two main interests here. One is to trace some implications for social theory, specifically in the status of the signifier "society." The second is to consider the possible contributions of a public social science to debates on multiculturalism and immigrant integration. Particularly in relation to recent forms of neonationalism in Western Europe, the question here is how the public(s) of social science relate to the public that is the nation.

A pivotal concept both in public debate and in social science is the concept of "society." Integration discourse hinges on the question who is or is not a legitimate part or member of "society." In the context of multiculturealism, "society" is thus a highly politicized and hardly neutral concept. We must take the non-neutrality of the concept of society a bit more serious than we usually have in social science. After all, most social scientists still situate their analyses within "society" as a kind of container of social life, existing out there. As the next section briefly illustrates, there are certainly those who critique the use of the concept of society. But the "alternative" is not to discard the concept as useless. Neither does not entail the replacement of "society" by "culture" (as traditionally in cultural anthropology or in cultural studies), nor does it lead to either Thatcherist negations of the social or Marxist fixations on the "real society" as made up of relations of production. Rather, it should consist of a theoretical *re-imagination* of the common sense concept of society that is able to uncover the complexities of the familiar and everyday *uses of society.*

In this chapter, then, I aim to illustrate what the (public) contributions to social theory can be of the foregoing analysis of the ways "multiculturalism" is denounced in Western European discourses of immigrant integration. I seek to propose a concept of "society" that is seen less in substantivist than in processual terms, and that appears, first of all, as a social *medium of separation and of social distance,* or, in other words, a medium of in- and exclusion or, better yet, of *sorting populations.* Reference to "society" separates and allows for mutual orientation. Such separation is immanent to various discourses in which that reference appears in the form of representation. So instead of assuming such integrated societies consisting of equally integrated individuals, I propose we take seriously the explicit public manifestations, invocations, and performative evocations of "society" that are at hand. Today, these are nowhere more salient than in debates on immigrant integration. It is integration discourse that allows the clearest view of the way the signifier "society" functions in social life.

Society: A Hypothesis the Social Sciences Do Not Need?

Michel Foucault may have been right in claiming that "we need to cut off the king's head. In political theory that has still to be done" (1994: 122). In social science as well, the prevailing image in prerevolutionary France of (political) society as an organic community still lingers on. But a sociology that discards the category of "society" for theoretical reasons must not forget the empirical relevance of that category as a form of social imagination. What is then forgotten is the *productivity* of "society." "Society" may not be the basic entity of social life, an encompassing home to all that is social, or at least a national address thereof. But it is, or rather does something, it is an active form of social imagination, and this activity should be accounted for in social theory. So, the problem with social theory and social science is that it has often assumed a bounded conception of society as a kind of thing-like container of social life. This is adequately put forward by Craig Calhoun:

> Part of the problem is that a great deal of modern social science has tacitly assumed that human beings normally live in one social world at a time. Modern social science has produced a notion of bounded and internally integrated societies and has treated both cross-border relations and subcultures as problematic. It has presumed that the individual consciousness is itself integral and that it requires a stable and consistent social environment. (1995: xix)

But does the solution to this problem lie in abandoning the concept? Should we then, faced with "societies" as zombies, go ghost busting? Is social theory aimed at myth breaking, at the unmasking and debunking of popular belief? Should our answer perhaps be similar to Laplace's, when Napoleon asked him which role God played in his *Méchanique celeste*: "Sire, je n'ai pas eu besoin de cette hypothèse"? That depends on the way "society" is imagined. In its meaning of a container concept or a basic category of social inquiry, certainly, it appears of no use in social theory. In its primary sense, when we describe "society" as a politically charged signifier or as a stake in everyday social struggles, it is certainly of use. In that sense, we stop looking at what happens *within* society, and start scrutinizing what happens *with* society, that is, what happens when "society" is used as a description. Against conception of society that are in the end based on the metaphysics of a social body, social theory could then not only be regarded as providing us with an *argumentum ad hominem*, such as the idea that society is a zombie, but also as constructively engaging with the realities within which "society" figures. One of those realities, and a very prominent one as I hope to have illustrated in earlier chapters, concerns the context of what is called "immigrant integration." Ideas of "society," and all the practices surrounding it, have very real effects that tend to be ignored if we were to decide not to give "society" much attention. In fact, that is precisely the way things are today: both the social science that takes "society" as a basic and largely unquestioned category and the social science that deems "society" a zombie remain blind to the reality effects of "society" in the context of immigrant integration discourses.

Simply regarding the concept of society as a zombie category and then leaving it at that involves some dangers. One danger would be the reification of a certain version of neoliberalism, in which "society" does not figure. On the one hand, I do not share the indignation at Margaret Thatcher's saying that "there is no such thing as society." Who could argue that there *is* such a "thing" and actually show us where it is? Sociologists' indignation at her interview had to do, alongside with some conservative consequences concerning the very real existence, according to Thatcher, of "individuals" and "families," with the fact that the Prime Minister denounced the basic object of research of a particular science. But on the other hand, there is some truth in Outhwaite's warning that neoliberal notions of "society" as illusory can have very serious political consequences (2006: 21). Mitchell Dean has formulated some of these consequences as follows:

> to regard the categories of state and society as zombies is ... dangerous. This is because the denial of the currency of such categories is linked to the view that extraordinary measures will become necessary for a time which is, for many, a truly exceptional time, that is, one in which the reign of the state and its sovereignty has been drowned under the great oceanic flows and surfaces of globalization. It is to suppress the hard edge of politics, including the deployment of violence, conducted by certain states in relation to international and domestic opponents. (2007: 23–24)

Of course, Dean is here speaking more of the category of the state than of society, but previous chapters have illustrated the role that idea(l)s of "society" play in policy measures, and the violent consequences this can have. Added to the dangers of speaking of "zombies" is, of course, the fact that ideas of "zombies" are still wedded to notions of "bodies." So something more needs to be done, because social theory should be able to give a convincing account of the way the concept of society *functions* in social life. It is clear that too often social science has been blind to this functioning precisely as a consequence of the fact that it took "society" to be its own master category, which deserved neither much conceptual explication (as it simply constituted and delimited a field of research) nor much analysis (as all analysis always already took place within the confines of "society"). Such analysis, however, is precisely what should be done by social science. Amid fears that "globalization" threatens "society" as the basic unit of socio-logical analysis, and amid its centrality to various processes of social sorting pertaining to cultural belonging and, simultaneously, economic opportunity, social science should try to climb out of its own theoret-ical iron cage and observe it from the outside. In fact, a social science truly engaged with the struggles that today characterize the social should take as much distance from "society" as possible. Between the options of involvement and detachment (Elias 1982), both should in fact be entertained: involvement with the functioning of "society" in social life as *object of analysis* and detachment vis-à-vis "society" as *basic category* and starting point of sociological analysis. Social theory should thus generate perspectives on the idea of "society" that allows us to see it in a different light. It should generate descriptions that plausibly highlight new aspects.

The Uses of Society

It is fruitful to focus on the imaginary character of "society." That is not to say that the existence of society is fiction, but that society exists *as* fiction. A society is a creative fiction, a map that claims to be a territory. The fiction of "society" is the fiction of an unbroken, self-contained togetherness placed under an identitarian marker. In that sense, "society" could be called a "confiction" – a fiction of a certain togetherness ("con"). It is what Gilles Deleuze, using concepts coined by Bergson, calls a *"fictive representation"* (*représentation fictive*) that has a *fonction fabulatrice* (Deleuze 1966: 113–114), which can be called a *fiction function* crucial to forms of social imagination. Such fictions are discursive constructs whose plausibility depends on their use. And that use is immanent to a discursive field through which certain discursive *programs* draw lines of orientation. Discursive pro-grams (such as culturism, secularism, and citizenship) unfold discursive lines on which (con)fictional imaginations rest.

Taking the fiction of society seriously means that talk of "inclusion" and "exclusion" in social science becomes problematic. After all, a strong focus on "exclusion" tends to reify "society" as a solid con-tainer that one can actually "be outside of," while others "remain inside." It is to ratify precisely the fictional account that the use of "society" claims as a neutral, descriptive truth. While a concern for "social exclusion" often springs from a political engagement and concern, its effects lead in the opposite direction of legitimating the fictional framing that should be the matter of concern. Alternatively, I argue that "inclusion" and "exclusion" are always already *modes of conclusion*. For those who are "excluded" are, by virtue of that very exclusion, relationally connected to what is "included." One can wonder what use such theoreticism is to the person experiencing exclusion, but I believe it is crucial nonetheless, should social science not partake in the well-meaning ratification of "exclusion" by endorsing the very idea that social distance amounts to actual social "exclusion." All the sympathy with the excluded perpetuates exclusion in the sense that it ratifies and legitimates the idea of a bounded social whole from which one *can* be "excluded." The social relation of exclusion as the negative mode of conclusion has hardly had attention in social theory, and this means that too often conceptions of "exclusion" have been adopted that reify the social body from which exclusion is thought to occur. That is not to say that what is called exclusion may not be detrimental to the person experiencing it, which is why it is important to consider it as the negative mode of conclusion. But it is important to recognize the fact that the excluded to not reside outside a clear and distinct social whole consisting of the "included." Conclusion thus entails the fact that any exclusion is always what Giorgio Agamben has termed an "including exclusion" (1998: 21; compare Luhmann 1995: 61). What is relevant is not to consider "society" as some form of transcendence, but rather to understand the way a "society" construes itself confictionally over against a residue to which it is immanently connected. Today this occurs by programming a certain conception of the national society over against a residual "outside society." This occurs through the observation of those "excluded from society" in terms of their "integration." When social science contributes to that, it operates as a machine for the production of difference. That means social theory needs to refuse all talk of "society" and its "outside," as well as all conceptualization of "exclusion," no matter how social democratic it might seem. Inclusion and exclusion rather need to be conceived as two confictional modes of conclusion, meaningful only in relation to a confiction whose reality should be described as that of a self-description, not as what that self-description claims to describe.

Immigrant Integration and the Governing of "Society"

The conclusion must be that it does not make sense to speak of a "society" without being able to identify that which is considered not a part of it, which is why discourses of immigrant integration are so important. There used to be a variety of other ways of constructing the national society's significant other, such as the identification of the proletariat, but the colonial projects and the development of capitalism largely included the working class in the national society. One nation could be pitted over against the colonial other, and at the same time, class conflict was muted by giving workers the status of members of society. Race is another ensemble of discourses and practices rendering society identifiable through the identification of its constitutive outside. Racially excluded were and are not wholly "excluded," their exclusion is the negative mode of conclusion, which does presuppose the existence of a strong social relationship, namely one giving shape to what is called "exclusion." Today, at least in Western Europe, a cluster of programs in which issues are connected with themes in light of what is called immigrant integration takes up the fiction function of society. This sheds light on what "society" actually *does*. For confictions do a certain work. When a confiction is considered in regard to the work it does or the mechanism it shapes, a confiction can be considered as a *medium*. I am using "medium" here in a sense adapted from Parsons and Luhmann, who spoke of "symbolically generalized media of communication." I prefer to speak here of a *medium of governing*. In the end, society is a productive fiction. The performativity of such descriptions lies in the real work they do or make possible. This work is not only a work of description, but also of aligning, of contraction, of social sorting. The intermediary step here, as it has in effect been throughout sociology when a "society" was posited, is the notion of a *population*. Society is a confictive identity whose invocation allows a form of governing a population. Immigrant integration imaginaries are therefore profoundly biopolitical. They have to do with the regulation of a population constituted as a collective body.

The concept of biopolitics has been put forward by Michel Foucault, who understood it as one form of biopower, which he described as the power over life. While up to the Classical Age the sovereign decided over life and death in the sense of a letting-live and a bringing-death, the mechanisms of power change in the Classical Age. Death now becomes the inverse of the right of the social body to secure and develop its own life (Foucault 1976: 179). Over against sovereign power as a power over death, biopower emerges as the dominant form of power, and this puts the power over life center stage. Power thus gains a specific "hold" on life during the eighteenth and nineteenth centuries (Foucault 1997a: 213). Central to biopower is the control of biological life. But a distinction is in order between what Foucault calls *disciplines* and *regulatory controls*. The former are characterized by an "anatomo-politique du corps humain," the latter by a "biopolitique de la population" (Foucault 1976: 183; 1997a: 216). Biopolitics, Foucault states, started first and foremost with the establishment of a link between economic and political processes with birth rates and mortality rates. For Foucault, biopolitics furthermore involves forms of social hygiene and a governing through techniques of "security." In his lectures at the Collège de France called *Naissance de la biopolitique* (which are mostly concerned with (neo-)liberalism), Foucault once again defines biopolitics. There, he describes "biopolitics" as "the attempt, starting from the eighteenth century, to rationalize the problems posed to governmental practice by phenomena characteristic of a set of living being forming a population: health, hygiene, birth rate, life expectancy, race" (2004b: 323). He then relates it strongly to the mode of governing peculiar to biopolitics, which he terms "governmentality" and of whose contemporary neoliberal communitarian shape I have briefly outlined in the previous chapter. While Foucault thus refers to biopolitics as the power over a population that tacks on to the biological characteristics of its members as a species, I prefer to speak of this literal biological form of power as a form of *zoèpolitics*. I thereby adopt the concept of *zoè* used by Giorgio Agamben (1998). Agamben uses it to denote bare, naked life, the life before it is entered into a community or *bios*. Because of this equation of community with this second Greek concept of life, *bios*, I apply biopolitics at the level of the collective of a population and take it to be the politics of a social body, thereby understanding the history of organicist attempts at forging unity out of heterogeneity as a history of biopolitics (Schinkel 2010). Thus, where "society" is invoked, a biopolitical ordering act occurs, although its outcome is by no means certain or guaranteed. This ordering involves a social sorting of populations. One might say that the idea that social life at large consists of a variety of "societies" is one way of ordering a global population, analogous to the ordering effectuated through citizenship, which occurs by dividing the global population into distinct chunks called nation-states (Hindess 2000).

It is here that the link between society as a (con)fictive self-description and its everyday effects is to be sought. The concept of population, which tacitly always was what most sociologists thought of when they assumed "societies" or did statistical analyses, is the intermediate term upon which governing operations are performed in the medium of society. This means that the invocation of "society" opens a space in which practices of social sorting take place. The very reproduction, stabilization, and generalization of the plausibility of "society" entail the continued plausibility of a certain way of ordering and of governing a population. When a confiction such as society is regarded as a medium of governing, that means that the differentiation between "society" and its residual "outside society" opens a space of attribution along the lines of inside/outside. In Luhmann's use of the theory of media, the invocation of the *medium* of society entails the actualization of the two-sided *form* inside/outside. Within the medium of society, which can be seen as a loosely coupled collection of elements, forms can be drawn and marked that constitute strict couplings. It is the strict coupling of elements within the medium of society that ultimately embodies the real work that "society" does. It is here that "society" gains the lived reality of being "external to" the individual yet exerting a "coercive force" upon it. That is to say that as soon as "society" is invoked, this opens up the possibility of relegating populations to its inside or to its residual outside. Immigrant integration is a marker that identifies persons relegated to society's outside. When immigrant integration is at stake, its subjects are marked as "outside." That does not mean we should take literally that there is a society and that they reside outside that society. Rather, what occurs is the negative mode of conclusion in which the space of "society" enables persons to be marked as "outside." And crucially, this takes place both in the case of "integration" and in the case of "lacking integration." As argued in Chapter 3, the dispensation of integration entails that the dividing line runs not between better or worse integration, but between being marked as integrated to some degree and not being marked in terms of integration at all. It is this social sorting that is the work performed by "society." And because of the work "society" does as a medium of social sorting and of governing, it is a concept that cannot be simply cast aside in sociology. "Integration" is a concept that helps the fiction of society to remain plausible, but it does so by marking immigrants as not belonging to it. The "social function" of "integration" is *to keep those who are to be integrated at a distance from society*, as this is one of very few remaining ways to plausibilize the very idea of "society." That means social scientists conducting analyses of "immigrant integration" exhibit a very low sense of responsibility in the concepts they assume. Before concluding by highlighting the connection of all this with familiar conceptions of nationalism, let's briefly return to that social science.

Revisiting the Social Science of Immigrant Integration: For a Public Social Science

The idea of a society bearing characteristics lacking in persons to-be-integrated explains the tautological nature of measurements of integration, in which society is delineated on the basis of measurements that presuppose its delineation. This tautological way of measuring is not a problem for concepts of society, as it is part of the very logic of the functioning of society. Like race, society is a way of grouping character-istics of a population and of assuming a deeper unity among them, which can then be discerned as distinct from populations lacking such characteristics. And given this tautologous nature of immigrant integra-tion research, is it any wonder that, as Peter Sloterdijk has said, soci-ology, having lost its former optimism, is extremely boring? Research after research spews similar integration statistics, all on the basis of unreflexive assumptions of what "integration" actually is and of what the status of the presupposed "society" is. However, there is a continu-ous feedback between input and output here. That is why, over the years, images of society change, for instance, in the direction of a more culturist substance. New images of society are taken up in measure-ments of integration, and the results lead to new or reinforced ways of delineating society. The programs in which society is articulated con-tinually morph, and new programs are added. Sexuality, for instance, was hardly considered a hallmark of modernity in the 1950s, at least not when it included sexual permissiveness and tolerance of homosexuality. Citizenship was considered, even up to the early 1990s, as a formal requirement for nation-state membership. It became a moral character-istic of membership of society when all sorts of populations gained entry to the nation-state but were yet observed as residual.

Thus, "society" is a signifier that continuously curves back on itself, that thereby always threatens to undermine itself, that unsettles and renews itself. Society itself, once it appears, functions as a medium for inside/outside imaginations. Its tautology can be regarded as a Möbius strip. It has no starting point, no primary point of entry. What is imagined as immigrant integration changes the imagination of society, the terrain within which integration is assumed to take effect. And vice versa, what is imagined as society defines the parameters along which integration can be assessed. In order to study the actual functioning of the signifier "society," one must therefore discard the linear causal view that construes "variables" that may or may not correlate (and that then illegitimately conceives of correlations as causal relations). Such linearity always necessarily *presupposes* society as a preexisting bounded entity. Integration is then a process that can be measured longitudinally by tracking the scores on a bundle of indicators referring to a fixed societal status quo. But the point is, rather, to conceptualize the social mesh in which "society" and the definition of "integration" appear as co-constitutive and are so entangled as to emerge discursively as media and forms contained in one another.

What the social science of immigrant integration needs most of all is a renewed sense of responsibility. Concepts such as "society," "integration," and "ethnicity" are far from neutral. They are extremely normative, naturalizing, and power-laden concepts. Recently, the Israeli historian Schlomo Sand (2011: 59) has commented similarly on the extreme lack of caution and intellectual responsibility with which many of his Israeli colleagues (but this is nothing specific to them alone) use a concept such as "ethnicity." The same goes for Western European social scientists involved in immigrant integration research. Right off the bat, such research assumes dualisms between "society" and "immigrants," and one stumbles over research into the most stereotypical of assumptions regarding religion, culture, or sexuality. Most problematic is the one-sided nature of this research, which is fixated upon immigrants only. The very notions of "benchmarks" and of "normal standards" that are so thoroughly suffused throughout empirical research of immigrant integration are highly normative constructs. Social science thereby follows in the footsteps of Durkheim, for whom integration was a political problem, or a problem whose solution was political (Nassehi 2006: 328). Interestingly, the use of counterfactual notions of society should be highly problematic for social science, as it thereby necessarily moves into a realm in which no empirical truth claims can hold. In this case, however, the counterfactual nature of the concepts used allows for their connection to a broader field of programs of problematization. What the social science of immigrant integration contributes to is the *purification of society*. It imagines society as a pure domain, which has no problems, since all its problems are part of its "outside." The use of counterfactual concepts indeed allows one to not stick to the facts. The conclusion must be that "society" is, in our times, a shrinking domain. Any social problem can now be coded in terms of "integration" and can thereby be relegated to an outside. The consequence of the purification performed by "immigrant integration" is that the fiction of "society" is plausibilized, but it is also increasingly marginalized. The day is to come when social scientists find out that "society" has ceased to exist because everyone deviates from the norms that supposedly define its membership. Until that day, social science does its part in contributing to the fiction function of the medium of society.

That is clearly a very *public role for social science*. But it is a role that, as previous chapters illustrated, runs parallel to prevailing (political) discourse in far too many ways. In particular the focus on the failures of "multiculturalism," and on the "effects" of "culture" and "ethnicity," as well as the concluding problematization of "immigrant integration" run parallel to a (bio)political agenda. The individualization of immigrant integration and its asymmetric dispensation run counter to making it, in Wright Mills's terms, a public issue. The social science of "integration," and specifically the research quangos involved therein, play a crucial role in fixing the opposition between "society" (where public issues reside) and the "outside society" (where private troubles abound). They function as what Latour (1987: 232–243) has called "centers of calculation." But they are influential to the extent that they feed into and are often connected to policy and political debate. They are sites for the *professionalized visualization or articulation of society* and could be called "ocular centers." The presence of their classificatory schemes in public discourse has by now made it nearly impossible – whatever one's political conviction – not to assume that "immigrants" are somehow at a remove from "society." They make both realms (inside/outside society) measurable and quantifiable, and they thereby make "society" observable my rendering its moral antipode identifiable. Integration research is the postcolonial equivalent "at home" of the Enlightenment and Romantic European travel writer, who, without much reflexive awareness, went abroad to document the exotic otherness of colonial subjects (see Thompson 2011).

To a surprising degree, then, this public role still very much appears in-line with the work of those critiqued by Wright Mills as "social pathologists." It is instructive to recall his critique of the concepts of "society" and "American culture" these scientists used from Chapter 3:

> The terms represent undifferential entities. Whatever they may indicate, it is systematically homogeneous. Uncritical use of such a term as "the" permits a writer the hidden assumption in politically crucial contexts of a homogeneous and harmonious whole. The large texture of "the society" will take care of itself, it is somehow and in the long run harmonious, it has a "strain toward consistency" running through it; or, if not this, then only co-operation of all is needed, or perhaps even a right moral feeling is taken as a solution. (Wright Mills 1969: 538)

When "social pathologists" or, in our day, social scientists measuring "immigrant integration" evaluate results, what happens is that "evaluations are ... translated into a time sequence; cultural lag is an assertion of unequal 'progress'" (Wright Mills 1969: 545). As we have seen, the difference is not only a temporal one (although the deferral of entry into "society" is potentially endless). It is also a spatial one, positing "immigrants" at a certain "distance from society." Mill's critique of "social pathologists" is especially striking when he states: "Social and moral elements are masked by a quasi-biological meaning of the term 'adaptation.' ... The idea of adjustment seems to be most directly applicable to a social scene in which, on the one hand, there is a society and, on the other, an individual immigrant" (549–550).

Similarly, this is reminiscent of the roots of social science in what Foucault (1994) called "social medicine." This, too, amounted to a strong public role, but it is not the public sociology that has more recently been promoted by people such as Michael Burawoy (2005), much inspired by the example of Wright Mills. What other public role is there for social science? No doubt the measurement of immigrant integration will continue despite the arguments against it, so what remains? What remains is the recognition, first of all, of the existence of a variety of publics. "The" public, like "society," doesn't exist as such. Publics need to be mobilized. Connections need to be forged, just as networks like the institutional networks between research quangos and policy makers need to be maintained. A public social science should therefore not pretend to be speaking to (or worse: for) "the public," but it should recognize that its own fragmented nature – for instance, between positivist integration measurement and critical social theory – can and needs to be expressed in connection with a variety of publics. Internal social scientific struggle and conflict can be translated into public struggle and conflict, thereby empowering those who struggle with classification schemes that tie them down to ethnic categories at an a priori remove from the true center of social life: "society." In my own experience with interventions in Dutch and Belgian (Flemish) public debate, what is striking is the number of people who feel that a thorough critique of dominant classifications and modes of discourse, for instance, by pointing out the contradictions and the logical frictions in conceptions of "immigrant integration," really helps them in coming to grips with a social imagination many experience as crippling. In many instances, people have come up to me after lecturing on the topics in this book saying they felt this gave them "ammunition" or "tools to understand their situation." For instance, people of immigrant descent, or people in "mixed marriages," who daily struggle with classifications that have become so pervasive they had stopped reading newspaper or watching the news often feel happy that social science can also deliver this kind of contribution. Publics emerge when knowledge controversies emerge. That means the internal schisms of social science need to be much more publicly visible. Critical social science is not only, as Burawoy assumes, an internal critique of social science (Calhoun 2005), but it has a much wider public contribution as a social critique that provides tools for alternative understandings outside dominant classificatory schemes.

Today, the problematization of immigrant integration is one of the most prominent ways of pointing at society and of thus mobilizing the medium of social sorting that society constitutes. There is an old Chinese saying that when a finger points at the moon, only the fool looks at the finger. But when the object of reference is of the fiction of "society," I prefer to be the fool. The social scientist must strive to be this public fool who, when people and politicians alike decree that "something really needs to be done about the integration of Muslims in society," continuously asks what that "society" was before we started talking about "integration" into it.

The Public versus the Nation: Immigrant Integration and the Emergence of Neonationalism in Western Europe

There is one public that figures prominently in integration discourses. Whenever "society" is at stake, it is always the *national society*, whatever relation this bears to nation-states in their formal sense. Fixating "society" is also a way of fixing the nation as a public. Throughout Western Europe, the preoccupation with immigrant integration has highly nationalist overtones. In France, the construction of a ministry connecting the issue with "national identity" was, of course, the most obvious sign of this. But everywhere, from Denmark to Austria, from France to the United Kingdom, nationalist political parties have done their share in putting and keeping immigrant integration at the top of the political agenda. In Belgium, the Flemish Bloc is an early example, beginning to be relevant in 1991. In Italy, Forza Italia, the Lega Nord, and the National Alliance have been influential. Austria has seen the rise of the Freedom Party, and Denmark and the Netherlands have been governed with necessary parliamentary support of extreme right parties. Moreover, Eastern European countries such as Czechia, Slovakia, and Hungary have seen the rise of right-wing nationalist parties. Not all these parties are on the political far right in the traditional sense. Some combine anti-immigrant stances with rather socialist proposals concerning issues of economic redistribution. Most have cast off their quasi-fascist characteristics, interestingly by redirecting anti-Semitism from targeting Jews to targeting Muslims, up until the point that the Front National and the Flemish Bloc took on Jews as prominent members because Israel could be regarded as a front-ally in the real battle of civilizations (Bunzl 2007: 42–43). Dutch populist politician Geert Wilders, for instance, is an unconditional supporter of Israel and its politics, and he holds that "Islam" is a "fascist" religion. Moreover, anti-immigration stances are usually combined with a strong emphasis on immigrant integration. This is interesting not because one might expect nationalists to oppose integration. The whole point of emphasizing "integration" is to *create* a gap that "integration" then supposedly bridges. In other words: the problematization of integration *plausibilizes* society, it does not *problematize* it, not even from a nationalist point of view. But it is important not to be blinded by the rise of anti-immigration parties and movements. The problematization of immigrant integration occurs in all political parties, from the left to the right. Long before the declarations on the "failure of multiculturalism," with which I opened this book, regular political parties were involved in defining goals of immigrant integration, in setting up debates on the issue, and in thereby rendering immigrants and their children visible as not properly a part of society. An exclusive focus on political extremes in this sense blots out the extremism of everyday taken-for-granted conceptions of "immigrant integration" from view.

Crucially, I have argued that what is at stake throughout Western Europe is the nineteenth-century notion of the *national society*, even when the substance of the "national" has been imagined as supranational (i.e., as "Western," "liberal," "European," "cosmopolitan," or "universal"). It is the nationalized imagination of society that immigrant integration helps reproduce, stabilize, and generalize. Interestingly, while each political context has thus sought to purify a national image of society, all have done very similar things. There is a strong analogy to the nationalism of the nineteenth century here. In his book on the subject, Calhoun notes how nationalism was something very international (1997: 20). It took place nearly everywhere and was thus a near-universal process of claiming particularity. And yet there is also a crucial difference between the nationalism of the nineteenth century and what happens in Western Europe (though not only there) today. Nationalism in the nineteenth century consisted largely of efforts at creating the nation, at rendering "the nation" plausible as a confiction. Eugen Weber (1976) has, for instance, analyzed how in the nineteenth century in France, an awareness of such a thing as a nation was raised and how "peasants" were turned "into Frenchmen." In Germany, therefore, Fichte's *Reden an die deutsche Nation* can be seen as an attempt to arouse awareness of nationality. Fichte called upon the nation, which didn't yet exist, to come into being (Sloterdijk 1998).

Western European neonationalism of the early twenty-first century in a sense traces an opposite path: it *defends* a nation that is presupposed to still exist in unscathed and relatively unchanged form. It is equally performative in the credibility that it is at times able to lend to such conceptions of the nation, but it is performative not with a view to *create* but to *preserve*. Current nationalism, which is therefore better called *neonationalism*, therefore differs radically in that it does not seek to construe the very plausibility of such a thing as a nation or a national society in the first place. It rather assumes the unquestionable exitence of such a national society, which it at the same time deems threatened and to whose rescue and defense it comes. Rather than, for the first time, construing the national society, it is involved in ensuring its confictive reproduction, stabilization, and generalization. It defends the nation from intrusions from outside, instead of having to align relations from the inside in order for there to even be a plausible confiction as "nation." That is why neonationalism becomes most explicit in issues concerning immigrant integration. It concerns the *defense* of the national society, which considers itself threatened. The "nation" assumed to overlap with "society" can only ever exist in the form of *paranoia*. Neonationalism constructs the nation by defending it, instead of by construing it for the first time. Neonationalism can, with plausibility, claim the prior existence of the nation. It does not have to promote the very awareness of a thing called "nation." What it does in defending it is to claim the overlap between the nation and society. So the discourse of nationalism is one way of interpreting what happens in immigrant integration discourses. But rather than in the nineteenth century, the "springtime of nations," it concerns a neonationalism that imagines an *overlap between society and the nation*. It defines society as a national society, and it subsequently defines society in cultural, often culturist, terms. Especially in contexts where explicit nationalism is often shrugged at, such as the Low Countries and the Scandinavian countries, and also, for different reasons, in Germany, it can thus depart with an overtly nationalist discourse in which the nation is glorified. But at the same time, it can assume a fictive overlap between nation and society, and, through a proto-scientific conceptualization in terms of immigrant integration and its requirements, it can prop up an image of the national society as defined by certain cultural habits and histories. The programs of modernity, citizenship, and culture amply provide themes that can be presented as "modern" and universal, exactly when defining particularist identities of national societies.

In contemporary Western Europe, what we see occurring is the staunch defence of the national society, coined out of an imagination that only really came into being in the eighteenth and nineteenth century but informed by an organicist imagination many centuries older. It involves the imagination of an overlap between nation and society, in which "nation" gives plausibility to the cultural boundaries of "society" even when it is, itself, defined by allusion to supranational idea(l)s (Westernness, Enlightenment, cosmopolitanism, and the like). This imagination is informed by a drive toward purification that holds that, regardless of the presence of immigrants and their children, "society" is really only that which conforms to a counterfactual ideal of a unified culture, an unequivocal citizenship and a universal modernity. Discourses of immigrant integration are the most significant neonationalist discourses occurring today. They involve purifying the fiction that is "society" from all that does not conform to the counterfactual fantasies emerging in the programs of culture, modernity, and citizenship. For social science, the task remains to rigorously analyze such imaginaries, and to vigorously resist becoming its agent.

The public role of social science, then, lies in the illustration of the contingency of conceptions of immigrant integration and of articulations of national societies. The many publics of social science extend beyond social science itself and policy, but include the immigrants whose integration is currently measured. Rather than assuming society to remain unchanged after their arrival (and "measure" their "distance to society"), a public social science recognizes that society is the result of a struggle between a variety of publics. That is what debates over multiculturalism primarily illustrate. A public social science does not only take sides by either incorporating policy conceptions of integration and citizenship or endorsing some version of multiculturalism. Rather, it provides all publics with the materials to recognize the contingency of their own position. Dominant social imaginaries are contingent actualizations of the real that tend to get naturalized and totalized. The task of social science is to contribute to the imagination of alternatives.

Bibliography

Abbott, A. 2001. *Time Matters: On Theory and Method*. Chicago: University of Chicago Press.

Abu-Lugod, L. 1986. *Veiled Sentiments: Honor and Poetry in a Bedouin Society*. Berkeley: University of California Press.

2006 [1991]. "Writing against Culture," in H. L. Moore and T. Sanders (eds.), *Anthropology in Theory: Issues in Epistemology*, pp. 466–479. Oxford: Blackwell.

Agamben, G. 1996. "Beyond Human Rights," in P. Virno and M. Hardt (eds.), *Radical Thought in Italy: A Potential Politics*, pp. 159–165. Minneapolis: University of Minnesota Press.

1998. *Homo Sacer: Sovereign Power and Bare Life*. Stanford: Stanford University Press.

Akan, M. 2009. "Laïcité and Multiculturalism: The Stasi Report in Context," *British Journal of Sociology* 60(2): 237–256.

Ali, S. and B. Gidley 2014. *Advancing Outcomes for All Minorities: Experiences of Mainstreaming Immigrant Integration Policy in the United Kingdom*. Brussels: Migration Policy Institute Europe.

Amiraux, V. and P. Simon 2006. "There Are No Minorities Here: Cultures of Scholarship and Public Debate on Immigrants and Integration in France," *International Journal of Comparative Sociology* 47(3–4): 191–215.

Anderson, B. 1991. *Imagined Communities: Reflections on the Origin and Spread of Nationalism*. London: Verso.

Appadurai, A. 1996. *Modernity at Large: Cultural Dimensions of Globalization*. Minneapolis: University of Minnesota Press.

Appiah, K. A. 1992. *In My Father's House: Africa in the Philosophy of Culture*. New York: Oxford University Press.

Arendt, H. 1978. *The Origins of Totalitarianism*. New York: Harcourt & Brace.

Aristotle 2013. *Politics*. Chicago: University of Chicago Press.

Asad, T. 2003. *Formations of the Secular: Christianity, Islam, Modernity*. Stanford: Stanford University Press.

Augé, M. 1999. *A Sense for the Other: The Timeliness and Relevance of Anthropology*. Stanford: Stanford University Press.

Augustine 1972. *The City of God*. Harmondsworth: Penguin.

Aumüller, J. 2009. *Assimilation: Kontroversen um ein migrationspolitisches Konzept*. Bielefeld: Transcript.

Back, L. , M. Keith, A. Khan, K. Shukra, and J. Solomos 2002. "The Return of Assimilationism: Race, Multiculturalism and New Labour," *Sociological Research Online* 7(2): www.socresonline.org.uk/7/2/back.html.

Badiou, A. 2005a. *Metapolitics*. London: Verso.

2005b. *Being and Event*. London: Continuum.

Baldwin, J. 1998. "The Fire Next Time," in *Collected Essays*, pp. 291–348. New York: Literary Classics of the United States.

Balibar, E. 1988. "Propositions on Citizenship," *Ethics* 98: 723–730.

1991. "Is There a Neo-Racism?" in E. Balibar and I. Wallerstein (eds.), *Race, Nation, Class: Ambiguous Identities*, pp. 17–28. London: Verso.

2002. *Droit de cité*. Paris: Presses Universitaires de France.

2004. *We, the People of Europe: Reflections on Transnational Citizenship*. Princeton: Princeton University Press.

Banton, M. 1977. *The Idea of Race*. London: Tavistock.

Barker, M. 1981. *The New Racism: Conservatives and the Ideology of the Tribe*. Frederick, MD: Aletheia Books.

Barsch, A. and P. M. Hejl (eds.) 2000. *Menschenbilder: Zur Pluralisierung der Vorstellung von der menschlichen Natur (1850–1914)*. Frankfurt am Main: Suhrkamp.

Bauböck, R. (ed.) 1994. *From Aliens to Citizens: Redefining the Status of Citizens in Europe*. Avebury: Aldershot.

Bauman, Z. 1989. *De moderne tijd en de holocaust*. Amsterdam: Boom.

1992. *Intimations of Postmodernity*. London: Routledge.

1996. *Contesting Culture: Discourses of Identity in Multi-ethnic London*. Cambridge: Cambridge University Press.

Beck, U. 2002a. *Macht und Gegenmacht im globalen Zeitalter: Neue weltpolitische Ökonomie*. Frankfurt am Main: Suhrkamp.

2002b. "The Terrorist Threat: World Risk Society Revisited," *Theory, Culture & Society* 19(4): 39–55.

Benz, W. and J. Houwink ten Cate (eds.) 1998. *Die Bürokratie der Okkupation: Strukturen der Herrschaft und Verwaltung im besetzten Europa*. Berlin: Metropol.

Benz, W., J. Houwink ten Cate, and G. Otto 1998. *Die Bürokratie der Okkupation: Strukturen der Herrschaft und Verwaltung im besetzten Europa*. Berlin: Metropol.

Benhabib, S. 2004. *The Rights of Others: Aliens, Residents and Citizens*. Cambridge: Cambridge University Press.

Berg, L. van den et al. 2006. *The Safe City: Safety and Urban Development in European Cities*. London: Ashgate.

Berg, M. A. van den and W. Schinkel 2009. "'Women from the Catacombs of the City.' Gender Notions in Dutch Culturist Discourse," *Innovation: European Journal of Social Science Research* 22(4): 393–410.

Berghe, P. L. van den 1968. *Race and Racism: A Comparative Perspective.* New York: Wiley.

    1970. *Race and Ethnicity: Essays in Comparative Sociology.* New York: Basic Books.

Bertossi, C. 2011. "National Models of Integration in Europe: A Comparative and Critical Analysis," *American Behavioral Scientist* 55(12): 1561–1580.

Bijl, R. and A. Verweij (eds.) 2012. *Measuring and Monitoring Immigrant Integration in Europe.* The Hague: SCP.

Bjornson, M. 2007. "Speaking of Citizenship: Language Ideologies in Dutch Citizenship Regimes," *Focaal – European Journal of Anthropology* 49: 65–80.

Black, A. 2001. *The History of Islamic Political Thought: From the Prophet to the Present.* Edinburgh: Edinburgh University Press.

Blackburn, R. 1997. *The Making of New World Slavery: From the Baroque to the Modern, 1492–1800.* London: Verso.

Blanchot, M. 1988. *L'espace littéraire.* Paris: Gallimard.

Blau, P. 1977. *Inequality and Heterogeneity: A Primitive Theory of Social Structure.* New York: Free Press.

Blom, J. C. H. 1989. "The Persecution of the Jews in the Netherlands: A Comparative Western European Perspective," *European History Quarterly* 19: 333–351.

Boas, F. 1910. "The Real Race Problem," *Crisis* 1(December): 22–25.

    1928. *Anthropology and Modern Life.* Mineola, NY: New York.

Boersma, S. and W. Schinkel 2015. "Imagining Society: Logics of Visualization in Images of Immigrant Integration," *Environment and Planning D: Society and Space* 33(6): 1043–1062.

Bogardus, E. 1925. "Social Distance and Its Origins," *Journal of Applied Sociology* 9: 216–226.

Bommes, M. 1996. "Die Beobachtung von Kultur," in C. Klingemann et al. (eds.), *Jahrbuch für Soziologiegeschichte 1994*, pp. 205–226. Springer.

Bosniak, L. 2006. *The Citizen and the Alien: Dilemmas of Contemporary Membership.* Princeton: Princeton University Press.

Boswell, C. 2009. *The Political Uses of Expert Knowledge: Immigration Policy and Social Research.* Cambridge: Cambridge University Press.

Bourdieu, P. 1975. "Méthode scientifique et hiérarchie sociale des objets," *Actes de la recherche en sciences sociales* 1(1): 4–6.

    1982. *Ce que parler veut dire: L'économie des échanges linguistiques.* Paris: Fayard.

Bowen, J. R. 2007a. A View from France on the Internal Complexity of National Models," *Journal of Ethnic and Migration Studies* **33**(6): 1003–1016.

2007b. *Why the French Don't Like Headscarves: Islam, the State, and Public Space*. Princeton: Princeton University Press.

Bracke, S. and N. Fadil 2009. "Tussen dogma en Realiteit: Secularisme, multiculturalisme en nationalisme in Vlaanderen," in K. Arnout et al. (eds.), *Een leeuw in een kooi: De grenzen van het multiculturele Vlaanderen*, pp. 93–110. Antwerp: Meulenhoff.

Brouwer, A. 2006. *Groene Amsterdammer* **130**(23), June 9: 5.

Brown, W. 2006a. *Regulating Aversion: Tolerance in the Age of Identity and Empire*. Princeton: Princeton University Press.

2006b. "American Nightmare: Neoliberalism, Neoconservatism, and De-Democratization," *Political Theory* **34**(6): 690–714.

Brubaker, R. 1989. *Immigration and the Politics of Citizenship in Europe and America*. Lanham, MD: University Press of America.

2001. "The Return of Assimilation?" *Ethnic and Racial Studies* **24**(4): 531–548.

2012. "Categories of Analysis and Categories of Practice: A Note on the Study of Muslims in European Countries of Immigration," *Ethnic and Racial Studies*, pp. 1–8.

Buck-Morss, S. 2000. *Dreamworld and Catastrophe: The Passing of Mass Utopia in East and West*. Cambridge, Mass. : MIT Press.

Bunzl, M. 2007. *Anti-Semitism and Islamophobia: Hatreds Old and New in Europe*. Chicago: Prickly Paradigm Press.

Burawoy, M. 2005. "2004 American Sociological Association Presidential Address: For Public Sociology," *British Journal of Sociology* **56**(2): 259–294.

Burguière, A. et al. (eds.) 1996. *A History of the Family*, 2 vols. Cambridge, Mass. : Belknap Harvard.

Buruma, I. 2006. *Murder in Amsterdam: The Death of Theo van Gogh and the Limits of Tolerance*. London: Penguin.

Bussemaker, J. 1998. "Vocabularies of Citizenship and Gender: The Netherlands," *Critical Social Policy* **18**(56): 333–354.

Butler, J. 2007. *Opgefokte taal: Een politiek van de performatief*. Amsterdam: Parrèsia.

2010. *Frames of War: When Is Life Grievable?* London: Verso.

Caillé, A. 2007. "Introduction to Symposium," *European Journal of Social Theory* **10**(2): 179–183.

Caldwell, C. 2009. *Reflections on the Revolution in Europe: Immigration, Islam and the West*. New York: Anchor Books.

Calhoun, C. 1995. *Critical Social Theory: Culture, History, and the Challenge of Difference*. Oxford: Blackwell.

1997. *Nationalism*. Minneapolis: University of Minnesota Press.

2003. "'Belonging' in the Cosmopolitan Imaginary," *Ethnicities* 3(4): 531–568.

2005. "The Promise of Public Sociology," *British Journal of Sociology* 56(3): 355–362.

2009. "Cosmopolitanism and Nationalism," in W. Schinkel (ed.), *Globalization and the State: Sociological Perspectives on the State of the State*, pp. 209–242.

Calhoun, C., M. Juergensmeyer, and J. VanAntwerpen (eds.) 2009. *Rethinking Secularism*. Oxford: Oxford University Press.

Cameron, D. 2011. "Speech at Munich Security Conference," www.british politicalspeech.org/speech-archive.htm?speech=329.

Carter, R. 2007. "Genes, Genomes and Genealogies: The Return of Scientific Racism?" *Ethnic and Racial Studies* 30(4): 546–556.

Casey, E. S. 2000. *Imagining: A Phenomenological Study*. Bloomington: Indiana University Press.

Castles, S. 2000. *Ethnicity and Globalization: From Migrant Worker to Transnational Citizen*. London: Sage.

Castles, S. and M. J. Miller 2003. *The Age of Migration: International Population Movements in the Modern World*. Basingstoke: Palgrave Macmillan.

Castoriadis, C. 1987. *The Imaginary Constitution of Society*. Cambridge: Polity Press.

1997. "Reflections on Racism," in *World in Fragments*, pp. 19–31. Stanford: Stanford University Press.

Cavalli-Sforza, L. L. 2000. *Genes, Peoples, and Languages*. New York: North Point Press.

CBS 2008. "Minder migratiehuwelijken Turken en Marokkanen," Webmagazine CBS: www.cbs.nl/nl-NL/menu/themas/dossiers/allochtonen/publi caties/artikelen/archief/2008/2008-2350-wm.htm (accessed September 7, 2015).

2014. *Jaarrapport Integratie 2014*. The Hague/Heerlen: Centraal Bureau voor de Statistiek.

CBS & WODC 2006. *Integratiekaart 2006*. The Hague: WODC.

Claessens, D. and K. Claessens 1979. *Kapitalismus als Kultur: Enstehung und Grundlagen der bürgerlichen Gesellschaft*. Frankfurt am Main: Suhrkamp.

Cliteur, P. 2007. *Moreel Esperanto: Naar een autonome ethiek*. Amsterdam: Arbeiderspers.

Collins, R. 2004. "Rituals of Solidarity and Security in the Wake of a Terrorist Attack," *Sociological Theory* 22(1): 53–87.

Comaroff, J. L. and J. Comaroff 2009. *Ethnicity, Inc.* Chicago: University of Chicago Press.

Dagevos, J. M., J. Iedema, and R. Schellingerhout 2005. "Gescheiden Werelden? De Etnische Signatuur van Vrijetijdscontacten van Minderheden," *Sociologie* 1: 52–69.

Dean, M. 1999. *Governmentality: Power and Rule in Modern Society.* Los Angeles: Sage.

2007. *Governing Societies: Political Perspectives on Domestic and International Rule.* Maidenhead: Open University Press.

Debord, G. 1994. *The Society of the Spectacle.* New York: Zone Books.

Delanty, G. 2007. "European Citizenship: A Critical Assessment," *Citizenship Studies* 11(3): 64–72.

Deleuze, G. 1966. *Le bergsonisme.* Paris: Presses Universitaires de France.

Derrida, J. 1974. *Of Grammatology.* Baltimore: Johns Hopkins University Press.

Derrida, J. 1981. "Plato's Pharmacy," in *Dissemination*, pp. 67–186. London: Continuum.

2003. "Autoimmunity: Real and Symbolic Suicides," in G. Borradori (ed.), *Philosophy in a Time of Terror: Dialogues with Jürgen Habermas and Jacques Derrida.* Chicago: University of Chicago Press.

2005. *Rogues: Two Essays on Reason.* Stanford: Stanford University Press.

Dewey, J. 1950. *Reconstruction in Philosophy.* New York: Random House.

Dijk, T. A. van 2002a. "Denying Racism: Elite Discourse and Racism," in P.Essed and D. T. Goldberg (eds.). *Race Critical Theories*, pp. 307–324. Oxford: Blackwell.

2002b. "Reflections on 'Denying Racism: Elite Discourse and Racism'," in P. Essed and D. T. Goldberg (eds.). *Race Critical Theories*, pp. 481–485. Oxford: Blackwell.

Douglas, M. 1966. *Purity and Danger: An Analysis of Concepts of Pollution and Taboo.* London: Routledge.

1996. *Natural Symbols: Explorations in Cosmology.* London: Routledge.

Dower, N. 2000. "The Idea of Global Citizenship – A Sympathetic Assessment," *Global Society* 14(4): 553–567.

Drachsler, J. 1921. *Intermarriage in New York City.* New York: Columbia University Press.

Driouichi, F. 2007. *De casus Inburgering en Nationaliteitswetgeving.* Amsterdam: Amsterdam University Press.

Dunn, J. 2005. *Setting the People Free: The Story of Democracy.* London: Atlantic Books.

Dutch Cabinet 2011. *Integratienota Integratie, binding, burgerschap*. The Hague.

2013. *Agenda integratie*. The Hague.

Duyvendak, J. W. and J. Uitermark 2006. *Ruimte maken voor straatburgerschap. Sociale Integratie ... straataanpak in de praktijk. Essay Mensen Maken de Stad*. Rotterdam: Project Sociale Integratie.

Duyvendak, W. G. J. and P. W. A. Scholten 2011. "Beyond National Models of Integration: The Coproduction of Integration Policy Frames in the Netherlands," *Journal of International Migration and Integration* 13(1).

Eberhardt, J. L. 2005. "Imagining Race," *American Psychologist* 60(2): 181–190.

ECRI 2008. *Third Report on the Netherlands*. Strasbourg: Council of Europe.

Elias, N. 1982. *Problemen van betrokkenheid en distantie*. Amsterdam: Meulenhoff.

Engbersen, G. B. M. and R. Gabriëls (eds.) 1995. *Sferen van integratie: Naar een gedifferentieerd allochtonenbeleid*. Amsterdam: Boom.

Engbersen, G. and J. de Haan 2006. "Sociologische perspectieven in de Nederlandse sociologie," in G. Engbersen and J. de Haan (eds.). *Balans en toekomst van de sociologie*. Amsterdam: Pallas Publications.

Entzinger, H. 1984. *Het Minderhedenbeleid*. Amsterdam: Boom.

2003. "The Rise and Fall of Multiculturalism: The Case of the Netherlands," in *Towards Assimilation and Citizenship: Immigrants in Liberal Nation-States*, pp. 59–86. Basingstoke: Palgrave Macmillan.

Erlanger, S. 2011. "Amid Rise of Multiculturalism, Dutch Confront Their Questions of Identity," *The New York Times*, August 14, p. A6.

Ersanilli, E. and R. Koopmans 2010. "Rewarding Integration? Citizenship Regulations and the Socio-Cultural Integration of Immigrants in the Netherlands, France and Germany," *Journal of Ethnic and Migration Studies* 36(5): 773–791.

Esposito, J. L. 2005. *Islam: The Straight Path*. Oxford: Oxford University Press.

Essed, P. 1991. *Understanding Everyday Racism: An Interdisciplinary Theory*. Newbury Park: Sage.

Essed, P. and D. T. Goldberg (eds.) 2002. *Race Critical Theories*. Oxford: Blackwell.

Essed, P. and K. Nimako 2006. "Designs and (Co)Incidents. Cultures of Scholarship and Public Policy on Immigrants/Minorities in the Netherlands," *International Journal of Comparative Sociology* 47(3–4): 281–312.

Essed, P. and S. Trienekens 2008. "'Who Wants to Feel White?' Race, Dutch Culture and Contested Identities," *Ethnic and Racial Studies* 31(1): 52–72.

Estonian Ministry of Culture 2011. *Estonian Integration Monitoring 2011*. Tartu: Praxis Center for Policy Studies, University of Tartu.

Etzioni, A. 1993. *The Spirit of Community*. New York: Crown Books.

Eyerman, R. 2008. *The Assassination of Theo van Gogh: From Social Drama to Cultural Trauma*. Durham: Duke University Press.

Ezrahi, Y. 2015. *Imagined Democracies: Necessary Political Fictions*. Cambridge: Cambridge University Press.

Falk, R. 2003. "Recasting Citizenship," in R. Robertson and K. A. White (eds.). *Globalization: Critical Concepts in Sociology, Volume III: Global Membership and Participation*, pp. 93–106. London: Routledge.

Fanon, F. 2006. *Pour la révolution africaine: Écrits politiques*. Paris: La Découverte.

Fassin, E. 2012. *Démocratie précaire*. Paris: La Découverte.

Favell, A. 2001a. "Integration Policy and Research in Europe: A Review and Critique," in T. A. Aleinikoff and D. Klusmeyer (eds.). *Citizenship Today: Global Perspectives and Practices*, pp. 349–399. Washington, DC: Brookings Institution & Carnegie Endowment for International Peace.

   2001b. *Philosophies of Integration: Immigration and the Idea of Citizenship in France and Britain*. Basingstoke: Palgrave.

   2003. "Integration Nations: The Nation-State and Research on Immigrants in Western Europe," *Comparative Social Research* 22: 13–42.

Fermin, A. 1997. *Nederlandse politieke partijen over minderhedenbeleid, 1977–1995*. Amsterdam: Thesis Publishers.

Fields, B. J. 1990. "Slavery, Race and Ideology in the United States of America," *New Left Review* 181(May/June): 95–118.

Finkielkraut, A. 1987. *La défaite de la pensée*. Paris: Gallimard.

Fiske, J. 1998. "Surveilling the City: Whiteness, the Black Man and Democratic Totalitarianism," *Theory, Culture & Society* 15(2): 67–88.

Fong, E. and W. W. Isajiw 2000. "Determinants of Friendship Choices in Multiethnic Society," *Sociological Forum* 15(2): 249–271.

Foner, N. 2005. *In a New Land: A Comparative View of Migration*. New York: NYU Press.

Fortuyn, P. 1997. *Tegen de islamitisering van onze cultuur [Against the islamicization of our culture]*. Utrecht: Bruna.

   2002a. *De puinhopen van acht jaar paars*. Uithoorn: Karakter Uitgevers.

   2002b. "Grens dicht voor islamiet," *De Volkskrant*, 9 February.

Foucault, M. 1971. *L'ordre du discours*. Paris: Gallimard.

   1976. *Histoire de la sexualité I: La volonté de savoir*. Paris: Gallimard.

1991. "Governmentality," in G. Burchell, C. Gordon, and P. Miller (eds.). *The Foucault Effect: Studies in Governmentality*, pp. 87–104. Chicago: University of Chicago Press.

1994. *Power: Essential Works of Michel Foucault 1954–1984*, Vol. 3 (ed. J. D. Faubion). London: Penguin Books.

1997a. *"Il faut défendre la société." Cours au Collège de France. 1976.* Paris: Gallimard.

1997b. "What Is Enlightenment?," in P. Rabinow (ed.). *The Foucault Reader*, pp. 32–50. New York: Pantheon Books.

2004a. *Sécurité, territoire, population: Cours au Collège de France, 1977–1978*. Paris: Seuil/Gallimard.

2004b. *Naissance de la biopolitique: Cours au Collège de France, 1978–1979*. Paris: Seuil/Gallimard.

Fraser, N. 1995. "From Redistribution to Recognition? Dilemmas of Justice in a Post-Socialist Age," *New Left Review* **212**: 68–93.

Fraser, N. and L. Gordon 1998. "Contract versus Charity: Why Is There No Social Citizenship in the United States?," in G. Shafir (ed.). *The Citizenship Debates: A Reader*. Minneapolis: University of Minnesota Press.

Frattini, F. 2007. "A Common Approach for European Policy on the Integration of Migrants – European Debate," Potsdam: Informal Meeting of EU Integration Ministers, May 10, 2007.

Fredrickson, G. M. 2002. *Racism: A Short History*. Princeton: Princeton University Press.

Fuchs, S. 2001. *Against Essentialism*. Cambridge, MA: Harvard University Press.

Fukuyama, F. 2005. "A Year of Living Dangerously," *The Wall Street Journal*, November 2.

Garfinkel, H. 1967. *Studies in Ethnomethodology*. Cambridge: Polity Press.

Garton Ash, T. 2006. "Islam in Europe," *New York Review of Books* **53**(15): 32–35.

Geertz, C. 2004. "What Is a State If It Is Not a Sovereign?," *Current Anthropology* **45**(5): 577–593.

Gellner, E. 1970. "Concepts and Society," in D. Emmett and A. Macintyre (eds.). *Sociological Theory and Philosophical Analysis*, pp. 115–149. London: Basingstoke.

Geschiere, P. 2009. *The Perils of Belonging: Autochthony, Citizenship and Exclusion in Africa and Europe*. Chicago: University of Chicago Press.

Ghorashi, H. 2003. "Ayaan Hirsi Ali: Daring or Dogmatic? Debates on Multiculturalism and Emancipation in the Netherlands." *Focaal: European Journal of Anthropology* **42**: 163–169.

Gilroy, P. 1992. "The End of Anti-Racism," in J. Donald and A. Rattansi (eds.). *"Race," Culture and Difference*. London: Sage, pp. 49–61.

2000. *Against Race: Imagining Political Culture Beyond the Colour Line.* Cambridge, MA: Harvard University Press.

Glick Schiller, N., A. Çagdar and T. C. Guldbrandsen 2008. "Beyond the Ethnic Lens: Locality, Globality, and Born-Again Incorporation," *American Ethnologist* 33(4): 612–633.

Gordon, M. M. 1964. *Assimilation in American Life: The Role of Race, Religion, and National Origins.* New York: Oxford University Press.

Gordon, P. 1989. *New Right, New Racism.* London: Searchlight.

Gorski, P. 2000. "Historicizing the Secularization Debate: Church, State and Society in Late Medieval and Early Modern Europe, ca. 1300 to 1700," *American Journal of Sociology* 65(1): 138–167.

Gossett, T. F. 1963. *Race: The History of an Idea in America.* New York: Schocken.

Gouda, F. 1995. *Dutch Culture Overseas: Colonial Practice in the Netherlands Indies 1900–1942.* Amsterdam: Amsterdam University Press.

Gowricharn, R. 1998. *Hollandse contrasten: Over de keerzijde van sociale integratie.* Apeldoorn/Leuven: Garant.

Grillo, R. 2003 "Cultural Essentialism and Cultural Anxiety," *Anthropological Theory* 3(2): 157–173.

2005. "Backlash Against Diversity? Identity and Cultural Politics in European Cities," Working Paper No. 14. Oxford: COMPAS.

2007. "An Excess of Alterity? Debating Difference in a Multicultural Society," *Ethnic and Racial Studies* 30(6): 979–998.

Guillaumin, C. 1995. *Racism, Sexism, Power and Ideology.* London: Routledge.

Gunsteren, H. R. van 1998. *A Theory of Citizenship: Organizing Plurality in Contemporary Societies.* Boulder: Westview Press.

Habermas, J. 1989 "Leefwereld en systeem," in *De nieuwe onoverzichtelijkheid en andere opstellen.* Amsterdam: Boom, pp. 148–167.

1996. *Die Einbeziehung des Anderen: Studien zur politischen Theorie.* Frankfurt am Main: Suhrkamp.

1998. *The Inclusion of the Other: Studies in Political Theory.* Cambridge, MA: MIT Press.

Hacking, I. 1990. *The Taming of Chance.* Cambridge: Cambridge University Press.

Hagelund, A. 2002. "Problematizing Culture: Discourses on Integration in Norway," *Journal of International Migration and Integration* 3(3–4): 401–415.

Hagendoorn, L., J. Veenman, and W. Vollebergh (eds.) 2003. *Integrating Immigrants in the Netherlands. Cultural versus Socio-Economic Integration.* Aldershot: Ashgate.

Hall, S. 1992. "Race, Culture, and Communications: Looking Backward and Forward at Cultural Studies," *Rethinking Marxism: A Journal of Economics, Culture & Society* 5(1): 10–18.

  1996. "New Ethnicities," in H. A. Baker, M. Diawara, and R. H. Lindeborg (eds.). *Black British Cultural Studies: A Reader*, pp. 163–172. Chicago: University of Chicago Press.

  2002. "Democracy, Globalization, and Difference," in O. Enwezor et al. (eds.): *Democracy Unrealized: Documenta11_Platform1*, pp. 21–35. Ostfildern-Ruit: Hatje Cantz.

Hammar, T. 1990. *Democracy and the Nation-State: Aliens, Denizens and Citizens in a World of International Migration*. Aldershot: Avebury.

Hartigan, J. Jr. 2005. *Odd Tribes: Toward a Cultural Analysis of White People*. Durham: Duke University Press.

Haut Conseil à l'Intégration 2009. *Études et intégration: Faire connaître les valeurs de la République: Les élus issus de l'immigration dans les conseils municipaux (2001–2008)*. Rapport au Premier Ministre.

Hegel, G. W. F. 1970. *Phänomenologie des Geistes*. Frankfurt am Main: Suhrkamp.

Heitmeyer, W. 1996. "Für türkische Jugendliche in Deutschland spielt der Islam eine wichtige Rolle," *Die Zeit* 35, August 23.

Hindess, B. 2000. "Citizenship in the International Management of Populations," *American Behavioural Scientist* 43(9): 486–97.

Hirsi Ali, A. 2002. "Integratie is een cultureel problem" [Integration Is a Cultural Problem], *NRC Handelsblad*, August 31, p. 7.

  2006. *The Caged Virgin: A Muslim Woman's Cry for Reason*. London: Free Press.

Hondius, D. 2011. "Access to the Netherlands of Enslaved and Free Black Africans: Exploring Legal and Social Historical Practices in the Sixteenth–Nineteenth Centuries," *Slavery & Abolition* 32(3): 377–395.

Hooghiemstra, E. 2003. *Trouwen over de grens: Achtergronden van partnerkeuze van Turken en Marokkanen in Nederland*. The Hague: SCP.

Horkheimer, M. and T. W. Adorno 1969. *Dialektik der Aufklärung: Philosophische Fragmente*. Frankfurt am Main: Fischer.

Houdt, F. van 2014. *Governing Citizens: The Government of Citizenship, Crime and Migration in the Netherlands*. Doctoral Dissertation, Erasmus University Rotterdam.

Houdt, F. van, S. Suvarierol, and W. Schinkel 2011. "Neoliberal Communitarian Citizenship: Current Trends towards 'Earned Citizenship' in the United Kingdom, France, and the Netherlands," *International Sociology* 26(3): 408–432.

Huis, I. van and A. de Regt 2005. "Tussen dwang en dialoog: Maatschappijoriëntatie in inburgeringscursussen," *Sociologie* 1(4): 382–406.

Huis, M. van 2007. "Partnertrends van allochtonen," *Bevolkingstrends, 4ᵉ kwartaal 2007*. CBS, pp. 25–31.

Husserl, E. 2006. *Phantasie und Bildbewußtsein*. Hamburg: Felix Meiner.

Ignazi, P. 1992. "The Silent Counter-Revolution. Hypotheses on the Emergence of Extreme Right-Wing Parties in Europe," *European Journal of Political Research* 22: 3–34.

Israel, J. I. 2001. *Radical Enlightenment: Philosophy and the Making of Modernity 1650–1750*. Oxford: Oxford University Press.

Jacobson, D. 1996. *Rights across Borders: Immigration and the Decline of Citizenship*. Baltimore: Johns Hopkins University Press.

Joppke, C. 2004. "The Retreat of Multiculturalism in the Liberal State: Theory and Policy," *British Journal of Sociology* 55(2): 237–257.

2007. "Beyond National Models: Civic Integration Policies for Immigrants in Western Europe," *West European Politics* 30(1): 1–22.

2009a. *Veil: Mirror of Identity*. Cambridge: Polity.

2009b. "Limits of Integration Policy: Britain and Her Muslims," *Journal of Ethnic and Migration Studies* 35(3): 453–472.

Kalmijn, M. and F. van Tubergen 2006. "Ethnic Intermarriage in the Netherlands: Confirmations and Refutations of Accepted Insights," *European Journal of Population* 22(4): 371–397.

Koomen, M. et al. 2013. "Discursive Framing and the Reproduction of Integration in the Public Sphere: A Comparative Analysis of France, the United Kingdom, the Netherlands and Germany," *Ethnicities* 13(2): 191–208.

Koopmans, R. 2004. "Zachte heelmeesters ... Een vergelijking van de resultaten van het Nederlandse en Duitse integratiebeleid en wat de WRR daaruit niet concludeert," *Migrantenstudies* 18(2): 87–92.

Koopmans, R. and P. Statham 2001. "How National Citizenship Shapes Transnationalism: A Comparative Analysis of Migrant Claims-Making in Germany, Great Britain and the Netherlands," *Revue Européenne des Migrations Internationales* 17(2): 63–100.

Koopmans, R. et al. 2005. *Contested Citizenship: Immigration and Cultural Diversity in Europe*. Minneapolis: University of Minnesota Press.

Koselleck, R. 1959. *Kritik und Krise: Eine Studie zur Pathogenese der bürgerlichen Welt*. Frankfurt am Main: Suhrkamp.

Kruyt, A. and J. Niessen 1997. "Integration," in H. Vermeulen (ed.). *Immigrant Policy for a Multicultural Society: A Comparative Study of Integration, Language and Religious Policy in Five Western European Countries*, pp. 15–55. Brussels: Migration Policy Group.

Kymlicka, W. 1995. *Multicultural Citizenship: A Liberal Theory of Minority Rights*. Oxford: Oxford University Press.

Kymlicka, W. and W. Norman 1994. "Return of the Citizen: A Survey of Recent Work on Citizenship Theory," *Ethics* 104(2): 352–381.

Laan Bouma-Doff, W. van der 2004. "Begrensd contact: De relatie tussen ruimtelijke segregatie van allochtonen en de mate van contact," *Mens & Maatschappij* 76(4): 348–366.

Laclau, E. 2000. "Identity and Hegemony: The Role of Universality in the Constitution of Political Logics," in J. Butler, E. Laclau, and S. Žižek. *Contingency, Hegemony, Universality: Contemporary Dialogues on the Left*, pp. 44–89. London: Verso.

Laclau, E. and C. Mouffe 2001. *Hegemony and Socialist Strategy: Towards a Radical Democratic Politics*. London: Verso.

Latour, B. 1987. *Science in Action: How to Follow Scientists and Engineers through Society*. Cambridge, MA: Harvard University Press.

1999. *Pandora's Hope: Essays on the Reality of Science Studies*. Cambridge, MA: Harvard University Press.

2004. *Politics of Nature: How to Bring the Sciences into Democracy*. Cambridge, MA: Harvard University Press.

2005. *Reassembling the Social: An Introduction to Actor-Network-Theory*. Oxford: Oxford University Press.

Law, S. 2009. "Seeing like a Survey," *Cultural Sociology* 3(2): 239–256.

Lechner, F. J. 2007a. "Redefining National Identity: Dutch Evidence on Global Patterns," *International Journal of Comparative Sociology* 48(4): 355–368.

2007b. *The Netherlands: Globalization and National Identity*. New York: Routledge.

Leeuw, M. de and S. Van Wichelen 2005. "'Please, Go and Wake Up!' Submission, Hirsi Ali and the 'War on Terror' in the Netherlands," *Feminist Media Studies* 5(3): 325–340.

Lentin, A. and G. Titley 2011. *The Crises of Multiculturalism: Racism in a Neoliberal Age*. London: Zed Books.

Lévi-Strauss, C. 1973a. *Tristes Tropiques*. Harmondsworth: Penguin.

1973b. *Structural Anthropology*, Vol. 2. Harmondsworth: Penguin.

Lijphart, A. 1975. *The Politics of Accommodation*. Berkeley: University of California Press.

Lister, R. 1998. "Vocabularies of Citizenship and Gender: The UK," *Critical Social Policy* 18(56): 309–331.

Lockwood, D. 1992. *Solidarity and Schism: 'The Problem of Disorder' in Durkheimian and Marxist Sociology*." Oxford: Clarendon Press.

Löffler, B. 2011. *Integration in Deutschland: Zwischen Assimilation und Multikulturalismus*. Munich: Oldenbourg.

Lucassen, L. and A. J. F. Köbben 1992. *Het partiële gelijk: Controverses over het onderwijs in de eigen taal en cultuur en de rol daarbij van beleid en wetenschap (1951–1991)*. Amsterdam: Swetz & Zeitlinger.

Luhmann, N. 1973. *Zweckbegriff und Systemrationalität: Über die Funktion von Zwecken in sozialen Systemen*. Frankfurt am Main: Suhrkamp.

1977. *Funktion der Religion*. Frankfurt am Main: Suhrkamp.

Luhmann, N. 1982. "The Differentiation of Society," in *The Differentiation of Society*, pp. 229–254. New York: Columbia University Press.

1984. *Soziale Systeme: Grundriß einer allgemeinen Theorie*. Frankfurt am Main: Suhrkamp.

1987. "Paradigmawechsel in der Systemtheorie: Ein Paradigma für Fortschritt?," in R. Herzog and R. Koselleck (eds.). *Epochenschwelle und Epochenbewußtsein*. Munich: Fink.

1990. *Die Wissenschaft der Gesellschaft*. Frankfurt am Main: Suhrkamp.

1991. *Soziologie des Risikos*. Berlin: Walter deGruyter.

1993. *Das Recht der Gesellschaft*. Frankfurt am Main: Suhrkamp.

1995. *Die Kunst der Gesellschaft*. Frankfurt am Main: Suhrkamp.

1997. *Die Gesellschaft der Gesellschaft*. Frankfurt am Main: Suhrkamp.

2000a. *Die Politik der Gesellschaft*. Frankfurt am Main: Suhrkamp.

2000b. *The Reality of the Mass Media*. Stanford: Stanford University Press.

2002. *Das Erziehungssystem der Gesellschaft*. Frankfurt am Main: Suhrkamp.

2004. *Ökologische Kommunikation: Kann die moderne Gesellschaft sich auf ökologische Gefährdungen einstellen?* Wiesbaden: Verlag für Sozialwissenschaften.

2005a. *Soziologische Aufklärung 1: Aufsätze zur Theorie sozialer Systeme*. Wiesbaden: Verlag für Sozialwissenschaften.

2005b. *Einführung in die Theorie der Gesellschaft*. Heidelberg: Carl Auer.

2006. *Beobachtungen der Moderne*. Wiesbaden: Verlag für Sozialwissenschaften.

Macionis, J. J. and K. Plummer 2008. *Sociology: A Global Introduction*. Essex: Pearson.

Maguire, M. W. 2006. *The Conversion of Imagination: From Pascal through Rousseau to Tocqueville*. Cambridge, MA: Harvard University Press.

Malcolm X 1964. *The Autobiography of Malcolm X: As Told to Alex Haley*. New York: Ballantine.

Marcson, S. 1950. "A Theory of Intermarriage and Assimilation," *Social Forces* **29**(1): 75–78.

Marshall, T. H. 1963. "Citizenship and Social Class," in M. S. Lipset (ed.). *Class, Citizenship, and Social Development: Essays by T. H. Marshall*, pp. 71–134. New York: Doubleday.

1992. *Citizenship and Social Class*. Concord, MA: Pluto Press.

Martinovic, B., F. Van Tubergen, and I. Maas 2009. "Changes in Immigrants' Social Integration during the Stay in the Host Country: The Case of Non-Western Immigrants in the Netherlands," *Social Science Research* **38**: 870–882.

Marx, K. and F. Engels 1969 [1848]. *Manifest der kommunistischen Partei.* Stuttgart: Reclam.

Massad, J. A. 2007. *Desiring Arabs.* Chicago: University of Chicago Press.

M'Charek, A. 2013. "Beyond Fact or Fiction: On the Materiality of Race in Practice," *Cultural Anthropology* 28(3): 420–442.

McConahay, J. B. 1986. "Modern Racism, Ambivalence, and the Modern Racism Scale," in J. Dovidio and S. Gaertner (eds.). *Prejudice, Discrimination, and Racism*, pp. 91–125. Orlando: Academic Press.

Mead, M. et al. 1968. *Science and the Concept of Race.* New York: Columbia University Press.

Mead, L. (ed.) 1997. *The New Paternalism: Supervisory Approaches to Poverty.* Washington, DC: Brookings Institution Press.

Meeteren, M. van 2005. Discoursen van integratie: De omslag in het politieke debat over integratie in Nederland. Master's thesis, Erasmus University Rotterdam.

Meeteren, M. van et al. 2008. *"Zonder Papieren." Over de positie van irreguliere migranten en de rol van het vreemdelingenbeleid in België.* Leuven: Acco.

Meier-Braun, K.-H. 2002. *Deutschland, Einwanderungsland.* Frankfurt am Main: Suhrkamp.

Merkel, A. 2010. "Sprache, Schlüssel zur Integration," from www.bundeskanzlerin.de/nn_679950/Content/DE/Artikel/2010/12/2010-12-09-integrationsbesuche-hh.html (accessed 28-04-2011; link no longer active). For a summary, see: www.bundesregierung.de/Content Archiv/DE/Archiv17/Artikel/2012/03/2012-03-08-bkin-bei-kmk.html (accessed September 7, 2015).

Merriam, C. E. 1931. *The Making of Citizens.* Chicago: University of Chicago Press.

Merton, R. K. 1968. *Social Theory and Social Structure.* New York: Free Press.

Miles, R. 1993. *Racism after "Race Relations."* London: Routledge.

Miller, P. and N. Rose 2008. *Governing the Present: Administering Economic, Social and Personal Life.* Cambridge: Polity Press.

Mills, C. W. 1969. "The Professional Ideology of Social Pathologists," in I. L. Horowitz (ed.). *Power, Politics and People*, pp. 525–552. New York: Oxford University Press.

Modood, T. 1997. "Introduction: The Politics of Multiculturalism in the New Europe," in T. Modood and P. Werbner (eds.), pp. 1–25.

2007. *Multiculturalism: A Civic Idea.* Cambridge: Polity Press.

Modood, T. and P. Werbner (eds.) 1997. *The Politics of Multiculturalism in the New Europe. Racism, Identity and Community.* London: Zed Books.

Modood, T. et al. (eds.) 2006. *Multiculturalism, Muslims and Citizenship: A European Approach*. London: Routledge.

Mouffe, C. 2005. *On the Political*. London: Routledge.

Myrdal, G. 1944. *An American Dilemma: The Negro Problem and Modern Democracy*. New York: Harper Brothers.

Nassehi, A. 2006. *Der soziologische Diskurs der Moderne*. Frankfurt am Main: Suhrkamp.

Nederveen Pieterse, J. 2001. *Development Theory: Deconstructions/Reconstructions*. London: Sage.

Netherlands Ministry of Education, Culture and Science (2008): *Gewoon homo zijn: Lesbisch- en homo-emancipatiebeleid 2008–2011*. The Hague.

Netherlands Ministry of Foreign Affairs 1994. *Contourennota Integratiebeleid Etnische Minderheden*. The Hague.

Netherlands Ministry of Interior Affairs 1994a. *Beleidsopvolging Minderhedendebat: Advies in opdracht van de Minister van Binnenlandse Zaken*. The Hague.

1994b. *Contourennota Integratiebeleid Etnische Minderheden*. The Hague.

Noordegraaf, M. 2008. "Meanings of Measurement: The Real Story behind the Rotterdam Safety Index," *Public Management Review* 10(2): 219–237.

Obdeijn, H. and M. Schrover 2008. *Komen en gaan: Immigratie en emigratie in Nederland vanaf 1950*. Amsterdam: Bert Bakker.

OECD and EU 2015. *Indicators of Immnigrant Integration 2015: Settling In*. Paris: OECD Publishing.

Omi, M. A. 2001. "The Changing Meaning of Race," in N. J. Smelser, W. J. Wilson, and F. Mitchell (eds.). *America Becoming: Racial Trends and Their Consequences*, Vol. 1. Washington, DC: National Academy Press.

Ong, A. 1996. "Cultural Citizenship as Subject-Making: Immigrants Negotiate Racial and Cultural Boundaries in the United States," *Current Anthropology* 37(5): 737–762.

Ossewaarde, R. 2006. *Eigen verantwoordelijkheid: bevrijding of beheersing?* Amsterdam: SWP.

Outhwaite, W. 2006. *The Future of Society*. Oxford: Blackwell.

Park, R. 1950 [1923]. "Our Racial Frontier on the Pacific," in E. C. Highes et al. (eds.). *Race and Culture: The Collected Papers of Robert Ezra Park*, Vol. 1, pp. 138–151. Glencoe, IL: Free Press.

Pascal, B. 1976. *Pensées*. Paris: Mercure de France.

Penninx, R. 1979. *Naar een algemeen etnisch minderhedenbeleid? Voorstudie WRR*. The Hague: Staatsuitgeverij.

Peters, B. 1993. *Die Integration moderner Gesellschaften.* Frankfurt am Main: Suhrkamp.

Phalet, K. and M. Swyngedouw 2003. "Measuring Immigrant Integration: The Case of Belgium," *Migration Studies* 40(152): 773–803.

Phillips, A. 2007. *Multiculturalism without Culture.* Princeton: Princeton University Press.

Plato 2003. *The Republic.* London: Penguin.

Poggi, G. 1965. "A Main Theme of Contemporary Sociological Analysis: Its Achievements and Limitations," *British Journal of Sociology* 16(4): 283–294.

Policar, A. 1990. "Racism and Its Mirror Image," *Telos* 83: 88–108.

Prak, M. 1997. "Burghers into Citizens: Urban and National Citizenship in the Netherlands during the Revolutionary Era (c. 1800)," *Theory & Society* 26(4): 403–420.

Pred, A. 2000. *Even in Sweden: Racisms, Racialized Spaces, and the Popular Geographical Imagination.* Berkeley: University of California Press.

Prins, B. 2000. *Voorbij de onschuld: Het debat over integratie in Nederland.* Amsterdam: Van Gennep.

Putnam, R. D. 2000. *Bowling Alone: The Collapse and Revival of American Community.* New York: Simon & Schuster.

Putnam, R. D. et al. 1993. *Making Democracy Work: Civic Traditions in Modern Italy.* Princeton: Princeton University Press.

Putten, N. van 2006. *Terug naar de stad: Een kleine geschiedenis van het grotestedenbeleid (Back to the City: A Brief History of the Large Cities Policy).* The Hague: Ministerie van Binnenlandse Zaken en Koninkrijksrelaties, Directie Grotestedenbeleid en Interbestuurlijke Betrekkingen.

Radcliffe-Brown, A. R. 1961. *Structure and Function in Primitive Societies.* New York: Free Press.

Rawls, J. 1993. *Political Liberalism.* New York: Columbia University Press.

Reekum, R. van 2014. *Out of Character: Debating Dutchness, Narrating Citizenship.* Doctoral Dissertation, University of Amsterdam.

Reekum, R. van, J. W. Duyvendak, and C. Bertossi 2012. "National Models of Integration and the Crisis of Multiculturalism: A Critical Comparative Perspective," *Patterns of Prejudice* 46(5): 417–426.

Robertson, R. 1995. Glocalization: Time-Space and Homogeneity-Heterogeneity, in M. Featherstone, S. Lash, and R. Robertson (eds.) *Global Modernities,* pp. 25–44. London: Sage.

Romeyn, E. 2014. "Anti-Semitism and Islamophobia: Spectropolitics and Immigration," *Theory, Culture & Society* 31(6): 77–101.

Roodenburg, H. , R. Euwals, and H. Rele 2003. "The New Second Generation: Segmented Assimilation and Its Variants among Post-1965 Immigrant Youth," *Annals* 530: 74–96.

Rose, N. 1994. "Medicine, History and the Present," in C. Jones and R. Porter (eds.). *Reassessing Foucault: Power, Medicine and the Body*, pp. 48–72. London: Routledge.

Rosenberg, N. et al. 2002. "Genetic Structure of Human Populations," *Science* 298: 2381–2385.

Rotterdam City Council 2003. *Rotterdam zet door: Op weg naar een stad in balans*. Rotterdam: Gemeente Rotterdam.

2006. *Rotterdamse Burgerschapscode (Rotterdam Citizenship Code)*. Rotterdam.

Runnymede Trust Commission 2000. *The Future of Multi-Ethnic Britain*. London: Profile.

Ruthven, M. 2004. *Fundamentalism: The Search for Meaning*. Oxford: Oxford University Press.

Said, E. W. 2003. *Orientalism*. London: Penguin.

San, M. van 1998. *Stelen en steken: Delinquent gedrag van Curaçaose jongens in Nederland*. Amsterdam: Amsterdam University Press.

Sand, J. 2003. *House and Home in Modern Japan: Architecture, Domestic Space, and Bourgeois Culture, 1880–1930*. Cambridge, MA: Harvard University Asia Center.

Sand, S. 2011. *Die Erfindung des Jüdischen Volkes: Israels Gründungs-mythos auf dem Prüfstand*. Berlin: List Verlag.

Sassen, S. 2006. *Territory, Authority, Rights: From Medieval to Global Assemblages*. Princeton: Princeton University Press.

Scheffer, P. 2000. "Het multiculturele drama," *NRC Handelsblad*, January 29.

Schinkel, W. 2007a. *Denken in een tijd van sociale hypochondrie: Aanzet tot een theorie voorbij de maatschappij*. Kampen: Klement.

2007b. "Sociological Discourse of the Relational: The Cases of Bourdieu & Latour," *Sociological Review* 55(4): 707–729.

2009. *Globalization and the State: Sociological Perspectives on the State of the State*. Basingstoke: Palgrave Macmillan.

2010. "From Zoèpolitics to Biopolitics: Citizenship and the Construction of Society," *European Journal of Social Theory* 13(2): 155–172.

2012. *De nieuwe democratie: Naar andere vormen van politiek*. Amsterdam: De Bezige Bij.

2015. "Woorden zijn maar woorden," *De Groene Amsterdammer* 139(4): 22–25.

Schinkel, W. and M. A. van den Berg 2011. "City of Exception: The Dutch Revanchist City and the Urban *Homo Sacer*," *Antipode* 43(5): 1911–1938.

Schinkel, W. and F. Van Houdt 2010. "The Double Helix of Cultural Assimilationism and Neoliberalism: Citizenship in Contemporary Governmentality," *British Journal of Sociology* 61(4): 696–715.

Schmitt, C. 2002. *Der Begriff des Politischen.* Berlin: Duncker & Humblot.

Schnapper, D. 2003. *La communauté des citoyens.* Paris: Gallimard.

Scott, J. C. 1998. *Seeing Like a State: How Certain Schemes to Improve the Human Condition Have Failed.* New Haven: Yale University Press.

Scott, J. W. 2009. "Sexularism: On Secularism and Gender Equality." Ursula Hirschman Annual Lecture on Gender and Europe. Florence, Italy, April 23, 2009. Florence: European University Institute.

SCP 2003. *Rapportage minderheden 2003.* The Hague: Netherlands Institute for Social Research.

2005. *Jaarrapport Integratie 2005.* The Hague: Netherlands Institute for Social Research.

2006. *Survey integratie minderheden 2006: Verantwoording van de opzet en de uitvoering van een survey onder Turken, Marokkanen, Surinamers, Antillianen en een autochtone vergelijkingsgroep.* The Hague: Netherlands Institute for Social Research.

2007a. *Explaining Social Exclusion: A Theoretical Model Tested in the Netherlands.* The Hague: Netherlands Institute for Social Research.

2007b. *Jaarrapport Integratie 2007.* The Hague: Netherlands Institute for Social Research.

2007c. *Interventies voor integratie: Het tegengaan van etnische concentratie en het bevorderen van interetnisch contact.* The Hague: Netherlands Institute for Social Research.

2009. *Jaarrapport Integratie 2009.* The Hague: Netherlands Institute for Social Research.

Shafir, G. (ed.) 1998. *The Citizenship Debates: A Reader.* Minneapolis: University of Minnesota Press.

Shalin, D. N. 2003. "George Herbert Mead," in G. Ritzer (ed.). *The Blackwell Companion to Major Classical Social Theorists.* Oxford: Blackwell.

Shapin, S. and S. Shaffer 1989. *Leviathan and the Air-Pump: Hobbes, Boyle, and the Experimental Life.* Princeton: Princeton University Press.

Shorto, R. 2010. "The Integrationist," *New York Times Magazine,* May 28.

Siebers, H. and M. J. J. Dennissen 2015. "Is It Cultural Racism? Discursive Exclusion and Oppression of Migrants in the Netherlands," *Current Sociology* 63(3): 470–489.

Simmel, G. 1995 [1903]. "Über räumliche Projektionen sozialer Formen," in *Aufsätze und Abhandlungen 1901–1908,* pp. 201–220. Frankfurt am Main: Suhrkamp.

Simon, P. 1999. "Nationality and Origins in French Statistics: Ambiguous Categories," *Population: An English Selection* 11: 193–220.

2003. "Les sciences socials françaises face aux catégories ethniques et raciales," *Annales de Démographie Historique* 1: 111–130.

Sloterdijk, P. 1998. *Der Starke Grund, zusammen zu sein: Erinnerungen an die Erfindung des Volkes.* Frankfurt am Main: Suhrkamp.

Small, S. and J. Solomos 2006. "Race, Immigration and Politics in Britain: Changing Policy Agendas and Conceptual Paradigms, 1940s–2000s," *International Journal of Comparative Sociology* 47(3–4): 235–257.

Smedley, A. 1993. *Race in North America: Origin and Evolution of a Worldview.* Boulder: Westview.

Smith, A. D. 1983. "Nationalism and Classical Social Theory," *British Journal of Sociology* 34(1): 19–38.

Smith, V. 2007. *Clean: A History of Personal Hygiene and Purity.* Oxford: Oxford University Press.

Snel, E. and G. Engbersen 1999. "Openheid en geslotenheid van de Nederlandse verzorgingsstaat: Over oude en nieuwe vormen van sociale ongelijkheid," in Trommel, W. and R. Van der Veen (ed.). *De Herverdeelde Samenleving: Ontwikkeling en herziening van de Nederlandse verzorgingsstaat,* pp. 261–290. Amsterdam: Amsterdam University Press.

Sniderman, P. M. and L. Hagendoorn 2007. *When Ways of Life Collide. Multiculturalism and Its Discontents in the Netherlands.* Princeton: Princeton University Press.

SOEP 2008. *Living in Germany: Survey 2008 on the Social Situation of Households.* Munich: TNS Infratest Sozialforschung.

Solomos, J. and L. Back 1996. *Racism and Society.* Basingstoke: Palgrave Macmillan.

Somers, M. 2008. *Genealogies of Citizenship. Markets, Statelessness, and the Right to Have Rights.* Cambridge: Cambridge University Press.

Soper, J. C. and J. S. Fetzer 2007. "Religious Institutions, Church–State History and Muslim Mobilisation in Britain, France and Germany," *Journal of Ethnic and Migration Studies* 33(6): 933–944.

Soysal, Y. N. 1994. *The Limits of Citizenship: Migrants and Postnational Membership in Europe.* Chicago: University of Chicago Press.

1997. "Changing Parameters of Citizenship and Claims-Making: Organized Islam in European Public Spheres," *Theory and Society* 26: 509–527.

Staring, R. 1998. "Scenes from a Fake Marriage: Notes on the Flip-side of Embeddedness' in K. Koser and H. Lutz (eds.). *The New Migration in Europe: Social Constructions and Social Realities,* pp. 224–241. London: Macmillan.

Stevin, S. 2001 [1590]. *Het burgherlick leven* (Vita Politica). Utrecht: Bijleveld.

Stewart, A. 1995. "Two Conceptions of Citizenship," *British Journal of Sociology* 46(1): 63–78.

Stocking, G. W. Jr. (ed.) 1974. *A Franz Boas Reader: The Shaping of American Anthropology, 1883–1911*. Chicago: University of Chicago Press.

Stolcke, V. 1995. "Talking Culture: New Boundaries, New Rhetorics of Exclusion in Europe," *Current Anthropology* 36(1): 1–24.

Stoler, A. L. 2002. *Carnal Knowledge and Imperial Power: Race and the Intimate in Colonial Rule*. Berkeley: University of California Press.

2009. *Along the Archival Grain: Epistemic Anxieties and Colonial Common Sense*. Princeton: Princeton University Press.

Tague, I. H. 2001. "Love, Honor, and Obedience: Fashionable Women and the Discourse of Marriage in the Early Eighteenth Century," *Journal of British Studies* 40(1): 76–106.

Taguieff, P.-A. 1990. "The New Cultural Racism in France," *Telos* 83: 109–122.

Taguieff, P.-A. 2010. *Le Racisme*. Paris: L'Harmattan.

Tarman, C. and D. O. Sears 2005. "The Conceptualization and Measurement of Symbolic Racism," *Journal of Politics* 67(3): 731–761.

Tawney, R. H. 1922. *Religion and the Rise of Capitalism*. Harmondsworth: Penguin.

Taylor, C. 1989. *Sources of the Self: The Making of the Modern Identity*. Cambridge: Cambridge University Press.

1994. "The Politics of Recognition," in A. Gutmann (ed.). *Multiculturalism: Examining the Politics of Recognition*, pp. 25–73. Princeton: Princeton University Press.

2004. *Modern Social Imaginaries*. Durham: Duke University Press.

2007. *A Secular Age*. Cambridge, MA: Harvard University Press.

The Hague City Council 2006. *Samen stad zijn: Burgers maken het verschil! Beleidskader Burgerschap*. (The Hague Policy Memorandum on Citizenship *Being the City Together: Citizens Make the Difference*). The Hague.

Thompson, C. 2011. *Travel Writing*. London: Routledge.

Thucydides 1954. *The Peloponnesian War*. London: Penguin.

Tillich, P. 1959. *Theology of Culture*. Oxford: Oxford University Press.

1961. *Wesen und Wandel des Glaubens*. Berlin: Ullstein.

Tilly, C. 1984. *Big Structures, Large Processes, Huge Comparisons*. New York: Russell Sage Foundation.

Tokmetzis, D. 2007. "Echte problemen zitten achter de voordeur: Verloedering in de Utrechtse wijk Overvecht moet door bewoners zelf worden bestreden," *NRC Handelsblad*, January 6–7, p. 3.

Torpey, J. 1998. "Coming and Going: On the State Monopolization of the Legitimate 'Means of Movement'," *Sociological Theory* 16(3): 239–259.

Touraine, A. 2003. "The Decline of the Social," *Comparative Sociology* 2(3): 463–474.

Touraine, A. 2007. "Sociology after Sociology," *European Journal of Social Theory* 10(2): 184–193.

Towns, A. 2002. "Paradoxes of (In)Equality: Something Is Rotten in the Gender Equal State of Sweden," *Cooperation and Conflict* 37(2): 157–179.

Tresch, J. 2012. *The Romantic Machine: Utopian Science and Technology after Napoleon.* Chicago: University of Chicago Press.

Tribalat, M. et al. 1996. *De l'immigration à l'assimilation: Enquête sur les populations d'origine étrangère en France.* Paris: La Découverte.

Tubergen, F. van 2004. *The Integration of Immigrants in Cross-National Perspective: Origin, Destination, and Community Effects.* Utrecht: ICS.

Tubergen, F. van and I. Maas 2007. "Ethnic Intermarriage among Immigrants in the Netherlands: An Analysis of Population Data," *Social Science Research* 36(3): 1065–1086.

Turner, B. 2001. "The Erosion of Citizenship," *British Journal of Sociology* 52(2): 189–209.

Tweede Kamer der Staten-Generaal 2005. *Jaarnota Integratiebeleid 2005. Tweede Kamer,* 30 304

2006. *Jaarnota Integratiebeleid 2006. Tweede Kamer,* 30 810.

Uitermark, J. 2010. *Dynamics of Power in Dutch Integration Politics.* Doctoral Dissertation, University of Amsterdam.

Uitermark, J. et al. 2005. "Reinventing Multiculturalism: Urban Citizenship and the Negotiation of Ethnic Diversity in Amsterdam," *International Journal of Urban and Regional Research* 29(3): 622–640.

Urry, J. 2000. *Sociology beyond Societies: Mobilities for the Twenty-First Century.* London: Routledge.

Veenman, J. 1995. *Onbekend maakt onbemind: Over de selectie van allochtonen op de arbeidsmarkt.* Assen: Van Gorcum.

Veer, P. van der 2006. "Pim Fortuyn, Theo van Gogh, and the Politics of Tolerance in the Netherlands," *Public Culture* 18(1): 111–124.

Verbrugge, A. 2004. *Tijd van onbehagen: Filosofische essays over een cultuur op drift.* Amsterdam: SUN.

Verhofstadt, D. 2006. *De derde feministische golf* ('The Third Feminist Wave'). Antwerp: Houtekiet.

Vermeulen, B. P. 2007. *Vrijheid, gelijkheid, burgerschap: Over verschuivende fundamenten van het Nederlandse minderhedenrecht en –beleid: immigratie, integratie, onderwijs en religie.* The Hague: SDU Uitgevers.

Vermeulen, H. and Penninx, R. (eds.) 2000. *Immigrant Integration: The Dutch Case.* Amsterdam: Het Spinhuis.

Verwey-Jonker Institute 2003. *Bronnenonderzoek Integratiebeleid.* The Hague: SDU.

Voegelin, E. 1998. *The History of the Race Idea: From Ray to Carus.* Baton Rouge: Louisiana State University Press.

VROM 2007. *Integratienota 2007–2011: Zorg dat je erbij hoort!* The Hague: Ministerie van VROM/WWI.

VVD 1994. *Beleidsnotitie van niet-westerse migranten in Nederland* [*Policy-paper on non-western immigrants in the Netherlands*].

Walzer, M. 1983. *Spheres of Justice: A Defense of Pluralism and Equality.* New York: Basic Books.

     1994. *Thick and Thin: Moral Argument at Home and Abroad.* Notre Dame, IN: University of Notre Dame Press.

Ward, L. 1921. "Sociology and the Social Sciences: The Social Organism and the Collective Mind," *American Journal of Sociology* 27(1): 1–21.

Weber, E. 1976. *Peasants into Frenchmen: The Modernization of Rural France, 1880–1914.* Stanford: Stanford University Press.

Weijters, G. and P. Scheepers 2003. "Verschillen in sociale integratie tussen etnische groepen: beschrijving en verklaring," *Mens & Maatschappij* 78(2): 144–157.

Weingart, P. 2000. "Biologie als Gesellschaftstheorie," in A. Barsch and P. M. Hejl (eds.). *Menschenbilder: Zur Pluralisierung der Vorstellung von der menschlichen Natur (1850–1914),* pp. 146–166. Frankfurt am Main: Suhrkamp.

Wekker, G. 2016. *White Innocence: Paradoxes of Colonialism and Race.* Durham: Duke University Press.

White, H. C. 2007. "Instituting Society, Our Mirage," *European Journal of Social Theory* 10(2): 194–199.

White, H. C. 2008. *Identity & Control: How Social Formations Emerge.* Princeton: Princeton University Press.

Wieviorka, M. 2005. *La différence: Identités culturelles: enjeux, débats et politiques.* Paris: Éditions de l'aube.

Wikan, U. 1995. *Mot en ny norsk underklasse: Innvandrere, kultur og integrasjon* ('Towards a New Norwegian Underclass. Immigrants, Culture and Integration'). Oslo: Gyldendal.

     1999. "Culture: A New Concept of Race," *Social Anthropology* 7(1): 57–64.

Wikan, U. 2002. *Generous Betrayal: Politics of Culture in the New Europe.* Chicago: University of Chicago Press.

Williams, R. 1983. *Keywords: A Vocabulary of Culture and Society.* London: Fontana Press.

Williams, V. J. Jr. 2006. *The Social Sciences and Theories of Race.* Urbana: University of Illinois Press.

Willke, H. 1993. *Systemtheorie*. Stuttgart: Fischer.

Wilson, W. J. 1980. *The Declining Significance of Race: Blacks and Changing American Institutions*. Chicago: University of Chicago Press.

Wimmer, A. and N. Glick Schiller 2002. "Methodological Nationalism and Beyond: Nation-State Building, Migration and the Social Sciences," *Global Networks* 2(4): 301–334.

   2003. "Methodological Nationalism, the Social Sciences, and the Study of Migration: An Essay in Historical Epistemology," *International Migration Review* 37(3): 576–610.

Winant, H. 2004. *The New Politics of Race: Globalism, Difference, Justice*. Minneapolis: University of Minnesota Press.

Wirth, L. 1938. *The Ghetto*. Chicago: University of Chicago Press.

Wittgenstein, L. 1984. *Philosophische Untersuchungen*. Frankfurt am Main: Suhrkamp.

Wolin, S. 2004. *Politics and Vision: Continuity and Innovation in Western Thought*. Princeton: Princeton University Press.

Wright Mills, C. 1959. *The Sociological Imagination*. Oxford: Oxford University Press.

   1969. "The Professional Ideology of Social Pathologists," in I. L. Horowitz (ed.). *Power, Politics and People*, pp. 525–552. New York: Oxford University Press.

WRR 1979. *Etnische minderheden: Rapport aan de regering*. The Hague: Staatsuitgeverij.

WRR [Dutch Scientific Council for Government Policy] 2001. *Nederland als immigratiesamenleving*. The Hague: SDU.

Yuval-Davis, N. 1997. *Gender and Nation*. London: Sage.

   1999. "The 'Multi-Layered Citizen.' Citizenship in the Age of Glocalization," *International Feminist Journal of Politics* 1(1): 119–136.

Žižek, S. 2000. *The Fragile Absolute or, Why Is the Christian Legacy Worth Fighting For?* London: Verso.

   2008. "Tolerance as an Ideological Category," *Critical Inquiry* 34: 660–682.

Zolberg, A. and Woon 1998. "Why 'Islam' Is like 'Spanish,'" *Politics and Society* 27(1): 5–38.

Zwaard, J. van der 2008. *Gelukzoekers: Vrouwelijke huwelijksmigranten in Nederland*. Amsterdam: Artemis & Co.

Index

Abbott, Andrew, 88
abortion, forced, 128–129
Abu Lughod, Lila, 136, 189
Adorno, T.W., 169
Agamben, Giorgio, 197, 223, 225
agranormativity, 138
allochthons
  autochthons compared to, 148
  autochthons' contact with, 94–95,
    109
  genealogization and, 150–151
  neo-liberal communitarianism for,
    153–154
  in Netherlands, 17, 65, 77, 89,
    148–151
  non-Western, 148–150
  in policy, 149–150
  western and non-western, 77
Allochthons Policy, 89, 148
*An American Dilemma. The Negro
    Problem and Modern
    Democracy* (Myrdal), 75
Amsterdam School for Social Science
    Research (ASSR), 85
Anderson, Benedict, 6–7
antagonism, 53–54, 59–60
anthropology, 135–136
Antilleans, 93, 129, 149, 172–173
anti-Semitism, 140–141
Appadurai, Arjun, 29, 170, 217
Arendt, Hannah, 194
Aristotle, 55, 198
Asad, Talal, 32
assimilation
  in culturism, 145
  marriage impact on, 175–177
  Mills on, 96
assimilationism
  in Europe, 21–22, 115

in France, 128
in integration, 76
in Netherlands, 21–23, 122–123,
  128, 130
racism compared to, 115
in UK, 128
ASSR. *See* Amsterdam School for Social
  Science Research
Augustine (St.), 41
autochthons, 94–95, 109, 148
autoimmunity, 189–191

Badiou, Alain, 217
Balibar, Étienne, 132–135, 153
Barker, Martin, 132
Barry, Brian, 160
Bauman, Zygmunt, 46–47, 138,
  184–185
Beck, Ulrich, 46, 206
Belgium, 79, 164–165, 232
Bergson, Henri, 222
biopolitics, 224–226
biopower, 212, 224–225
Blanchot, M., 10–11
Blau, Peter, 95
Blom, J.C.H., 81
Boas, Franz, 135, 196
the body
  as illegible, 185–187
  Muslims and, 185–188
  national society and, 166
  religion in, 188–189
Bogardus, Emory, 75
Bolkestein, Frits, 123
Boswell, Christina, 68–69, 88
Bourdieu, Pierre, 69, 90, 131
Bowen, John, 188
Boyle, Robert, 183
Breivik, A., 160–161

Brown, Wendy, 29, 152–153, 168–169
Brubaker, Rogers, 128, 164
Burawoy, Michael, 84–85, 87, 195, 230–231
burger, 193. *See also* citizenship
burqa-bill, 19–20, 171, 184
Butler, Judith, 17, 165–167, 173

Caldwell, Christopher, 161
Calhoun, Craig, 32, 65, 170, 233
Cameron, David, 70, 156–157, 181
Castoriadis, Cornelius, 7–9, 28, 41, 116, 131, 134
Charlie Hebdo, 185
Cicero, 198
citizenship, 34, 227
 active, 193–194, 199, 204, 208, 211, 217
 culture in, 33
 formal, 198
 in France, 213
 globalization impact on, 194
 in governmentality, 192
 in The Hague, 209–211
 individual responsibility in, 200, 211
 integration and, 82, 192, 200–202
 in integration discourse, 197
 loyalty and, 200
 moral, 198–199, 202, 215, 217
 moralization of, 33, 199, 203–204, 211, 216–217
 nation relation to, 196
 nation-state and, 33, 197
 in neo-liberal communitarianism, 212–213, 216
 in Netherlands, 193, 199–204
 in political philosophy, 194–195
 as program, 193
 regionalization of, 204–206
 in Rotterdam, 206–209
 secularism in, 32
 in social science, 195
 society relation to, 194, 196–197, 216–217
 state relation to, 196–197, 217
 Taylor on, 216
 in UK, 213
 virtualization of, 202–204, 216–217
class, 153, 169–170

Coleman, James, 86
colonialism
 in Indonesia, 71–72
 in integration, 70–74
 Netherlands and, 71–72
 racism in, 140
Comaroff, J., 194
Comaroff, J.L., 194
communitarianism, neo-liberal, 153–154, 216
 for allochthons, 153–154
 citizenship in, 212–213, 216
 as de-individualizing individualization, 213–214
 in France, 213
 individual responsibility in, 213–215
 responsibilization in, 215
 in UK, 213
concept
 assembling, 36
 container, 36
 coordinating, 43
conclusion, 147, 222–223
confiction, 222–224
contacts, 106
 for allochthons, 94–95, 109
 for autochthons, 94–95, 109
 measurement of, 92–96
 Moroccans and, 93–94
 SCP on, 92–94
cosmopolitanism, 170
crime, 19–22, 101, 107, 127, 147, 149
critical theory, 11–12
culturalism, 134–136
culture
 in citizenship, 33
 dominant, 30–31, 117–118
 culturism on, 167
 of Enlightenment, 167–168
 hierarchization of, 139–140
 immigrant, culturism on, 167
 in integration discourse, 30, 116–117, 120–121
 in integration imaginaries, 29–30
 Islamic, 127–128
 in liberal democracies, 30–31
 in liberal subjecthood, 214
 Mills on, 144–145
 modernity in, 31
 particularist, 30

culture (cont.)
  as program, 100
  in racism, 132–134
  society and, 117, 143–144, 154–155
Culture & Equality (Barry), 160
culturism
  agranormativity in, 138
  anti-racism in, 141–143
  assimilation in, 145
  culturalism compared to, 134–136
  de-individualizing individualization
    in, 145
  on dominant culture, 167
  Enlightenment in, 167–169
  in Europe, 128–129
  feminism in, 170–171
  in France, 144
  on immigrant culture, 167
  in integration discourse, 123–124,
    130–131
  in Netherlands, 140–142, 167
  racism compared to, 31, 116,
    137–139
  racism in, 136–137, 139–141
  society and, 151–152
  terranormativity in, 139–141

*Déclaration des droits de l'homme et du
    citoyen*, 198
DeLanda, Manuel, 40–41
Deleuze, Gilles, 36, 222
Denmark, 118
deparadoxization, 191
depoliticization, 152–153
deprivation, economic, 153–154
Derrida, Jacques, 43, 58, 189–190
Descartes, René, 188
Dewey, John, 41–42
diagrammars, 21–27, 100, 107–108
Die Gesellschaft der Gesellschaft
    (Luhmann), 110
discourse. *See also* imaginaries
  disagreements in, 24
  dominant, 24–25
  Foucault on, 23–24
  imaginaries and, 28
  integration, 23–26
    autoimmunity in, 190–191
    citizenship in, 197
    culture in, 30, 116–117, 120–121

culturism in, 123–124, 130–131
  ethnicity in, 28–29
  modernity in, 166–167
  in Netherlands, 121–131, 180
  society impacted by, 69–70
  professional, 69
  social imagination and, 24–25
dispensation
  of ethnicity, 102–103, 151
  of integration, 3, 103–104
diversity, 29
Douglas, Mary, 37–38, 179, 185
Drachsler, Julius, 175, 177
Durkheim, Emile, 21, 29–30, 43–44,
    56–57, 74, 228
Dutch Scientific Council for
    Government Policy (WRR), 89,
    148

ECRI. *See* European Committee on
    Racism and Equality
emancipation, 97–98, 172
Engbersen, Godfried, 205–206
Engels, F., 141
Enlightenment
  culture of, 167–168
  in culturism, 167–169
  Foucault on, 169
  Horkheimer and Adorno on, 169
  Luhmann on, 169
  as tolerance, 168
Entzinger, Han, 89–90, 200
ERCOMER. *See* European Research
    Centre on Migration and Ethnic
    Relations
Essed, Philomena, 84, 105
Estonia, 99
Ethnic Minorities Policy, 89, 122, 126
ethnicity
  Appadurai on, 29
  dispensation of, 102–103, 151
  in integration discourse, 28–29
  in policy, 128–130, 149
  in research, 102–103, 141–142
  statistics on, 79–80
EU. *See* European Union
Europe, 16–17
  assimilationism in, 21–22, 115
  culturism in, 128–129
  immigrants in, 1–2

integration in, 4, 11, 82–83
multiculturalism in, 6
multiculturealism in, 161
Muslims in, 164
racism in, 115–116
European Committee on Racism and
    Equality (ECRI), 19
European Research Centre on
    Migration and Ethnic Relations
    (ERCOMER), 86
European Union (EU), 82
exclusion, 134, 145–148, 222–224
extremism, Islamist, 156
Eyerman, Ron, 125–126
Ezrahi, Y., 6

Fanon, Frantz, 133
Favell, Adrian, 70
feminism, 170–171
Fichte, Johann Gottlieb, 233
Finkielkraut, Alain, 160
Fiske, J., 113–143
Fortuyn, Pim, 21, 124–125, 206
Foucault, Michel, 13, 65, 87, 157,
    169, 192–193, 212, 224–226,
    230
  on discourse, 23–24
  on governmentality, 87, 212, 215
France, 79–80, 128, 144, 158, 163,
    165, 181, 213
  multiculturalism in, 158–160
  nationalism in, 232–233
  republicanism in, 79, 159, 163
Fraser, Nancy, 153
Fredrickson, George, 115
freedom of speech, 185
Fukuyama, Francis, 162
functional differentiation, 56, 64

Garfinkel, H., 3–4, 104
Geertz, Clifford, 46
Gellner, E., 42
gender
  in integration, 164–165, 180
  in Sweden, 164
genealogization, 104–105, 150–151
Germany, 69–70, 80, 118, 158–160,
    171
Gilroy, P., 131
globalization, 46–49, 194

glocalization, 205
Gordon, P., 132
Gorski, Philip, 169
Gouda, Frances, 71–72
governing
  populations, 224, 226
  society as medium of, 25–26, 29,
    224, 226–227
governmentality, 87, 192, 212, 215

Habermas, Jürgen, 75, 189
The Hague, 209–211
Hall, S., 137
Harrison, Faye, 136
Hartigan, John, 103, 136
Hegel, G.W.F., 44
hegemony, 51–52
*Hegemony and Socialist Strategy.
    Towards a Radical Democratic
    Politics* (Laclau and Mouffe),
    51
Hindess, Barry, 212
Hirsi Ali, Ayaan, 123, 189
Hobbes, Thomas, 183
*Home Office Policy Advice Minority
    Debate*, 89
homosexuality, 165–167, 173–175
Hondius, Dienke, 71, 113–114
Hooghiemstra, E, 179
Horkheimer, T.W., 169
Huntington, Samuel, 161, 182
Husserl, E., 6

ICS. *See* Interuniversity Centre for
    Social Science Theory and
    Methodology
image, 10
imaginaries
  Blanchot on, 10–11
  discourse and, 28
  integration, 4, 11–23, 27–28
  culture in, 29–30
  social, 6–11
    Castoriadis on, 7–9
    social systems in, 9–10
    Taylor on, 7–9, 28
imagination, 6–11
  Plato on, 6–7
  social, 10
    discourse and, 24–25

imagination (cont.)
  integration as form of, 73, 83–84,
    109
  Luhmann on, 73
  society as form of, 42–43, 49–50,
    66–67
Imagined Communities (Anderson), 6
Imagined Democracies (Ezrahi), 6
immigrants, 1–4
  culture of, culturism on, 167
  in Europe, Western, 1–2
  genealogization of, 104
  integration impact on, 14–15
  in national society, 1–2
  in nation-state, 2
  in Sweden, 164
  unmasking of, 3
immigration
  income demands for, 129
  in nation-state, 172–173
  in Netherlands, 16–19, 21–22, 129
  in social science, 2
  society impacted by, 1–2
import brides, 175–180, 190–191.
    See also marriage
*Indicators of Immigrant Integration
    2015*, 68
individualization, de-individualizing,
    101–102, 145, 213–214
Indonesia, 71–72
instability, 58–59
*Integratienota 2007–2011 (Integration
    Memorandum 2007–2011)*,
    201, 204
integration, 1–4
  assimilationism in, 76
  in Belgium, 79
  biopolitics in, 224
  citizenship and, 82, 192, 200–202
  colonialism in, 70–74
  as coordinating concept, 43
  crime and, 21–22, 101, 107, 127,
    147
  de-individualizing individualization
    of, 101–102
  in Denmark, 118
  diagrammar of, 21–27, 100,
    107–108
  discourse, 23–26
    autoimmunity in, 190–191

citizenship in, 197
culture in, 30, 116–117, 120–121
culturism in, 123–124, 130–131
ethnicity in, 28–29
modernity in, 166–167
in Netherlands, 121–131, 180
society impacted by, 69–70
dispensation of, 3, 103–104
Durkheim on, 44, 74
in Estonia, 99
in EU, 82
in Europe, 4, 11, 82–83
in France, 79–80, 213
gender in, 164–165, 180
genealogization of, 104–105,
    150–151
in Germany, 69–70, 80, 118, 171
Habermas on, 75
in The Hague, 209–210
imaginaries of, 4, 11–23, 27–28
  culture in, 29–30
immigrants impacted by, 14–15
Luhmann on, 59–60, 110
Malcolm X on, 11
measurement of, 78–99
in mereological metaphysics, 56
modernity in, 31
in moral monitoring, 2–3
multiculturalism in, 218
Nassehi on, 75
in national society, 4, 70, 78–84, 233
nationalism and, 232, 234–235
in Netherlands, 4, 15–23, 69, 76–78,
    80–81, 84–90, 119–131,
    181–182
in Norway, 69, 118–119
operationalization of, 76–78
organicism in, 35–36, 74, 96
Parsons on, 74–76
policy, 108, 118
  marriage in, 176, 179–180
  in Netherlands, 119–121, 171,
    176, 179–180
  women in, 171
in programs, 26–27
religion in, 4, 164–165, 181–182
in social hypochondria, 62–63,
    65–66
as social imagination, 73, 83–84, 109

in social science, 4–5, 13–14, 39,
72–78, 84–90, 108–109,
228–230
in society, 4–21, 72–74, 103,
224–228
socio-cultural
measurement of, 90–99
modernity in, 92
modernization as measure of,
98–99
SCP on, 91–92, 105–107
structural, 76–77, 106
in Sweden, 119
system/environment for, 109–111
temporalization of, 107
in UK, 80, 119, 213
women in, 173
Integration, bonding, citizenship,
201–202
Interuniversity Centre for Social Science
Theory and Methodology (ICS),
85–89
Islam
culture and, 127–128
extremism and, 156
in France, 158, 181
nation-state relation to, 182–183
in Netherlands, 181–182, 208–209
secularism and, 183, 188
islamophobia, 140–141, 183–185
Israel, 232
Israel, Jonathan, 169
issues, programs and, 27
Italy, 232

Janmaat, Hans, 20
Joppke, Christian, 143–144,
160–161

Kant, Immanuel, 11, 190
Kok, Wim, 125
Komrij, Gerrit, 174
Koopmans, Ruud, 113
Koselleck, Reinhart, 168

Lacan, Jacques, 52–55
Laclau, E., 51–54
Latour, Bruno, 50–51
Lévi-Strauss, C., 135
liberal democracies, 30–31

liberalism
Brown on, 29, 169
Cameron on, 157
class in, 169–170
difference in, 29
freedom of speech in, 185
in Netherlands, 29
neutralization of, 169–170
religion in, 186
secularism in, 186
Taylor on, 64–65
loyalty, 178–179, 200
Luhmann, Niklas, 13, 45, 59–60,
73–74, 110–111, 169, 191, 226
on functional differentiation, 56, 64
on integration, 59–60, 110
on organicism, 36, 54–60
on semantics, 25–27
on social systems, 9–10, 58–60
on system/environment, 57–58,
109–111

Macionis, J.J., 42
Maguire, M.E., 6–7
Malcolm X, 11
Marcson, Simon, 175–177
marriage
assimilation impacted by, 175–177
as economic, 177–178, 190–191
fake, 177–178
in integration policy, 176,
179–180
loyalty and, 178–179
migration, 172, 175
transnational, 176–180
Marshall, T.H., 33, 192, 196
Marx, K, 141
M'Charek, Amade, 132
measurement
of contacts, 92–96
of integration, 78–99
of modernity, 96–99
of secularization, 97
of socio-cultural integration,
90–99
of socio-economic position,
100–101
mechanicism, 37
medium
confiction as, 224

medium (cont.)
    of governing, society as, 25–26, 29,
        224, 226–227
    Luhmann on, 226
*Memorandum Integration Policy
    Ethnic Minorities
    (Contourennota Integratiebeleid
    Etnische Minderheden)*,
        200–201
Merkel, Angela, 158, 171, 181
Merton, Robert, 3
metaphysics, mereological, 37, 45,
    55–56
Migrant Integration Policy Index
    (MIPEX), 82
migrants. *See also* immigrants
    economic deprivation among,
        153, 154
    self-organizations among, 153
Mills, C. Wright, 96, 144–145, 229
    on social pathologists, 36, 39, 111,
        230
    on society, 230
minority research industry, 84–90
MIPEX. *See* Migrant Integration Policy
    Index
Mitchell, W.J.T., 116
modernity
    Asad on, 32
    Calhoun on, 65
    in culture, 31
    homosexuality and, 173–175
    in integration, 31
    in integration, socio-cultural, 92
    in integration discourse, 166–167
    measurement of, 96–99
    national societies articulated through,
        163–164
    in Netherlands, 31, 98–99, 102
    as program, 32, 100
    religion and, 31, 165
    SCP on, 96
    sexuality and, 165, 227
    as Western, 31
modernization
    emancipation as measure of, 97–98
    SCP on, 97
    secularization as measure of, 97
    socio-cultural integration measured
        by, 98–99

moral monitoring, 2–3, 74
morality, 59
moralization, citizenship and, 33, 56,
        199, 203–204, 211, 216–217
Moroccans, 127, 141, 149, 176–177
    contacts and, 93–94
    criminalization of, 19–20, 127, 149
Morocco, 127
Mouffe, Chantal, 51–54, 125
The Multicultural Drama (Scheffer),
        18–19, 125–126
multiculturalism
    denouncement of, 5–6, 156–158,
        181
    in Europe, 6
    in France, 158–160
    in Germany, 158–160
    in integration, 218
    multiculturerealism and, 6, 12
    as nationalism, 163
    in Netherlands, 18–19, 22–23,

        122–126, 130, 162
    in UK, 156–157, 159
multicultureralism
    in Europe, 161
    in France, 163
    multiculturalism and, 6, 12
    in Netherlands, 18–19, 22, 123–126,
        130
    in Norway, 163
    in social science, 218
    in Sweden, 163
Muslims
    the body and, 185–188
    in Europe, 164
    in France, 165
    in Netherlands, 4–20, 29, 127–128,
        173
    in Norway, 164
    in UK, 144
Myrdal, G., 75

Nassehi, Armin, 75
nation
    citizenship relation to, 196
    self-referentiality of, 213–214
    society relation to, 196–197
nationalism
    in Belgium, 232

Calhoun on, 233
in France, 232–233
integration and, 232, 234–235
in Italy, 232
multiculturalism as, 163
national society defended by,
  233–235
neo, 233–234
nationality, 142–143
nation-state
citizenship and, 33, 197
immigrants in, 2
immigration in, 172–173
Islam relation to, 182–183
religion relation to, 182–183, 189
sexuality relation to, 172–173, 189
nature, society and, 50–51
Netherlands, 16–17
allochthons in, 17, 65, 77, 89,
  148–151
Antilleans in, 93, 129, 149, 172–173
assimilationism in, 21–23, 122–123,
  128, 130
Butler on, 17, 165–167, 173
citizenship in, 193, 199–204
colonialism and, 71–72
culturism in, 140–142, 167
homosexuality in, 165–167, 173–175
immigration in, 16–19, 21–22, 129
import brides in, 177–178
integration discourse in, 121–131,
  180
integration in, 4, 15–23, 69, 76–78,
  80–81, 84–90, 119–131,
  181–182
integration policy in, 119–121, 171,
  176, 179–180
Islam in, 181–182, 208–209
liberalism in, 29
minority research industry in, 84–90
modernity in, 31, 98–99, 102
on modernization, 97
Moroccans in, 19–20, 93–94, 127,
  141, 149, 176–177
multiculturalism in, 18–19, 22–23,
  122–126, 130, 162
multiculturealism in, 18–19, 22,
  123–126, 130
Muslims in, 4–20, 29, 127–128, 173
pillarization in, 81

populism in, 124–125
racism in, 114–145
religion in, 142
slave trade in, 113
social science in, 84–90
sociology in, 85–86
statistics in, 81–82
Netherlands Institute for Social
  Research (SCP)
on contacts, 92–94
government affiliation of, 86–87
ICS relationship with, 88–89
on integration, socio-cultural, 91–92,
  105–107
on modernity, 96
on modernization, 97
on SIM-survey, 90
networks, 49–50
neutrality, liberal, 181
Nimako, K., 84
Norway, 69, 118–119, 163–164

Ong, Aihwa, 192–193
operationalization, integration and,
  76–78
order, 61–62
organicism
Castoriadis on, 41
in integration, 35–36, 74, 96
Luhmann on, 36, 54–60
as mereological, 37
Mills on, 111
Plato on, 63–64
in social science, 36, 38, 63–64
in social theory, 36
in sociology, 39–41
Taylor on, 35

Pandora's Hope (Latour), 50–51
Parsons, Talcott, 29–30, 74–76
Pascal, B., 63
passing, 104–105
paternalism, new, 211
Penninx, Rinus, 89, 122
Pericles, 198
Phillips, Anne, 159
philosophy, political, 194–195
pillarization, 81
Plato, 6–7, 55–56, 63–64
Plummer, K., 42

Poggi, Gianfranco, 58
policy
 allochthons in, 149–150
 ethnicity in, 128–130, 149
 integration, 108, 118
  marriage in, 176, 179–180
  in Netherlands, 119–121, 171,
   176, 179–180
  women in, 171
 research in, 68–69, 87–90
 in Rotterdam, 206–207
 social science and, 15–16
polis, 55–56
politesse, 79
*The Political Uses of Expert
 Knowledge. Immigration Policy
 and Social Research* (Boswell),
 68
politics, emancipatory, 14
The Politics of Recognition (Taylor),
 216
populations, governing of, 224, 226
populism, 124–125
positivism, 85–86
Prins, Baukje, 178
programs
 citizenship as, 193
 culture as, 100
 diagrammar expressing, 26
 integration in, 26–27
 issues in, 27
 modernity as, 32, 100
 race as, 116
 themes in, 27
Proudhon, Pierre-Joseph, 41
public sphere, 189
publics, 230–231
purgatory, cultural, 144
Purple Coalition, 125

race, 116, 131–132
racism
 anthropology on, 135–136
 assimilationism compared to, 115
 Blut-variant, 139–140
 Boden-variant, 139–140
 in colonialism, 140
 cultural, 132–134
 in culturism, 136–137, 139–141
 culturism against, 141–143

culturism compared to, 31, 116,
  137–139
 in Europe, 115–116
 as hidden, 134
 neo, 132–133
 in Netherlands, 114–145
 social science on, 131–133
 terranormativity in, 137
Rawls, John, 196, 214
reality effects, 69
Reden an die deutsche Nation (Fichte),
  233
regionalization, citizenship and,
  204–206
religion
 in the body, 188–189
 Derrida on, 189–190
 in integration, 4, 164–165, 181–182
 in liberal neutrality, 181
 in liberalism, 186
 modernity and, 31, 165
 in national society, 165–166
 nation-state relation to, 182–183,
  189
 in Netherlands, 142
 secularism relation to, 32
 sexuality and, 165
 as surface phenomenon, 184,
  187–188
republicanism, 79, 159, 163
research
 ethnicity in, 102–103, 141–142
 in policy, 68–69, 87–90
 quango, 86
responsibility, individual
 in citizenship, 200, 211
 in neo-liberal communitarianism,
  213–215
responsibilization, 215
Robertson, Roland, 205
Robespierre, Maximilien, 198
Rose, Nikolas, 38
Rotterdam, 206–209
Rotterdam Citizenship Code,
  207–209
Rotterdam Law, 207
Rutte, Mark, 114

Said, Edward, 128
Sand, Schlomo, 228

Sarkozy, Nicolas, 158, 163, 181
Sassen, Saskia, 33
Scheffer, Paul, 18–19, 125–126
Schmitt, Carl, 53
Scientific Research and Documentation
    Centre of the Netherlands
    Ministry of Justice (WODC),
    86
Scott, James, 70
Scott, Joan Wallace, 32, 165
SCP. *See* Netherlands Institute for
    Social Research
secularism
    Asad on, 32
    autoimmunity in, 190
    Calhoun on, 32
    in citizenship, 32
    Islam and, 183, 188
    in liberal neutrality, 181
    in liberalism, 186
    religion relation to, 32
    Taylor on, 169, 180–181
secularization, 97
Seeing Like a State (Scott), 70
Seeing Through Race (Mitchell), 116
self-organizations, 153
semantics, 25–27
sexuality
    modernity and, 165, 227
    in national society, 165–166
    nation-state relation to, 172–173,
        189
    religion and, 165
sexularism, 165
Shaffer, S., 183
Shapin, S., 183
Simmel, Georg, 172
SIM-survey. *See* Survey Integration
    Minorities
slave trade, 113
Sloterdijk, Peter, 227
the social
    hegemony in, 51–52
    Laclau on, 51–52
    Mouffe on, 51–52
social body, 63, 178–179
social contract, 63
social hypochondria, 193, 215
    contingency negated by, 64
    functional differentiation and, 64

integration in, 62–63, 65–66
national society and, 214
social pathologists, 36, 39, 111,
    230
social science
    citizenship in, 195
    in France, 79–80
    immigration in, 2
    integration in, 4–5, 13–14, 39,
        72–78, 84–90, 108–109,
        228–230
    Mills on, 36
    multiculturealism in, 218
    in Netherlands, 84–90
    organicism in, 36, 38, 63–64
    Parsons on, 29–30
    policy and, 15–16
    public role of, 229–231, 235
    on race, 131–132
    on racism, 131–133
    society and, 12–13, 218–222
social systems
    instability as ground of, 58–59
    Luhmann on, 9–10, 58–60
    in social imaginaries, 9–10
social theory
    exclusion in, 145–147
    Luhmann on, 45
    organicism in, 36
    society in, 43–45
socialization, 43–44
society, 49–51, 219
    Augustine on, 41
    Bauman on, 46–47
    Beck on, 46
    beginnings of, 63
    biopolitics and, 225–226
    Castoriadis on, 28
    citizenship relation to, 194, 196–197,
        216–217
    conception of, 37–38
    and conclusion, 222–223
    as confiction, 222–223
    as container concept, 36
    culturalization of, 48
    culture and, 117, 143–144, 154–155
    culturism and, 151–152
    deparadoxization in, 191
    Dewey on, 41–42
    Durkheim on, 21, 29–30, 228

society (cont.)
  Dutch, as modern, 98–99, 102
  economization of, 48
  ends of, 63–64
  exclusion and, 146–148, 222–223
  Foucault on, 65
  Gellner on, 42
  globalization impact on, 46–49
  imagination of, 6–11
  immigration impact on, 1–2
  integration discourse impacting,
      69, 70
  integration in, 4–21, 72–74, 103,
      224–228
  Laclau on, 52–54
  Latour on, 50–51
  Luhmann on, 54–60
  as medium of governing, 25–26, 29,
      224, 226–227
  Mills on, 230
  modern, 8
  morality in, 59
  Mouffe on, 52–54
  nation relation to, 196–197
  national, 166
    the body and, 166
    exclusion in, 224
    immigrants in, 1–2
    integration in, 4, 70, 78–84, 233
    modernity articulating, 163–164
    nationalism defending, 233–235
    religion in, 165–166
    sexuality in, 165–166
    social hypochondria and, 214
    state relation to, 216–217
  nature relation to, 50–51
  network compared to, 49–50
  order in, 61–62
  paradoxes of, 60–62
  political use of, 51–54
  Proudhon on, 41
  as social body, 63
  social imagination, as form of,
      42–43, 49–50, 66–67
  social science and, 12–13, 218–222
  in social theory, 43–45
  in sociology, 12, 37, 60–61
  state defining, 118, 217
  supplement needed for, 43
  Taylor on, 8, 28

temporalization of, 62
Tilly on, 49
Touraine on, 48–49
unity in, 61–62
White on, 49
wholeness in, 38–39, 45
socio-economic position, 100–101
sociology
  in Netherlands, 85–86
  organicism in, 39–41
  positivism in, 85–86
  society in, 12, 37, 60–61
Sociology: A Global Introduction
      (Macionis and Plummer), 42
Somers, Margaret, 145–146
Spencer, Herbert, 74
state
  citizenship relation to, 196–197, 217
  control of movement by, 175
  national society relation to, 216–217
  society defined by, 118, 217
statistics
  on ethnicity, 79–80
  in Netherlands, 81–82
Stolcke, Verena, 135
Stoler, Ann, 72, 104, 133
subjecthood, liberal, 214
supplement
  Derrida on, 43, 58
  society needing, 43
surface phenomenon, religion as, 184,
      187–188
Survey Integration Minorities (SIM-
      survey), 87–88, 90
Sweden, 119, 163–164
system/environment
  for integration, 109–111
  Luhmann on, 57–58, 109–111
systems theorists, 42

Taguieff, Pierre-André, 134, 136, 144
Taylor, Charles
  on citizenship, 216
  on liberalism, 64–65
  on organicism, 35
  on secularism, 169, 180–181
  on social imaginaries, 7–9, 28
  on society, 8, 28
temporalization
  of integration, 107

of society, 62
terranormativity, 137, 139–141
terrorism, 156–157
themes, programs and, 27
Thucydides, 198
Tilly, Charles, 12, 49
tolerance
    Brown on, 152, 168
    Enlightenment as, 168
Torpey, John, 175
Touraine, Alain, 48–49
Towards a New Norwegian Underclass
    (Wikan), 164
Towns, Ann, 163
Tribalat, Michèle, 80
Turner, Jonathan, 40

Uitermark, J., 23–24
umma, 182–183
United Kingdom (UK), 80, 119, 128,
    144, 156–157, 159, 213
unity
    Luhmann on, 111
    in society, 61–62
Urry, J., 46

van Dijk, Teun, 105, 112–113
van Gogh, Theo, 20–22, 127,
    183–184
van Houdt, Friso, 192, 212–213

Van Kemenade, Jos, 122–123
van Reekum, Rogier, 12
veil, debate on, 183
virtualization, citizenship and,
    202–204, 216–217
Voltaire, 168, 190

Weber, Eugen, 233
Weber, Max, 64, 69
Wekker, Gloria, 116
White, Harrison, 49
whiteness, 103
Wieviorka, Michel, 153
Wikan, Unni, 164
Wikileaks, 17
Wilders, Geert, 19–20, 171, 232
Willke, Helmut, 75–76
WODC. *See* Scientific Research and
    Documentation Centre of the
    Netherlands Ministry of Justice
Wolin, Sheldon, 39, 214
women
    in integration, 173
    in integration policy, 171
    in public sphere, 189
WRR. *See* Dutch Scientific Council for
    Government Policy

Žižek, S., 11–12
zoèpolitics, 225